Brown. L. | Eagles of the world.
'77

EAGLES

OF THE WORLD

LESLIE BROWN

EAGLES
OF THE WORLD

DAVID & CHARLES
Newton Abbot . London . Vancouver

To Emil and Lois, in memory of a million good times together.

ISBN 0 7153 72696

© Leslie Brown 1976

Set in 11 on 12pt Plantin
and printed in Great Britain
by Alden and Mowbray, Oxford
for David & Charles (Publishers) Limited
Brunel House Newton Abbot Devon

Published in Canada
by Douglas David & Charles Limited
1875 Welch Street North Vancouver BC

Contents

Preface

For thousands of years eagles have fascinated and impressed mankind. Nor is it hard to understand why, for a big eagle in masterful flight combines grandeur and grace in a manner no bird can eclipse. Other, smaller masters of flight, such as swifts, can evidently fly rings round a big eagle; and that matchless flier, the Peregrine Falcon, frequently pesters eagles. The falcon knows, however, that to come within range of the clutching talons means instant death, and many eagles can evade what is to them a tiresome gadfly presence without difficulty. At rest, no bird can match the regal pose of an eagle's head between the shoulders formed by folding those great wings, or the piercing stare of yellow eyes, while the foot and talons are at once eloquent of its size and power over other, lesser creatures. It is at the top of the avian tree, and big eagles are the world's most formidable birds.

I am told that the eagles which aroused in the ancients of the Bible a sense of wonder may actually have been vultures; but the way of an eagle in the air will still draw a gasp of admiration or pleasure from many a watcher who might not, these days, feel quite the same wonder about serpents on rocks, much less about men and maids who are, quite frankly, merely boring. Eagles have a long history in fable and legend. Icarus sought to emulate them; and maybe it was an eagle, not a vulture, that fed regularly on Prometheus' liver until killed by Hercules. Several eagles are national emblems, and they appear in heraldic attitudes (appropriately, threat display) on many a gatepost and coat of arms. Nowadays they advertise safari firms, insurance companies, motor tyres and children's magazines. One may think the eagle demeaned by some such uses; but to me these, too, speak of the abiding wonder of an eagle for mankind.

Wonder, tinged with awe, leads rare enthusiasts to seek out eagles and study them. They are few, because this is no easy field of work. The late David Lack told me once that they were ornithologically unrewarding because you could not get statistical results from them! Leaders in the field were the old bird photographers; and I am old enough to remember the late Captain C. W. R. Knight and his Golden Eagle, Mr Ramshaw, and the joy and excitement that possessed me when the great bird flew round the hall and came back to land on his fist. Nor would I have exchanged those old natural history films which exposed the secrets of the Golden Eagle's home life for any Hollywood epic. I myself began studying eagles at the age of nineteen, in fact as soon as I was big and indepedent enough to cover alone the necessary ground in Scotland; and I have never looked back. From time to time the best of us, for one reason or another, deviate to study flamingoes, pelicans or even—oh horror!—small passerines. But we always return to eagles in the end; I know of no real eagle man who has given up, except through infirmity or lack of time—for time is of the essence.

Many years ago I wrote: 'This is no easy bird to know; he does not come to any bird table.' And, in the main, that is still true, though some eagles are commoner and easier to observe than others. It generally means hard slogging over wild, rough country, a challenge in itself. Most of the real devotees to date have been large, tough, male carnivores; but lately the distaff side has been represented by a most distinguished observer, a slim, slight vegetarian at that. All such long-standing eagle watchers speak a language few others can understand. We may speak of such and such a bird; and we mean only one bird, an eagle of some sort.

This single-mindedness is needed to achieve results in a challenging field of research. Nowadays I suppose 'dedication' (which I regard as a singularly odious term, so let no one apply it to me) would be the 'in' word. An eagle enthusiast must be something of a solitary, in keeping with the magnificent but elusive birds he seeks; but that need not make him a misanthrope. We don't often meet; but when we do our tongues wag from morn to night, or whenever we draw breath on the inevitable steep hill. Thus one learns, and sharpens one's wits against those of a kindred spirit.

One man's lifetime is not long enough to learn all about eagles, and I often wish that when I was younger I had had the money and the freedom from earning a living that would have let me spend all my days in this pursuit. Unfortunately, the wherewithal to buy the traditional bottle of whisky is still needed. I do not ordinarily wish to travel beyond the Iron Curtain—I'd soon be shot if I did, because I'd give my guide the slip and be found, with binoculars, in some forbidden mountain valley. But I'd like to learn about the huge Steller's Sea Eagle of Kamschatka, and watch a trained Berkut chase a wolf—just to see properly how it did it. I'd like, too, to see the mighty Harpy of the Amazon, and some of the gay little forest hawk eagles of the far East. I may do some of these things yet; but on the whole I feel that it is better to stick to ground I know, and concentrate on elaborating knowledge from an already solid base. I know of no place other than one small mountain in the Embu District of Kenya where a small group of eagles has been continuously recorded for twenty-seven years; here I have learned all that is known of natural wild lifespans, and many other things. Nor do I know of any other large group of big eagles that has been as assiduously watched for a decade as the Verreaux's Eagles of the Matopos Hills in Rhodesia.

I therefore make no apology for extensive reference to African eagles here, for research on eagles is as advanced, more so in many respects, in tropical Africa as anywhere in the world. Moreover, the varied, often common and tame African eagles, still living relatively unmolested natural lives, can illumine our knowledge of the scarce, persecuted remnants of a few species which are all that most temperate developed countries can boast. No eagles are easier to study than African Fish Eagles, which consequently provide a unique opportunity for really detailed work, and are even now the best-known eagles in the world.

Would-be enthusiasts in this field tend to try to gravitate to Africa these days, partly because of the other outstanding natural history attractions of, especially, East Africa. While I do not deny that there is still much to learn here, one of my objects has been to demonstrate how relatively little is known about even magnificent large eagles in South America and tropical Asia east to New Guinea. I hope that any ornithologists living in these areas who may hanker after the Matopos or the Serengeti will now see how ripe and easily plucked are the fruits ready to hand—and pluck them.

I have tried here to marshal under different heads, so that anyone interested in a particular aspect or group can go straight to it, the state of our knowledge of every eagle in the world. Limitations of space mean that much interesting illustrative detail must be omitted. It will be obvious that many eagles are still relatively unknown, whereas others have been exhaustively studied for many years. This does not, of course, mean that there is nothing left to learn—I still see something new every day when I go to watch fish eagles, the best-known of all species because they can easily be watched all day and because they *must* kill their prey in the open where one can see exactly what they do. But there are a good many quite common species whose nests are unknown or barely described, and whose way of life, prey and mode of hunting have never been studied at all. Those who want to add to our knowledge might dedicate their energies to some of these, rather than follow in well-trodden paths.

The time has come, too, for eagle watchers to turn from the comparatively well-known aspects of breeding biology and the statistics of survival to the more difficult and challenging work of following an eagle through the day, finding out how often and how it kills, and so on. No one knows better than I the fascination of sitting in a hide at close quarters to watch an eagle at the nest—I believe I may still hold the record for the number of species so photographed. I know, too, that no eagle is properly appreciated if watched only at long range; everyone should look, eyeball to eyeball, into that piercing eye. Nevertheless, aided by electronic gadgetry (which I should instantly break), there is now a great opportunity to develop new fields of work; some has started. Even anatomists, collectors and falconers could help—and the latter should, to justify what they do. We know far too little about wing structures and wing-loading, which must control the flying performance of any flying machine, eagles included. We need a new good comparative study of eagles' eyes, to tell us, for instance, the exact limits of their visual acuity, and why snake eagles' eyes are so often yellow.

This book is intended, not as the voice of an oracle or the last word—for no one knows better than I that it is not—but as a springboard for new research, and a basis for argument and discourse. As I have said, eagle watchers tend to talk long and vehemently when they can. Long may this continue, for only thus can we sharpen each other's wits to learn what remains to be learned—and it is plenty.

Part I The Species of Eagles

1 Introducing Eagles

In 1800, an eagle might have been thought of as a large, powerful and unusually rapacious bird, capable of carrying off babies, credited with enormous strength and savagery, and endowed with extraordinary powers of flight. Of course, none ever did carry off babies; but such a concept fitted well enough the very large European Golden and Sea Eagle, or the American Bald Eagle, and could be stretched to include the smaller Lesser and Greater Spotted Eagles, Imperial and Tawny Eagles, perhaps even Bonelli's Eagle.

However, it was later recognised that there were also very small eagles, such as the Booted Eagle, some even smaller than buzzards (*Buteo* spp). In the far East, very small eagles were found, such as the relatively tiny Wallace's Hawk Eagle; and some very small species of snake eagles, such as the Nicobar Island Snake Eagle and the tiny Nias Island race of the Crested Serpent Eagle. Most of these small species are still comparatively little known; but it is clear even from a skin that the Nias Island race of the Crested Serpent Eagle is closely related to the typical Crested Serpent Eagle of India, twice its size, and possibly five times as heavy. Such small birds would probably not have been called eagles by a committee including, say, Aristotle, Linnaeus and Cuvier; but later scientists recognised that they were related to other much larger species, and so called them eagles.

Thus an eagle is nowadays best described, rather ambiguously, as a large or very large diurnal raptor which is not a kite, buzzard, vulture, hawk or falcon. The distinction between, especially, buzzards and eagles is tenuous. Some of the largest buzzards are bigger than small eagles, while some birds that anyone would call eagles are, systematically, just overgrown rapacious buzzards. The 'near buzzard' or Buteonine eagles actually include both the largest species in the world, the Harpy (probably the most formidable living bird) and the Philippine Monkey-eating Eagle. No one would suggest that Wallace's Hawk Eagle could carry off a baby; but a Harpy certainly could.

This rather elastic definition of eagles includes fifty-nine species in four groups, not very closely related to one another. They are:

1. The sea, fish, fishing eagles and Vulturine Fish Eagle of the genera *Haliaeetus*, *Ichthyophaga* and *Gypohierax*. All are large to very large, Steller's Sea Eagle being almost as big as a Harpy. All are mainly or entirely aquatic, feeding largely on fish and water birds, except the unique vegetarian Vulturine Fish Eagle, which feeds on oil-palm fruit. The sea and fish eagles are most obviously related to the oriental kites of the genus *Haliastur*, especially the sacred Indian Brahminy Kite. The Vulturine Fish Eagle may link this group with the Old World vultures through *Neophron*, the Egyptian Vulture. However, it is so unlike the Egyptian Vulture in habits that it is best to keep an open mind on the subject.

2. The snake eagles or serpent eagles, of the genera *Circaetus*, *Terathopius*, *Spilornis*, *Dryotriorchis*, and *Eutriorchis*. All but *Spilornis* are European or African, especially African, though the European Snake Eagle extends from southern France east to China. *Spilornis* is found in the tropical East and East Indies; but does not cross Wallace's line into Australasia.

Systematically, snake eagles are a specialised group, not obviously related to others. They appear rather closely related to the curious African Harrier Hawks, *Polyboroides*. In the accepted classification they follow the Old World vultures, to which they are certainly not closely related. Their specialised diet, mainly of snakes, includes also lizards and frogs. One very aberrant member, the magnificent African Bateleur, the almost tail-less original design for a flying wing, has a more catholic diet than the other snake eagles, but is nevertheless best placed in this group.

3. The buzzard-like or Buteonine eagles of South America, New Guinea and the Philippines, in the genera *Harpyhaliaetus*, *Harpia*, *Morphnus*, *Harpyopsis*, and *Pithecophaga*. Systematically, these seem the culmination of the buzzard line of evolution. They are all very large or enormous species, living mainly in forests and preying on large mammals such as monkeys and sloths; but the Solitary Eagles *Harpyhaliaetus* may also live in open country, and eat some snakes.

Most of these eagles have been little studied, except the magnificent Philippine Monkey-eating Eagle, not only the second largest eagle in the world, but also by far the most threatened, with less than a hundred wild individuals. Our ignorance of their ways seems strange, since several are huge, magnificent and alluringly rare. It results from their dense, often inaccessible, tropical forest habitat, and the fact that they live in countries lacking enthusiastic observers.

4. The 'true' or booted eagles, which differ from all others so far mentioned in having the legs, not bare and scaled, but feathered to the toes below the tarsal joint. I should prefer to call them 'trousered' rather than 'booted' since, to me, boots are worn on the feet. At some stage the ancestors of these eagles may have diverged from the buzzard stock to evolve some distinctive features. They are often swifter and more rapacious than buzzards, killing larger prey in proportion to their weight, and in better style.

Booted eagles vary from tiny species weighing less than $17\frac{1}{2}$ oz (500g) to huge birds such as the African Martial Eagle and the Asian Golden Eagle or Berkut, weighing almost as much as a Harpy Eagle and probably much more active and swift in flight. The twenty-nine species compose the genera *Ictinaetus, Aquila, Hieraaetus, Spizastur, Spizaetus* (including *Lophaetus*), *Stephanoaetus, Oroaetus* and *Polemaetus*. Some authorities would amalgamate *Hieraaetus* with *Spizastur*, and the last three with *Spizaetus*; or even simply call all *Aquila*. However, the *Aquila* eagles differ in bodily proportions, immature plumages, voice and habits; and the Crowned and Martial Eagles (*Stephanoaetus* and *Polemaetus*) are at least twice as big as most *Spizaetus* species.

Booted eagles feed on anything from termites and small birds to quite large mammals and carrion. They inhabit every type of terrain from desert to tropical forest, arctic to equatorial, plains to mountain peaks. The most markedly aberrant member of the group is the Indian Black Eagle *Ictinaetus*, which some consider resembles a kite with feathered tarsi; however, until it is better known it remains in this group.

Although many eagles have been studied intensively for so long that their way of life is, considering the difficulties involved, relatively well known, there is still plenty left to learn. The nests of a total of fourteen out of fifty-nine species have never been described, and only a few species, not always the most magnificent, have really been studied in detail.

For convenience I define the state of our knowledge of eagles at five levels.

1. Intimately known. The general habits, diurnal behaviour, food preferences and breeding biology are thoroughly understood, with a long series of observations at nests in the same area for many successive years.

2. Very well known. The general distribution, habits,

migrations, food preferences, etc are understood; and detailed observations are available for the breeding cycle at one nest at least.

3. Well known. There is a good general idea of distribution, abundance, food and general habits, but with little specific detail. The nest, clutch size, etc is described but no complete description of even one breeding cycle is available.

4. Little known. Very few published observations are available, only a few records of food taken, and only odd descriptions of nests and eggs, without any sustained observations.

5. Unknown, or sketchily known. The nest has never been found, the status of the bird is obscure, and almost nothing is recorded of its habits and food preferences.

One can further subdivide these categories of knowledge to cover more specific aspects of an eagle's life; for instance, its general habits; its behaviour from dawn to dark; hunting methods; food preferences (often a very important point for conservationists); its breeding biology, and survival and longevity (including moults and immature plumages). Only if we have a good idea of all these aspects of eagle behaviour can we say that a particular species is well known. An eagle whose breeding habits have been much studied (because this is relatively easy) may have been little studied away from the nest.

Appendix 1 contains a list of the world's eagles in systematic order, with a summary of the present state of our knowledge on these six aspects of their biology. If the level of knowledge is thus assessed for each separate aspect, at five levels for which 2-10 points can be given, we can quantify our knowledge more accurately. It then becomes clear how very few are really well known, and how the much greater proportion are little known. Even the continued existence of one still almost unknown snake eagle may be in doubt.

The maximum number of points attainable is 60. No eagle, on present available published knowledge, attains this. The best-known species, all round, is the African Fish Eagle, with 56 points; perhaps it should get 58 because its food preferences are actually very well known. Next come Verreaux's Eagle and the Golden Eagle, each with 54/60. Although better known in several respects than any other species, their detailed diurnal behaviour and hunting methods are not well enough described. The Golden Eagle's breeding behaviour is better known than appears in published accounts.

Five other eagles attain the low 50s; the Bald Eagle, the

European Snake Eagle, Wahlberg's Eagle, Bonelli's Eagle (with its African race) and the Crowned Eagle. Some more study of diurnal behaviour, hunting methods, breeding biology and, especially, survival would place Bonelli's near the top. The European Snake Eagle loses on survival and longevity; but probably more is known about this than is published. The Crowned Eagle, in some ways better known than any other, loses points on hunting methods and diurnal behaviour, principally because of the difficulty of locating and watching it in thick forest. Wahlberg's Eagle loses on general habits because we do not really know where it spends half the year.

Thus only eight out of fifty-nine eagle species attain more than 50 out of a possible 60 points. Eleven more, one sea eagle, three snake eagles (one a race of the European) and seven booted eagles attain between 40 and 50 points. All the rest are below 40; and one sea eagle, seven snake eagles, two harpy group eagles, and eight booted or true eagles (eighteen altogether) get less than 20, even on a fairly generous estimate of present knowledge. Thus about one-third of all the world's eagles are very little known. Many of these are relatively small forest species, the most difficult to study; and political events, and lack of interest by the people of some countries have also affected our ignorance of these groups.

Of course, no eagle should really attain top marks in any category because we cannot say that no problems remain; research is never complete. However, I hope Appendix 1 assesses quite realistically and objectively the state of our present knowledge; and directs attention to geographical areas and aspects of behaviour in particular species where our knowledge is weakest. In this way it may help enthusiasts in the future to avoid duplication of work already done, and enable them to concentrate on acquiring the new knowledge so badly needed for many eagles.

2 Sea and Fish Eagles

The eleven sea and fish eagles form a very distinct group, superficially and in habits resembling some other eagles, but probably most nearly related to the scavenging Asian and Australasian kites of the genus *Haliastur*, notably the sacred Indian Brahminy Kite. One systematist has described the African Fish Eagle as 'only a great big Brahminy Kite'. Having known the Brahminy Kite since my boyhood, and having studied the African Fish Eagle intensively, I can assert that, despite the superficial similarity of chestnut and white plumage, the African Fish Eagle resembles other large fish eagles more than the Brahminy Kite. Nevertheless, the African and other fish and sea eagles do in some ways behave like kites; notably in their highly piratical habits, and in certain stages of their nuptial displays.

Head of American Bald Eagle (*P. Morris, Ardea Photographics*)

The eight members of the genus *Haliaeetus* include all the 'typical' sea and fish eagles. Only one, the American Bald Eagle, inhabits the New World. Of the other seven, four—the European Sea Eagle, White-tailed Eagle or Erne, Pallas' Sea Eagle, Steller's Sea Eagle and the White-bellied Sea Eagle—inhabit Europe and Asia, the White-bellied extending to Australasia. Two, the African Fish Eagle and the Madagascar Fish Eagle, inhabit the Ethiopian region, being commonest in the tropical parts; and one, Sanford's Sea Eagle, inhabits the Solomon Islands.

Three species, Steller's, the European and the Bald Eagle, are very large or enormous, spanning 7ft (2.14m) or more and weighing 8lb 12oz to 17lb 8oz (4-8kg). Steller's Sea Eagle would compete with the huge South American Harpy for the title of the world's most impressive bird of prey, for a female weighs 18lb 9oz (8.5kg). The other five members of this genus are large, but not enormous. The impressive and beautiful African Fish Eagle is yet one of the smaller, spanning about 6½ft (2m) and weighing 4lb 6oz to 7lb 10oz (2-3.5kg) according to sex.

Only three, the European Sea Eagle, the American Bald Eagle and the African Fish Eagle, are very well known or better, the African Fish Eagle being probably the best-known eagle in the world, perhaps because it is so easy to watch. However, there is as yet no really good published account of the breeding behaviour of any of these species. All three, especially the African Fish Eagle, have had their population dynamics studied in depth, stimulated in recent times by the threat of extinction of the Erne and Bald Eagle in parts of their range.

The enormous, magnificent Steller's Sea Eagle, the White-bellied Sea Eagle and Pallas' Sea Eagle are only fairly well known and Sanford's Sea Eagle is practically unknown; its nest has never been found and little is recorded of its habits, though it appears more likely than other sea eagles to live inland in forest and prey on mammals. There is, therefore, plenty of scope left for research on the less well-known members of the genus.

The two so-called fishing eagles of the genus *Ichthyophaga* inhabit India, Malaysia and Indonesia. Smaller than true sea or fish eagles, they are still large birds, the larger Grey-headed Fishing Eagle weighing 3lb 8oz to 5lb 14oz (1.6-2.7kg), comparable to a male African Fish Eagle. Neither is well known; no long-term breeding studies nor any good population data exist; however, there is no reason to suppose that either species is endangered. Any keen observer in

Malaysia or Indonesia could, in a year or two, add greatly to our knowledge of fishing eagles.

The African Vulturine Fish Eagle or Palm-nut Vulture is a unique, aberrant, mainly vegetarian bird of prey which subsists largely on the fatty pericarp of oil-palm fruits. Possibly its immediate ancestors scavenged and caught small fish in coastal creeks, flood-plain swamps and large rivers. Here they may have learned to pick up the fallen oil-palm nuts, then spread inland, finally into forested areas where there may be little water but abundant oil palms. With few exceptions, which may not be breeding birds, the range of this extraordinary raptor is today closely coincident with that of the oil palm, but again it is a bird that has never been fully studied.

The Vulturine Fish Eagle is sometimes called the Palm-nut Vulture because of its bare face; and it may possibly link the sea eagles with the Old World vultures through the genus *Neophron*, the Egyptian Vulture, which superficially resembles the Vulturine Fish Eagle in its black and white adult plumage and dark brown immature. However, the Egyptian Vulture lives mainly in deserts or arid country, nests in holes in cliffs, and is so unlike the Vulturine Fish Eagle in its other habits that it would be unwise to dogmatise on possible links between the two.

Vulturine Fish Eagles resemble vultures in having a very long incubation period in relation to their size, and somewhat scavenging habits, but more thorough comparative studies are needed to establish true relationships. Both the bare face and the scavenging habits are shared by other raptors not closely related: for instance the South American Caracaras and the African Harrier Hawk *Polyboroides*. A bare face may merely be associated with eating oily or messy food, and need not indicate any close relationship with vultures. To me, the Vulturine Fish Eagle seems more like a true fish eagle than a vulture.

Although only three of eleven in this group are very well known or better, enough is known about all except Sanford's Sea Eagle to say that all (even the unique Vulturine Fish Eagle) are inclined to prefer the neighbourhood of water and will feed on fish when they can, augmenting this fishy diet with water birds and carrion, especially the three large northern species in winter. They seldom stay long in arid areas, but they may migrate over such areas, though rarely lingering there; and they sometimes roost in winter in unlikely places. The most 'landlocked' of all is Pallas' Sea Eagle, inhabiting the rivers, lakes and swamps of central Asia and found even on the mountainous, arid Tibetan plateau, as long as there are lakes and fish. In winter it migrates to, for instance, the Caspian Sea.

Besides catching their own fish, sea and fish eagles feed much on dead cast-up fish, dependence on this varying according to species and locality. The American Bald Eagle and Steller's Sea Eagle both feed in winter on abundant dead and dying Pacific salmon kelts. In contrast, the African Fish Eagle catches most of its own fish; it may even ignore a putrid dead one. It varies its diet with the adults and young of water birds; and may come to carrion far from water in the African bush.

Fish and sea eagles are less spectacular in their fishing methods than are Ospreys, normally snatching fish close to the surface in a neat sweeping movement which lifts the fish with the eagle's momentum. For this reason they may select fish species which are inclined to bask near the surface or are forced to come to the surface for air such as catfish and African lungfish. The White-bellied Sea Eagle takes many highly venomous sea snakes, since these, too, must surface to breathe. Deep-swimming, active fish such as healthy salmon or trout, or bottom-feeders, are practically immune from fish eagles. Rarely, the eagles may plunge right in with a dramatic splash or, more often, they descend gently like a parachute until they can finally drop on a fish near the surface.

What little is known of the habits of fishing eagles of the genus *Ichthyophaga* suggests that they are even more confined to aquatic habits than members of the genus *Haliaeetus*. They are apparently even less likely than true fish and sea eagles to catch fish by a spectacular plunge, but perhaps more likely to take dead or cast-up fish. Apparently they do not take young or adult water birds.

Sea and fish eagles also frequently pirate the catch of other fishing birds, such as pelicans, storks or herons, and especially Ospreys, which must often catch several fish before they can keep one. This piratical habit seems unrecorded in fishing eagles (*Ichthyophaga*). Piracy can be almost compulsive, carried so far in the African Fish Eagle that it will even pirate another bird's prey when not itself hungry; parents will rob their own young; an incubating bird will leave its nest to pursue another fish eagle; and one of a pair will even rob its mate. This piratical habit is also very strongly developed among kites.

The sea and fish eagles (*Haliaeetus*) often take the young and adults of water birds, and the European Sea Eagle takes diving ducks, especially eiders, and auks. Adult water birds

African Fish Eagle, the world's best known eagle *(Norman Myers)*

may escape the eagle's attack by flying; or they may dive, in which case the eagle has only to soar above and force them to dive repeatedly to catch them at will. Diving ducks, such as eiders, are apparently more vulnerable than more powerful underwater swimmers such as cormorants. The African Fish Eagle seldom takes water birds when fish is available; but on alkaline lakes lacking fish it becomes a pure bird-eater killing, for instance, adults of both species of flamingoes. It takes many young from breeding colonies of herons, storks, spoonbills, darters and cormorants; but seldom catches active adult water birds.

Carrion, such as dead cast-up fish, whales, seals and so on, is important winter diet for the three large northern species. Many may congregate round a dead whale and feed on it for weeks. The survival of Bald Eagles in Alaska has probably been assisted in recent years by human rubbish dumps, doubtless rich in discarded portions of hot dogs and hamburgers and even the T-bones of specially flown-in Texas steaks. In tropical climates carrion tends to be rather a last resort; it does not normally keep so well, or last so long in the presence of other scavengers such as hyenas. Even here it may be important for immatures; immature African Fish Eagles are more likely to be found at carrion than are adults. The carrion-eating habit has lately been put to good use in Sweden and East Germany by inducing the few remaining European Sea Eagles to come to pesticide-free carcases put out for them, a desperate measure to try to save the remnant of a dwindling population.

It seems likely that all sea and fish eagles, and fishing eagles, obtain their prey relatively easily. These birds probably spend most of each day perched or loafing; and if they fly it may not be to hunt, but to soar or display. This is further discussed under hunting methods, Chapter 11.

All that the mainly vegetarian Vulturine Fish Eagle normally has to do is to locate a ripe bunch of oil-palm nuts, walk hand-over-hand up the palm frond, and feed on the fruit at will. The same oil palms are visited day after day and the bird sometimes directly competes with human oil-palm growers. However, there are generally enough wild palms to satisfy the bird. Although it can use alternative food supplies such as small fish, crabs, molluscs and carrion the Vulturine Fish Eagle is never common in areas without abundant oil palms. It used to be thought that its peculiar diet was due to an unusually high demand for vitamin A; but captive birds manage quite well without palm fruit.

All fish and sea eagles, fishing eagles and the Vulturine Fish Eagle breed in trees where available. In northern latitudes the Erne and Bald Eagle may breed on sea cliffs, on outlying skerries, or even on the ground. Certain tree species may be selected. Most nests of the African Fish Eagle are in large figs with smooth scaling bark, thorny Euphorbias with acid milky latex, or Acacias with both smooth bark and always ferocious thorns. A dead tree standing in water may be used if available; shade for the young is apparently less important than inaccessibility. Such site selection may help to avoid attacks by animals such as ratels or genet cats at night, or the persecution of monkeys and baboons.

In wooded areas the nests of sea eagles are the largest made by any raptor, consistently larger, related to the size of the bird, even than those of the larger booted eagles. However in the treeless interior of Iceland, European Sea Eagles cannot

African Fish Eagle calling (*Clem Haagner, Ardea Photographics*)

make big nests for lack of material; they then may breed in a scrape on top of a column of rock, adding only a few bits of vegetation and feathers. The normal huge nests are often situated in the largest available trees, may be visible for miles in, for instance, an isolated tall tree growing in mangroves or low forest, and are easy to find, or even to observe from the air, as they are very often open to the sky. If undisturbed, the site continues to be occupied by a succession of different birds for many years, perhaps even for centuries. Pairs normally have one to three nests; but often only one.

Fish eagles and sea eagles are more likely than any others to perform the spectacular whirling or spinning nuptial displays with the feet locked together. They tend to lay rather larger clutches of eggs than other large eagles, two being usual and three common. They also tend to rear larger broods, perhaps because the young are less aggressive to one another than those of some other eagles. This implies, as a corollary, that the average wild life-span of sea eagles is shorter than in eagles that lay only one egg and rear smaller broods. However, for most species there is not enough good long-term data available to dogmatise on such points; and much data recently gathered for northern species is also suspect because it is affected by human interference, or pesticides, or both.

Two species, the European Sea Eagle and the American Bald Eagle, have decreased greatly, or have been exterminated in parts of their range, since 1800. The European Sea Eagle was exterminated in Britain by gamekeepers and egg collectors, in that order of menace, by 1916. There is little hope of the species re-establishing itself naturally because the Scandinavian population is largely sedentary in winter (unlike that of the Osprey, which has re-established itself in Britain but is migratory). The sea eagle can only be re-established in Britain by a long, costly and probably unpopular reintroduction programme.

Since 1950 there has been a further sharp decline in the populations of American Bald Eagles and European Sea Eagles, especially in Florida, central North America, Sweden and Germany. The Bald Eagle has locally become extinct. The decline is attributed largely to pollution of inland waters with organochlorine and mercury pesticides, the latter especially in Sweden. The eagles absorb these poisons from their prey. In the 1960s, Swedish Baltic Sea Eagles contained sixty times as much mercury in their feathers as in the nineteenth century, while Bald Eagles have been killed experimentally by feeding them diets rich in DDT. Lately the decline seems to have halted or slowed; but the Swedish and German population of European Sea Eagles is now very small and threatened. In the far north of Europe and North America, in Lapland and Alaska and also in part of Florida, the populations of both species are healthy and not declining.

Contact with civilised man and pollution spells doom for sea eagles. Although pesticides deservedly receive most of the blame for the decline, other human activities have contributed. Breeding grounds are more than ever disturbed by large numbers of people in pleasure craft or fishing; and active illegal persecution by killing and egg collecting has not entirely ceased.

To what degree other species are affected is not fully known, but fears have been expressed for the survival of Steller's Sea Eagle, one race of which has certainly become rare. Pallas' Sea Eagle, in view of the heavy level of contamination in such waters as the Caspian Sea, could also be in trouble. Recent studies of African Fish Eagles at Lake Naivasha, however, have indicated very low levels of pesticide residues in the food chains at present, and no reduction in breeding success. This species is certainly not in danger. The most likely to be endangered, on first principles, are the island species, the Madagascar Fish Eagle and Sanford's Sea Eagle. However, Madagascar is a very large island,

and the eagle is apparently quite common in extensive mangrove swamps. The Solomon Islands are little developed, so that probably neither of these species is in immediate danger of extinction. The Vulturine Fish Eagle and both species of fishing eagles are wide-ranging and apparently not at present threatened, despite events such as the Vietnam War in part of their habitat.

The species at present most in need of research is Sanford's Sea Eagle. Where does it nest? And does it depart from normal sea-eagle habits and subsist largely on forest mammals? The Vulturine Fish Eagle, easy to study in many West African countries, also deserves more research. Is it or is it not a link between fish eagles and vultures? In fact is it a fish eagle at all? We do not know the answer to this question, or to many others one could pose concerning this group of eagles.

3 Snake Eagles

The snake or serpent eagles are another highly specialised group of large birds of prey not obviously closely related to other eagles or, for that matter, to any other birds of prey. They are certainly not closely related to Old World vultures (which they follow in the accepted classification), and may be more closely related to the curious African Harrier Hawk *Polyboroides* and the South American Crane Hawk *Geranospiza*, which in turn follow them; but resemblances to these birds may only be superficial.

Some species of snake eagles are called harrier eagles because of a fancied resemblance to harriers of the genus *Circus* in flight. However, observation shows this to be absurd. Harriers habitually hunt close to the ground, alternately flapping and gliding. Snake eagles may also fly by alternately flapping and gliding—so do other eagles when they cannot soar; but most snake eagles normally hunt from perches, and two that do not, the European Snake Eagle (with its African races) and the unique and aberrant Bateleur, hunt respectively by hovering and by swift gliding to and fro. Neither in the least resembles the behaviour of harriers. Since all snake eagles mainly feed on snakes, the misleading name 'harrier eagle' should be abandoned; they should be called snake or serpent eagles, as several already are.

The twelve species of snake eagles compose five genera: *Circaetus* (four); *Terathopius* (one); *Spilornis* (five); *Dryotriorchis* (one); and *Eutriorchis* (one). All but the eastern serpent eagles *Spilornis* inhabit Europe, Asia and the Ethiopian region. None occurs in America or Australia. The

Madagascar Serpent Eagle *Eutriorchis astur* inhabits Madagascar. The European Short-toed or Serpent Eagle *Circaetus g. gallicus* extends from south Europe east to China; and it has two other races in tropical Africa, Beaudouin's Snake Eagle *C. g. beaudouini* and the Black-breasted Snake Eagle *C. g. pectoralis*. Although some persist in calling these separate species, the fact that the last two interbreed and all three form mixed pairs shows that it is best to regard them as races.

All species of the eastern genus *Spilornis* are obviously closely allied. The most widespread, the Crested Serpent

A female Brown Snake Eagle near nest with a still-writhing Yellow-bellied Grass Snake in her bill
(Peter Steyn)

Eagle *S. cheela,* has no less than twenty-one races, varying enormously in size, of which five are continental and the remainder, including some of the smallest eagles, are found on various East Indian islands. The other four species are very like the Crested Serpent Eagle; one, the Philippine Serpent Eagle *S. philippensis,* is often regarded as a race of *S. cheela.* All live in islands of Indonesia, the Philippines and the Andaman and Nicobar groups. Except for the rare and little-known Andaman Serpent Eagle *S. elgini* (which overlaps with a race of the Crested Serpent Eagle *S. c. davisoni*), no two occur in the same island. In the Andamans, where these two species occur together, they are ecologically separated.

The Congo Serpent Eagle *Dryotriorchis spectabilis* and the Madagascar Serpent Eagle are so little known that their precise relationships are obscure. Both are, however, obviously snake eagles; and the Madagascar Serpent Eagle resembles the eastern *Spilornis* more than the African *Circaetus* species. Both inhabit dense forest; and the eyes of the Congo Serpent Eagle are very large, probably adapted for vision in dim light.

The most aberrant of all snake eagles is the magnificent, unique Bateleur *Terathopius ecaudatus.* The black, white and chestnut adult plumage, with scarlet feet and face, is completely unlike that of any other snake eagle. The young, however, is brown, rather resembling a young Brown Snake Eagle *Circaetus cinereus,* distinguishable by its longer, barred tail and yellow eye. Further, the Bateleur is aerodynamically highly specialised, the adult especially having very long wings and practically no tail—the feet project beyond the stump in flight; the tail of the young is relatively longer. Resembling a design for an original flying wing, the magnificent adult glides swiftly and continuously across the African savannas and plains, using hunting methods totally different from any other snake eagle, or any other bird of prey. The very long wings contain more secondary feathers than those of all but a few large vultures; and alone among snake eagles, both adult and immature Bateleurs have soft brown eyes. However, recent research on the breeding behaviour of the Bateleur shows that the young develops like a young Brown Snake Eagle. Other anatomical similarities, and a raucous crowing voice like that of several *Circaetus* species, show that the Bateleur is best regarded as an aberrant, specialised snake eagle.

All snake eagles, including the Bateleur and *Spilornis,* have certain common anatomical features which may relate to their mode of hunting and preferred prey. Their heads are rather large, cowled or crested, less strikingly so in forest-loving species. All have short, stubby, strong toes, apparently well adapted for grasping and rapidly killing slim, writhing snakes: if one passes a piece of plastic hose through one's fingers, one realises that short thick toes are more efficient for grasping such quarry than are, for instance, the long thin toes of a sparrowhawk or harrier. All but the Bateleur have large, often brilliant, bright or pale yellow eyes, even in immature plumage.

The fact that the Bateleur is the only snake eagle which does not habitually feed mainly on snakes suggests that these brilliant yellow eyes may relate to a reptilian diet. Perhaps they denote unusually keen vision, since reptiles are often well camouflaged. The fact that immatures have them when they leave the nest suggests that they have nothing to do with nuptial display or aggression.

The best-known of all snake eagles is the European Snake Eagle. Through a classic study by Yves Boudouint it is intimately known at the nest; its hunting methods and survival rate are less well documented, though probably more is known than has been published. Its African race, the Black-breasted Snake Eagle, is also well known, as are the Brown Snake Eagle and Bateleur. The African Smaller Banded and the Southern Banded Snake Eagles are little known. Although the Crested Serpent Eagle is quite common and often obvious in much of its continental range, it has only once been studied in any detail at the nest. The Philippine Serpent Eagle, Celebes Serpent Eagle, Nicobar Serpent Eagle and Andaman Serpent Eagle are all very little known. The nests and eggs of these four, and those of the Congo and Madagascar Serpent Eagles, have never been described. There is therefore plenty of scope for research on this group, especially on the common eastern species.

Enough is known, however, to show that they all (excepting the Bateleur) habitually feed on snakes, some lizards and some frogs. The Bateleur varies this diet by killing many birds and some mammals, by taking carrion, and by pirating prey from other large birds such as vultures. Since they depend mainly on snakes, lizards and frogs, all the snake eagles are birds of the tropics or subtropics and of low altitudes, mainly in plains, forests and savannas, but also in deserts (where reptiles can be common). Breeding in the southern temperate zone, the European Snake Eagle migrates to the tropics in winter. Even in the tropics, cold nights at high altitudes limit or eliminate reptiles and frogs above about 8,000ft (2,440m) so that one sees no hunting snake eagles on high mountains—except the aberrant Bateleur, which catches rats on moorlands at 13,000ft (3,965m).

As long as they can find snakes and lizards, snake eagles have adapted to every habitat from open desert to dense, dimly-lit tropical forest. They are perhaps commonest in mixed forest, woodland and savannas. The European Snake Eagle and its African races occur on open heaths in Europe, open scrubby country, deserts, grass plains and light woodland, but not in dense woodland or forest. The eastern *Spilornis* species occur mainly in woodland or forest, but also among cultivation. Snakes are most abundant in relatively lush vegetation, though lizards are common in deserts. Their cryptic coloration, slim forms, stealthy movements and, in deserts, nocturnal habits may, however, make them hard to find even where they are common.

In a mosaic of African habitats, four species may occur together, for instance the Black-breasted, Brown, and Smaller Banded Snake Eagles and the Bateleur. They are then ecologically separated by mode of hunting and habitat preference. The Black-breasted Snake Eagle hunts mainly in open country, by hovering; the Brown Snake Eagle in denser woodland from perches; the Smaller Banded Snake Eagle in heavy riverine woodland from perches; and the Bateleur by streaking across the sky, ignoring the others. The ranges of the Smaller Banded and Southern Banded Snake Eagles, which prefer similar habitats of heavy woodland, do not overlap. The Andaman Serpent Eagle and the Andaman Island race of the Crested Serpent Eagle occur together; but one inhabits the interior forests and the other coastal mangrove swamps. Thus competition for available prey is minimised.

Most snake eagles hunt from perches, often within heavy cover. The regular hovering of the European Snake Eagle and its African races amounts to aerial perching over open country. The Brown Snake Eagle soars and perches in the open more often than the Smaller Banded, which frequents heavier woodland. In the east, Crested Serpent Eagles are usually seen perched in woodland or forest when hunting. So far as is known the forest-loving species, such as the Congo Serpent Eagle and other eastern *Spilornis* species, also habitually hunt from perches.

Snake eagles seldom take any other prey but snakes; even the Bateleur eats many snakes. A captive snake eagle may not be excited by the presence of a rat in its cage, but is immediately interested in a piece of writhing rope or hose. Quite how a snake eagle catches a snake is not very clear. Small ones are probably snatched into the air, and are then unable to strike effectively even if venomous. The snake eagle shifts its foothold along the body, as one might pass a piece of tubing through closed fists, and eventually grips and mangles the potentially dangerous fanged head, usually with its bill. Large snakes must be killed on the ground, but here too the head is crushed as soon as possible. Snake eagles seem able to avoid danger from formidable, striking snakes by agility and by their thick feathers. The snake gets only a mouthful of feathers and does not inject its venom, to which snake eagles are not immune, into the bloodstream.

In Europe, where the common venomous snakes are sluggish, cryptically-coloured vipers, snake eagles habitually feed on and perhaps actually select harmless slim-bodied but more conspicuous grass or water snakes. In Africa, however, many such slim snakes are mambas and cobras, both venomous and formidable. Snake eagles certainly do kill these, and even kill large, thick-bodied, highly venomous vipers such as puff adders. Here, then, there is evidently no selection of non-venomous prey.

Small snakes are simply swallowed whole; many are light for their length, and even a long one can easily be lifted and swallowed in the air. The eagle feeds the snake in inch by inch, usually head first, till all but a bit of the tail has disappeared. Larger snakes must be carried in the feet, and very large ones partly or wholly dismembered and eaten where they are killed. The fact that a snake is venomous does not hurt the eagle that swallows it, for provided that it has no wounds in mouth or throat the venom cannot enter the bloodstream, and is easily digested—as is the whole snake, bones and all, except the scales.

To watch a snake eagle feed its sitting mate or young is one of the great highlights of an eagle watcher's experience. The bringer of prey arrives at the nest with several inches of snake, often still wriggling, protruding from its beak. It offers this to mate or offspring, which seizes it in its beak. Then one leans back, the other pulls, and out comes a foot or so of snake. The process, irresistibly reminding those who have suffered such an indignity of a stomach tube, is repeated as often as necessary, till finally the snake lies in the nest. It is then picked up and swallowed, head first again, by sitting adult or young. Very large snakes must be torn up and fed to small chicks; but owing, presumably, to their unique ability to pack a snake straight down into the gut it is astonishing how large a snake a downy eaglet will engulf.

Most snake eagles apparently require large hunting ranges,

and are accordingly uncommon. The European Snake Eagle and the eastern Crested Serpent Eagle appear to differ from this general rule. Two pairs of European Snake Eagles have been known to nest 150yd (135.25m) apart, though a more usual distance between pairs is 1,000-2,000yd (915-1,830m). However, since the nests of European Snake Eagles are built where suitable trees grow on slopes, the actual hunting range of open country may be much larger than the 2-3 square miles (5.18-7 77sq km) suggested by the interval between nests. The larger African snake eagles, the Black-breasted and the Brown Snake Eagle, certainly require more than 10 (25.9) perhaps up to 50 (129.5) square miles (km) per pair, while the more aerial Bateleur, despite a more varied diet, probably needs 50-70 square miles (129.5-181.3sq km). The Bateleur is *seen* far more than the others because of its aerial habits; but it may not actually be more numerous than other species which spend most of their time perched.

The area required by pairs of Crested Serpent Eagles in one area of mangrove swamp in Malaya was small. Twenty pairs were found in a few square miles. Such a density is probably unusual for this species, judging by experience in India, where this species seems only a little more numerous than some African snake eagles.

In the breeding season, even otherwise secretive snake eagles often make themselves obvious by noisy nuptial displays. The voices of the Brown, Smaller Banded and Southern Banded Snake Eagles, and of the Bateleur, are deep, raucous and crowing, attracting attention to the bird at long range, whether perched or, more often, soaring. The eastern Crested Serpent Eagles soar and utter a loud, high-pitched scream. The voice of the European Snake Eagle and of its two African races is, however, mellow and whistling, not nearly so loud. There is apparently a direct connection between loud raucous voices and frequent calling, and habitat in dense woodland or forest. Young in the nest are all apt to squall loudly, betraying the site, otherwise hard to locate.

Other notable features of the breeding season in snake eagles include some unusual displays; the making of very small nests, normally new each year; the laying of single eggs, large for the size of the bird; long incubation and fledging periods relative to size; and, so far as is known, a low overall reproductive rate. Their breeding habits are, in fact, strikingly different from those of most other eagles.

Snake eagles are the only eagles known to perform true distraction displays, and those seldom. Such displays have been seen in the European Snake Eagle; and curious bowing and wing-jerking antics by Bateleurs near the nest, apparently aggressive, are more likely to be attempts to distract. Bateleurs are also, occasionally, seen to perform the most astonishing 360 degree rolls in flight, which one would not believe physically possible unless actually witnessed. Several rolls in quick succession making a loud clapping sound, audible 2 miles (3.2km) away, may be a unique advertisement display.

Nests are normally small, slight structures, built in the crowns of trees, in southern Europe usually stunted pines, in Africa mainly on flat-topped acacias, or in the even more formidable circular crowns of Euphorbia fronds, defended by both thorns and acid latex. Again, the Bateleur is an exception, building a more solid nest or sometimes using the empty nest of a much larger eagle. Crested Serpent Eagles also build small, slight, leafy nests, generally within the canopy of a tree. These small nests are not usually used for more than a year, being built afresh, often in the same general area but sometimes at some distance from the previous year's. The small nests, frequent changes of site and secretive habits of the sitting bird makes snake eagles' nests more difficult to find than those of any other eagles.

No snake eagle is known to lay more than one egg; reputed clutches of two may be wrongly identified. The eggs are large, rounded, white or whitish, and normally unmarked. Normally only the female incubates, fed on the nest by the male, who may incubate briefly if at all, and only by day. Incubation periods are normally long, forty-seven days in the European Snake Eagle, and fifty or more in the other species accurately observed, including the Bateleur. However incubation periods in Crested Serpent Eagles are apparently much shorter, estimates varying from twenty-eight to thirty-five days; but really accurate data are lacking for any eastern snake eagle.

In all species so far well studied, including the Bateleur, the development of the young is similar. The very large head is obvious in the early downy stage. The feathers grow in first on the back, head and upper surface of the wings, apparently an adaptation to the very open nest site, usually right on top of a tree in the full blaze of the sun. The belly and tail region remain unfeathered much later than in most eagles and the fact that the Bateleur has a similar mode of plumage development strongly supports the view that its origins are with the snake eagles. Fledging periods are invariably long for the size of the bird, 70-75 days in the European Snake Eagle, 90-110 days in the African *Circaetus* species and the Bateleur. In the Crested Serpent Eagle the variation is said to be 60-120 days, scarcely credible. Early in the fledging period the female stays on the nest with the young, but once the latter's body is covered with feathers it is left alone in the nest, and both parents visit it at long intervals bringing snakes; they may not even roost nearby. Since the young can swallow large snakes whole, unaided, if more than one snake is brought during the day no more parental visits may occur for several days.

To a human observer the antics of young snake eagles are comical. Much less active generally than other young eagles, they make their first flights with extreme caution, and only when nearly mature. Gingerly spreading their wings on a breeze, they slowly rise a few feet, then often collapse back into the nest, apparently shaken by their experience. Even after they leave the nest they may squat on a branch, perfectly visible, but futilely performing instinctive defensive behaviour which serves to conceal them while still in the nest.

The extraordinary Bateleur again differs in its nesting habits. It builds a large nest, usually in a shaded fork, and uses it year after year. Such a nest is often close to a path, road or river bed, along which humans may walk. However, the Bateleur, although apparently not disturbed by people passing close, bitterly resents any attempt to climb to the nest, performing aggressive displays and diving at the intruder with loudly flapping wings. Attempts to photograph the Bateleur at the nest by the usual method of constructing a hide have always caused acute alarm or actual desertion; photography of the Bateleur at the nest should not therefore be attempted.Other snake eagles are no more difficult to photograph in this way than any other bird of prey.

All evidence suggests that snake eagles have a low reproductive rate and must, accordingly, be long-lived. Some pairs do not breed every year; the egg is invariably a singleton; and the overall replacement rate of young fledged per pair is low or very low. Full data are not published for the European Snake Eagle, but scanty African data suggest a replacement rate of 0.1-0.6 young per pair per annum, averaging about one young per pair per three years. If this low replacement rate is coupled with normal high mortality of around 75 per cent before sexual maturity, few adult replacements can be available each year. This could be serious in such areas as France, where the European Snake Eagle is senselessly persecuted; however, here the replacement rate may be higher than in the tropical African species.

Age to maturity has only been studied in the aberrant and

specialised Bateleur. Moult studies of captive Bateleurs suggest they are not fully mature till at least seven, perhaps eight years old. The proportion of immatures in the whole population is about 31 per cent, from which the average age of adults is calculated at 16.1 years, or 23.1 years altogether. No good data are available for any other species; but a young Black-breasted Snake Eagle which died when two years old suggested that it would have become mature when about four. One recent observer claims that the Crested Serpent Eagle can breed in its second year; but this is so unlike any other species that it needs confirmation.

The European Snake Eagle is the only species ever persecuted, and only in part of its range, France and southern Europe. Such persecution is pointless, because the bird is completely harmless to any human interests. Only one species, the Madagascar Serpent Eagle, is acutely threatened with extinction, and this by the destruction of its forest habitat. It has not been seen by any observer in Madagascar for several years, and may even have gone into oblivion unnoticed. However, like all forest snake eagles, it is hard to find, so there is hope that it survives. The Southern Banded Snake Eagle, which has limited, mainly coastal and lowland forest habitat is not acutely threatened at present. Possibly some small island races of the Crested Serpent Eagle may also be threatened; but nothing is known about them.

Their unique diet, anatomical and behavioural peculiarities, and the details of their breeding cycle set the snake eagles apart from any other birds called eagles. Fish and sea eagles, harpies and booted eagles are far more like one another than any snake eagles. In fact, if some snake eagles were not evidently in the eagle size-range one would not call them eagles at all. The extraordinary Bateleur, always thought of as a magnificent eagle, shows more similarities to snake eagles than to others. It is to be hoped especially that some of the relatively common but little-known eastern Serpent Eagles of the genus *Spilornis* will soon be given the detailed study they deserve.

4 The Harpy Group

The six eagles included here are, systematically, very large and sometimes exceptionally powerful and rapacious buzzards, anatomically allied to the widespread genus *Buteo* by their bare tarsus and other characters. They are sometimes called Buteonine eagles, and appear the culmination of a line of evolution in the Buzzard group, best represented in the

Americas. However, neither the gigantic Harpy Eagle nor the fractionally smaller Philippine Monkey-eating Eagle could ever be thought of as buzzards, whatever their anatomical relationships.

All six are large or very large, strikingly coloured eagles of tropical forest or savanna, similarities of habit suggesting a common origin despite peculiar geographical distribution. Four, the Harpy itself, the Guiana Crested Eagle and the Black and Crowned Solitary Eagles, inhabit South America. The New Guinea Harpy Eagle lives there; and the Philippine Monkey-eating Eagle is found in some of the larger Philippine Islands. This distribution suggests no close relationship between the last two and the first four, though they are anatomically similar; they have been too little studied to permit sound conclusions based on comparative behaviour.

The two Solitary Eagles most resemble big buzzards; they indeed precede the genus *Buteo* in the accepted sequence of classification. The Black Solitary Eagle mainly inhabits Mexican mountain forests; the Crowned Solitary Eagle more open country in Brazil, Argentina and Uruguay. Little is recorded of their habits, but both are apparently sluggish birds, feeding on mammals and snakes caught on the ground, so at least partly replacing snake eagles in South America. The Black Solitary Eagle nests in trees, but the nest of the relatively common and tame Crowned Solitary Eagle, which in Argentina sometimes perches on roadside telephone poles, is unknown. These two birds epitomise how little is known about even the more spectacular South American birds of prey.

The Harpy and Guiana Crested Eagle are both magnificent crested species inhabiting tropical forests, with the short wings and long tails characteristic of forest raptors. The Harpy is unquestionably the world's most powerful raptor, and accordingly the world's most formidable bird. A male is impressive enough, weighing 9-10lb (4.4kg), a female huge, weighing 15-20lb (6.7-9kg) with a tarsus as thick as a child's wrist; she is about as big as a bird of prey can be while still able to fly easily. Jim Fowler, who kept one, observed graphically that the problem was not to get her to come to his fist but to be sufficiently braced and padded to withstand the impact of her arrival. The Philippine Monkey-eating Eagle is only a fraction smaller and slimmer than the Harpy, a male weighing 10lb (4.65kg). It can evidently be no problem for either of these huge eagles to kill the monkeys on which they often feed. What little is known about the Harpy, however, suggests that it flies among the treetops with astonishing

Monkey-eating Eagle from the Phillippines (*P. Morris, Ardea Photographics*)

agility, gliding at 40-50mph. Captive Harpies in zoos can be positively dangerous to their keepers.

The Guiana Crested Eagle is much smaller, slimmer and lighter, a female weighing 3lb 13oz (1.75kg), less than half the weight of a Golden Eagle. It apparently complements the Harpy in its range of prey, feeding on smaller monkeys, other arboreal mammals, perhaps birds. Aerodynamically it should theoretically be much more agile than the Harpy. Despite the difficulty of observing eagles in tropical forest it is astonishing that neither the Harpy nor the Guiana Crested Eagle has been much studied, especially as the Guiana Crested Eagle occurs on islands in the Panama Canal where it could be studied by North American naturalists.

The New Guinea Harpy Eagle does not resemble the true Harpy other than in bodily form. It is smaller, dark grey and white, with the flight feathers of wing and tail strikingly barred; these barred feathers are used in ornamental head-dresses. This almost unknown species is believed to feed on forest wallabies and other mammals.

The most famous and best-known of this group, the Philippine Monkey-eating Eagle, is the second largest and by far the most acutely threatened of all the world's eagles, reduced to less than 100 in the wild state. Long in demand as a trophy in the Philippines, and thoughtlessly over-collected for zoos, it has been further reduced by destruction of forest habitat by a rocketing human population and wasteful agricultural methods. Although the remnant population is now the subject of a special World Wildlife Fund programme, seeking to provide better protection in the wild and restore captives to a natural existence, this magnificent bird can never again become abundant because too much of the forest habitat has already been destroyed.

All members of this group, so far as is known, naturally breed in trees; but Harpies can also be induced to breed in captivity. The only nests described of the Black Solitary Eagle, Guiana Crested Eagle and the New Guinea Harpy Eagle were in tall forest trees. Only one egg of the Guiana Crested Eagle has been (doubtfully) described. The only member of the group studied in any detail at the nest is the Philippine Monkey-eating Eagle, though the enormous tree nests of the Harpy have also been watched for short periods.

As might be expected, the Harpy and Philippine Monkey-eating Eagles have very long incubation and fledging periods. Eggs of the Harpy in captivity hatch in fifty-four to fifty-six days; but incubation in wild Philippine Monkey-eating Eagles is recorded at sixty days, and the fledging period in this species is 105 days. Captive Harpy chicks have all died before reaching maturity, but probably take about the same time to fly. Such very long incubation and fledging periods suggest that these huge birds might not be able to breed annually in the wild state, by analogy with the forest-loving Crowned Eagle of Africa, which breeds only once every two years near the Equator. Studies at one wild Harpy's nest suggest that, like the Crowned Eagle, the young is fed by the parents for many months after it leaves the nest, so precluding annual breeding if the eaglet is successfully reared. This suggests a very low replacement rate, less than one eaglet per pair in two years; and a long wild life-span.

As a group, these great Buteonine eagles are the least studied of any. They all apparently live mainly on mammals, perhaps on some birds and snakes. If their voices are known, they are buzzard-like mews or screams. Our lack of detailed knowledge of them, even of the acutely threatened Philippine Monkey-eating Eagle and the gigantic Harpy, is the more curious because they include the largest and most powerful of all birds of prey.

5 True or Booted Eagles

These differ from all others so far mentioned in having the tarsus feathered to the toes, not bare and scaly. The evolutionary advantage of this is obscure; but it is certainly not an adaptation to cold, as in the only other raptor so equipped, the Arctic-breeding Rough-legged Buzzard *Buteo lagopus*. The sheath of leg feathers in these eagles is as dense in equatorial forests as in Alaska. In some, the feathers lie close, resembling stovepipe trousers, sometimes gaily barred; in others, it is like a pair of baggy breeches or plus-fours.

The thirty species compose eight genera: *Ictinaetus* (one); *Aquila* (nine); *Hieraaetus* (five); *Spizastur* (one); *Spizaetus* (eleven); and one each in *Stephanoaetus, Oroaetus* and *Polemaetus*. Occurring almost worldwide, they are most abundant and varied in Europe, Asia and Africa. Only one, the Golden Eagle, occurs in North America; four in Central and South America; and three in Australia and New Guinea.

This large and highly variable group conveniently divides into two subgroups, with *Ictinaetus* and *Aquila* in one, and all the rest in the other. The second group, with generally shorter wings and longer tails, are collectively known as hawk eagles, though in fact the distinction is sometimes tenuous. These subgroups are also separated by habits. *Ictinaetus* and all but perhaps one species of *Aquila* feed on small, weak, helpless creatures or carrion to some extent, as well as killing their own larger prey. No hawk eagle, so far as is known, eats carrion; apparently all take mainly full-grown live prey.

The Indian Black Eagle is the most aberrant member of the first subgroup, one of the most curious known eagles. It is sometimes thought to be a large aberrant kite with feathered tarsi, as its juvenile plumage is kite-like and its habits are peculiar. However, to me it seems most like an aberrant member of the genus *Aquila*, unlike a true kite such as *Milvus*. This eagle habitually soars slowly over forests and mountainsides, killing small animals, especially taking young birds in their nests. It has unusually long, soft, slightly emarginated primaries, widely separated when spread, and probably has relatively low wing-loading, which would assist slow soaring and methodical searching for nests of young birds. Its claws are long, thin and gently curving, resulting in a wide-spreading foot with little grasping power, well adapted for snatching in flight an entire birds' nest with young, but un-suited to killing large live prey, which the Black Eagle seldom does. The hunting behaviour of this eagle is not really kite-like, but resembles rather the slow methodical searching of the African Harrier Hawk, *Polyboroides*.

The nine members of the genus *Aquila* occur in North and Central America, Europe, Asia, Africa, New Guinea and Australia. Two of them are somewhat aberrant. Gurney's Eagle, very little known, is apparently an *Aquila* adapted to forest life by developing shorter wings and an unusually long tail. The smallest, Wahlberg's Eagle of Africa, weighing 2lb 3oz (1kg) or less, differs from all others in regularly laying only one egg; having a whistling, not clucking voice; and in not eating any carrion as far as is known. It is placed in *Aquila* partly because it is brown, with juvenile plumage similar to that of the adult. Its nearest relative is sometimes thought to be the Lesser Spotted Eagle, also rather small and with close-fitting stovepipe trousers on long legs. However, the Lesser Spotted Eagle feeds to some extent on carrion, insects, frogs and other helpless creatures; regularly lays two eggs; and has a clucking or yapping voice.

The other seven *Aquila* species are large to very large, weighing 3lb 4oz to 11lb (1.5-5.5kg). All except Verreaux's Eagle (in which the adult is coal black and white) are brown or dark brown in both adult and immature plumage. The Holarctic Golden Eagle, the African Verreaux's Eagle, the Australian Wedge-tailed Eagle and Gurney's Eagle form a 'superspecies' of rather closely related large eagles feeding on medium-sized mammals for preference. The European Im-perial Eagle is somewhat smaller, but still a large mammal-eater. The Lesser and Greater Spotted Eagles, and the Tawny or Steppe Eagle are all smaller, all brown, and in adult plumage notoriously difficult to distinguish in the field. The Steppe and Tawny Eagles are sometimes regarded as separate species, *Aquila nipalensis* and *A. rapax* respectively; but the consensus of opinion is that, despite differences in size and plumage, all are races of the Tawny Eagle *A. rapax*. Steppe Eagles may be twice the weight of tropical African or Indian Tawny Eagles.

Although they are found in a variety of habitats, from heavy woodland to steppe and subdesert, and from the Arctic to the Equator, *Aquila* eagles are more generalised, less specialised than hawk eagles. Excepting Gurney's Eagle, they have moderately long wings and rather long tails; they regularly lay two eggs (except Wahlberg's) and have barking or clucking voices. Except in Verreaux's Eagle, the immature plumage resembles the adult more or less closely; and even in Verreaux's Eagle the pattern of moult into adult plumage resembles that of the Golden Eagle.

These eagles include both the most numerous and many of the best-known of the world's eagles. Reference to Appendix 1 shows that three, the Golden Eagle, Verreaux's and Wahlberg's obtain more than 50/60 points; another four species (including five forms) have 40/50 points; the Greater Spotted Eagle is well known; and only Gurney's Eagle practically unknown. Probably the reason for this is that of all eagles the genus *Aquila* is the most easily observed in Europe, Australia and North America, while Verreaux's Eagle and Wahlberg's have also been intensively studied in Africa. Lack of knowledge of Gurney's Eagle reflects the inaccessibility and difficulty of its forest habitat in New Guinea.

The Golden Eagle is probably the most numerous large eagle in the world, and the Tawny and Steppe Eagles (regarding them as conspecific) the most numerous of all. This may seem strange because the Golden Eagle has been regarded as heading for extinction in North America and parts of Europe, mainly because of needless persecution by sheep ranchers. In 1964 its numbers in America were estimated at 10,000; but more recent counts revealed 10,000 wintering in Montana alone, so thast there might be 50-100,000 in Western USA, perhaps even 200,000 in North and Central America. Since Golden Eagles also occur in huge tracts of mountainous country in Europe, Asia south to the Himalayas, and northwest Africa, they could well number half a million. There are about 280 pairs, or 700 birds, including immatures, in Britain. The only eagle of its size occurring in comparable numbers is the Australian Wedge-tailed Eagle. A crude estimate, based on 10 square miles (25.9sq km) per pair, and with 80 per cent of Australia and Tasmania possible habitat, would mean 600,000-700,000 including immatures: this figure may be too high.

The Tawny and Steppe Eagles inhabit enormous tracts of open grassland, mountainous country and savannas from central Europe east to southern Siberia, Africa and India. In Africa alone their range is probably 5 million square miles (12.95 million sq km), with perhaps 250,000 pairs. In winter, migrant Steppe Eagles are several times as numerous in East

Tawny Eagle—a big booted eagle
(Norman Myers)

Africa as the resident Tawny Eagles, so this eagle is probably the only one likely to exceed a million. Probably the reasons for its success are its lack of specialisation, adaptability to a variety of habitat and prey, and nomadic or migratory habits where necessary. The northern populations of Golden Eagles migrate to warmer climates in winter, and the east European and central Asian races of the Steppe Eagle migrate to Africa or India; even resident races of the Tawny Eagle are somewhat nomadic in Africa. Such movements evade harsh winter conditions, and also enable many members of such species to congregate in areas where some food supply, such as locusts, or mole rats, may be temporarily abundant.

Although Golden Eagles prefer medium-sized mammals, they feed on everything from a frog or a small bird to a dead sheep or deer. Tawny Eagles, still more catholic in diet, feed on everything from termites and locusts to dead elephants, though they can also catch rats, snakes, game birds or even hares. They are also strongly piratical, prepared to rob other birds of prey from kestrels and kites to much larger Martial Eagles, even Lammergeiers. They eat carrion regularly and are the only eagles which normally associate with man—in north Africa and India. This lack of specialisation and adaptability leads to abundance. Some other species of *Aquila*, the Lesser and Greater Spotted Eagles, and in tropical Africa Wahlberg's, are also migratory, but are more dependent on one habitat, woodland or forest. Verreaux's Eagle is almost exactly the shape and size of a Golden Eagle; but resides only on rocky hills, and 99 per cent or more of its prey is rock hyrax. Verreaux's Eagle is almost as tied to the range of rock hyrax as the Vulturine Fish Eagle is tied to that of the oil palm.

The twenty species called hawk eagles are collectively much more varied than *Aquila* and *Ictinaetus*, but individually much more specialised in habitat and food preferences. In size they vary from the enormous Martial Eagle of Africa, with females weighing more than 14lb (6.5kg), to the smallest eagles ever weighed, the New Guinea race of the Australasian Little Eagle, an immature weighing less than 1lb (500g). Wallace's Hawk Eagle may be still smaller and lighter; and a male European Booted Eagle weighs less than 1lb 4oz (600g). Thus a female Martial Eagle is about thirteen times the weight of the smallest hawk eagles, while in the genus *Aquila* the largest Siberian Golden Eagle would not be more than eight times the weight of a male Wahlberg's Eagle.

Systematically, hawk eagles are still rather confused; and the current arrangement in numerous genera is unsatisfactory. The former accepted genera *Lophaetus* and *Cassinaetus* have now been merged with *Spizaetus*, though some consider *Lophaetus* nearer to *Aquila*. There appears no ground for this except that the immature Long-crested Eagle is like the adult; it otherwise resembles some eastern *Spizaetus* species. The well-known Old World genus *Hieraaetus* may shortly be merged in the practically unknown American genus *Spizastur*. It is morphologically similar, and *Spizastur* is apparently the older name, so Old World ornithologists may just have to tear their hair once again at the rules of international nomenclature. Some authorities would also merge the large monotypic genera *Polemaetus*, *Oroaetus* and *Stephanoaetus* in *Spizaetus*; there are similarities, but all are large or very large, and *Polemaetus* at least is relatively long-winged and short-tailed. There is some justification for systematic revision; but not to the extent of including all in two genera, *Spizastur* and *Spizaetus*, or even, as some have advocated, merging all in *Aquila*.

Although so variable, hawk eagles share certain features. The immature plumage is either strikingly or markedly different from that of the adult. In the most extreme cases, such as the Crowned Eagle *Stephanoaetus* and several *Spizaetus*, one would not think the young the same species if one saw it alone. In *Hieraaetus* the differences are not so great; and in the Long-crested Eagle *Lophaetus* they are slight. Many hawk eagles regularly lay only one egg, whereas all but one *Aquila* regularly lay two. All those whose voices are known whistle, utter mellow fluting calls or scream loudly; none utters a 'typical *Aquila* cluck'. Finally, none are at present known to take any carrion, though this may well be recorded in the future. The largest species, most likely to take carrion because they feed on large mammals, apparently do not.

Many hawk eagles live in forest or dense woodland, and consequently have relatively short rounded wings and long tails, resembling the Goshawk *Accipiter gentilis* in proportions—hence 'hawk eagle'. Only the huge Martial Eagle truly prefers open country. Its tail is less than half the standard wing length, whereas in the forest-loving Crowned Eagle, nearly as large, the tail length is three-quarters that of the wing. Some *Spizaetus* species have relatively even longer tails, that of the South American Tyrant Hawk Eagle being four-fifths of the wing length. Members of the genus *Hieraaetus*, preferring dense woodland and light forest, have tails 50-60 per cent of the wing length. These differences in proportion in hawk eagles demonstrate nicely that such variations are more a matter of habitat than genetic in origin. Likewise, in *Aquila*, the Golden Eagle's tail is less than half the wing length; but in the forest-loving Gurney's Eagle it is two-thirds of the wing length.

The forest habitat, which makes hawk eagles exceptionally difficult to observe, and the fact that many species live in tropical forests of Indonesia, Malaysia or South America (where good observations are few), result in many being little known. Bonelli's Eagle, its African race the African Hawk Eagle and the Crowned Eagle are the only three of twenty-one forms which obtain more than 50/60 points. Only two others exceed 40 points; one the huge Martial Eagle (which has accordingly attracted many enthusiasts), the other the unaccountably rare and small Ayres' Hawk Eagle, which is known only because I have been able to observe two pairs, one for twenty-six years. Ten forms, nearly half, obtain 20/60 points or less.

However, we do know that hawk eagles prey on a larger range of animals than do *Aquila* species, most of which prefer small or medium-sized mammals and eat carrion. The largest of all, the Martial Eagle, feeds mainly on game birds, with some large mammals. The most powerful of all, the Crowned Eagle, feeds on forest mammals, up to four times its own weight. Bonelli's and the African Hawk Eagle, taking a range of prey similar to that of the much larger Martial and Golden Eagles, are probably the most potent predators relative to their size of any eagles. Ayres' Hawk Eagle feeds on small birds, with a few mammals. The small eastern *Spizaetus* species apparently feed on mammals and birds; the rather large Mountain Hawk Eagle *S. nipalensis* can at least kill jungle fowl. Some may take reptiles such as iguanas in South America. Even the small species do not, apparently, take insects, and are not seen on the ground eating swarming termites like several *Aquila* species. None is known to indulge in piracy, or to eat carrion. In the pursuit of their prey some, notably Bonelli's and Ayres' Hawk Eagle, are exceedingly swift and dashing; Ayres' Hawk Eagle combines the speed of a Peregrine Falcon with the manoeuvrability of a Goshawk. Given these abilities, it is astonishing that it is so rare throughout its range, for its prey is abundant.

Only one hawk eagle, the Booted Eagle, is truly migratory. It summers in southern Europe, arriving rather late in the year in April, and breeds from Morocco and Spain east to India. After breeding it departs and winters south to South Africa, though is seldom seen in most of its African winter range. To everyone's astonishment, it has recently been found breeding in small numbers in South Africa. In Europe it breeds from April to June, in South Africa from October to December; in both areas, rather late in the summer. The only other well-known species of hawk eagle breeding in temperate climates, Bonelli's Eagle, remains in its haunts year round, roosting all winter near the nest site. The tropical forest species, as far as is known, remain in their territories the whole year round; they have no reason to move.

In their nesting habits, the hawk eagles and those of the genus *Aquila* and *Ictinaetus* are similar. All make large nests, which they use for several or many years. In the larger species, such as the Golden, Martial and Crowned Eagles, the nests become huge, and the site is used for many years, even centuries, as long as the birds remain undisturbed. The smaller species, such as the African Long-crested Eagle, may move more often, but one pair of the even smaller Ayres' Hawk Eagle has occupied the same site for twenty-six years. In such long-established nest sites the same area, or even the same nest, is occupied by a succession of different individuals. The site, occupied by a pair, is constant, but individuals change.

Most species nest in trees; only a few breed on cliffs. These include the Golden Eagle, which sometimes breeds in trees even when cliffs are available, but usually seems to prefer cliffs even when tall trees are available. Verreaux's Eagle is the most confirmed cliff-breeder of all; only three nests in trees have been recorded. Bonelli's Eagle normally breeds on cliffs, sometimes in trees; the African Hawk Eagle habitually breeds in trees, ocasionally on cliffs. The Booted Eagle nests in large trees in tall woodlands, but in north Africa breeds in cliffs. All the forest species, so far as is known, nest in tall forest trees.

Most species of *Aquila* lay two eggs, sometimes one, occasionally three; authentic clutches of four are recorded in the Imperial and Golden Eagle. The aberrant Indian Black Eagle and Wahlberg's Eagle normally lay one, occasionally two eggs. Among hawk eagles, clutches are generally smaller, often only one, sometimes two; only Bonelli's and the African Hawk Eagle are known to lay three. The largest of all, the Martial Eagle, never lays more than one; and two small *Hieraaetus* and several *Spizaetus* species normally or regularly lay only one. Whether this smaller clutch is of genetic origin, or whether it reflects the general trend towards smaller clutches in tropical species than in related temperate-zone species is obscure; probably a bit of both.

Hawk eagles thus start with a built-in tendency to rear fewer young than eagles of the genus *Aquila* (except Wahlberg's Eagle). However, even in species which regularly lay more than one egg, the second-hatched young bird is normally either dominated by the elder so that it cannot get food, or is actually killed by it. In some species this fratricide is invariable; in others two young, very rarely three (in Golden and Imperial Eagles) are reared. Even in those species where two are sometimes reared, the younger of two hatched succumbs in about four out of five cases. This has nothing to do with size or, apparently, with ferocity. In Bonelli's Eagle, one of the fiercest, two young are often reared; but in the comparatively inoffensive Lesser Spotted Eagle the younger almost always succumbs. The Golden

Eagle is almost the same size as Verreaux's and both prefer mammals; but in the Golden Eagle two young are quite often reared, while in Verreaux's only one brood of two is known among more than 500 recorded cases.

Incubation periods in booted eagles are about the same length, almost irrespective of size. That of Ayres' Hawk Eagle, forty-six days, is actually longer than that of the much larger Golden Eagle. The recorded range is from forty-one to forty-nine days in most known species, the only accurate wild records of less than forty days being thirty-seven to thirty-nine days in Bonelli's Eagle. There is only a slight observed tendency for longer incubation periods relative to size in these eagles in the tropics as compared to temperate zones; that of Verreaux's Eagle is almost exactly the same as that of its temperate counterpart, the Golden Eagle. Fledging periods, in total days, are, however, markedly longer in tropical species than in temperate species. That of Verreaux's Eagle is ninety to ninety-five days compared to sixty-five to seventy-five in the Golden Eagle; and the small Ayres' Eagle has a fledging period of seventy-five days, much longer than the larger Bonelli's Eagle recorded at fifty-seven days in France.

In well-studied species the breeding potential is still further reduced by non-breeding in some years; that is, the birds are present in their territory, build up the nest, but do not lay. In the Crowned Eagle, the breeding potential is automatically halved by an extremely long post-fledging period of nine to eleven months. If an eaglet is successfully reared to independence the birds can only breed once every two years. The potential is still further reduced by natural losses, to about two young in five years. It is claimed that this is only true in tropical climates, and that in South Africa Crowned Eagles breed every year; but really good South African data are lacking. In the apparently rather closely related Martial Eagle the relatively short post-fledging period of the eaglet permits the adults to breed in successive years. In Ayres' Eagle the breeding rate of young reared per attempt is even lower, perhaps because these birds seem unusually inept nest-builders. However, this conclusion rests on only two pairs observed in one area by me, and needs confirmation from elsewhere.

Longevity is presumably related to the number of young reared per nest and the number of these that reach maturity. Accordingly, most of the hawk eagles, even small species, should be longer-lived than eagles of the genus *Aquila*. In the hawk eagles, with their very striking barred plumage, in-

Ayres' Hawk Eagle—a small booted eagle *(author)*

dividuals can be recognised from year to year, and their actual life-spans as breeding adults recorded. Such observations are almost impossible in the more uniform-coloured *Aquila* species without colour-ringing individuals. Observations on plumage are supported by behaviour; one Crowned Eagle breeding near my house grew so used to me that she would attack me without any hesitation. Such actual records indicate that the large Crowned Eagle lives as an adult in the wild state for about eleven years, but that the smaller Ayres' Eagle lives for only about six years. That being so, it is extremely odd that Ayres' Eagle has a still lower breeding rate than the Crowned Eagle; possibly this is the explanation of its rarity throughout its range. In captivity the smaller hawk eagles certainly have shorter lives than the larger species, which can exceed forty years in captivity, but probably do not live much more than ten years in the wild.

An additional reason for our relatively advanced knowledge of some booted eagles is the fact that they, more than others, have been accused of threatening human interests, generally by taking lambs or game birds or both. This has led to intensive study of some species, notably the Golden Eagle and Wedge-tailed Eagle (the latter not yet published). Such studies, involving counts of the number of pairs in any area of country, their prey preferences and breeding rates, have in turn led to fears that some species might be threatened by extinction, at least locally, through direct persecution by humans, casual interference, the effects of pesticides, or combinations of all these. In some local areas, for instance in the Golden Eagle in Scotland and parts of America, the effect of such factors on survival is serious. In Scotland the breeding potential of the Golden Eagle is reduced from about 0.83 to 0.56 young per pair per annum by human interference of one sort and another, though the threat of pesticides in this case has receded. However, no species of booted eagle is really threatened by direct human interference. The species most likely to be threatened with extinction are some of the small, forest-loving eastern hawk eagles, confined to one or a few islands. Exploding human populations, leading to destruction of forests for agriculture, threaten at least two, possibly three, small booted eagles.

Although more is known about booted eagles than most other groups, there is still plenty left to learn. The well-known species are generally the large, strongly predatory ones that have accordingly attracted enthusiasts' attention. Smaller, less fierce species, even in accessible areas, have been less studied. If the African Long-crested Eagle, black, with a brilliant golden eye and long waving crest, were twice its size, it would be among the world's most spectacular eagles. As it is, though common and easily observed, it is much less well known than some rarer, larger species. Our ignorance is most marked in small forest species which may be both secretive and not especially grand, though some of them are more beautifully plumaged than any other eagles. Such species seem destined to remain largely unknown for many years to come.

Part II Physical Characters, Senses and Adaptation for Predation

6 Size and Weight

Considering that the size and power of an eagle is one of its most striking features, it is surprising how little accurate detail is recorded. From museum study skins only certain measurements can be obtained which normally give no accurate idea of span or body size; and few eagles are weighed when shot. However, from the many live eagles in the hands of falconers or in zoos, painlessly anaesthetised, all needed bodily dimensions and weights could be taken. Eagles in zoos are often overfed, and too fat; but they could provide at least some reasonable data.

If eagles must be shot or kept, any collector, zoo keeper or falconer should collect the following additional vital statistics besides standard wing, tail and tarsus measurements: (i) the weight (allowing for obvious crop contents); (ii) the wingspan; and (iii) the surface area of a complete spread wing and the expanded tail. Certain organs, notably the eyes, should be preserved in study collections for detailed examination later.

Although an eagle's wingspan is one of the commonest points of interest, few accurate records exist. There is a broad but not constant relationship between the standard wing measurement (from the carpal joint to the tip of the primaries) and wingspan. With the length of the wing the breadth of the chord (from the leading to the trailing edge of the wing) should be recorded to give the aspect ratio, which fundamentally affects the flight of any bird. Wings of high aspect ratio, very long, with a short chord, such as those of albatrosses, are the most efficient for gliding and soaring; but such very long, narrow wings would hamper eagles in cover or near the ground, where most hunt and kill.

From the weight and surface area, wing-loading and other details which must be crucial to flight performance, and therefore to an eagle's hunting ability, can be calculated. The energy developed by an eagle moving at any given speed is calculated from the formula Mv^2: M=mass or weight:

v=velocity (eg 10lb travelling at 20ft/sec=10×400= 4,000ft/lb). An African Fish Eagle, swooping at about 20mph (32kph; 30ft/sec, 9m/sec) develops energy of over 5,000 foot pounds, more than the muzzle energy of a bullet from a heavy rifle. A female Harpy at the same speed develops 13,500 foot pounds. From such figures one can visualise better the effect of an eagle's impact upon unsuspecting stricken prey.

Even the largest eagles are not as big as many believe. It is doubtful if any regularly spans over 8ft (2.4m), and most span less, often much less. The world's largest eagles are the Harpy and Philippine Monkey-eating Eagle, and the slightly smaller Steller's Sea Eagle; but accurate wingspan records are lacking. As both Harpy and Monkey-eater are short-winged forest species, resembling in proportions the African Crowned Eagle, neither would span more than 8ft (2.4m).

Next in the size scale is the European Sea Eagle, for which we have a good series of records for both sexes. Twenty-one females weigh between 10lb 2oz and 15lb 1oz (4.6-6.85kg), averaging 12lb 7oz (5.67kg); and thirteen males weigh between 7lb 14oz and 11lb 14oz (3.62-5.43kg), averaging 11lb 6oz (5.22kg). Fourteen females span between 7ft 5in and 8ft 8½in (2.26-2.65m), averaging 7ft 9¾in (2.379m); seven males span between 6ft 10¾in and 7ft 8in (2.1-2.336m), averaging 7ft 3¾in (2.226m). Only the largest females span 8ft (2.4m). Their wing-loading is about 0.68g/sq cm and their weight to wingspan ratio is 2.4g/mm in females and 2.34g/mm in males; even males are very large and ponderous birds. If Steller's Sea Eagle had similar proportions then, on the basis of recorded wing lengths (females 24-24⅜in, 61-62cm, cf 24-28⅛in, 61-71.4cm), this great bird would span no more than a European Sea Eagle. Captive Steller's Eagles, however, seem stouter, heavier and relatively shorter-winged than European Sea Eagles. Steller's is certainly heavier, females weighing 14lb 14oz to 19lb 14oz (6.8-8.97kg). Its weight to span ratio might thus be about 3.3g/mm; so that one might deduce that it would be more sluggish, less agile than even a female European Sea Eagle. A good idea of the relative proportions could be obtained in half an hour by anaesthetising and measuring a Steller's Sea Eagle in a zoo.

The best available series of measurements for any other large eagle concern the Australian Wedge-tailed Eagle. Forty-three (not accurately sexed) weighed 5lb 8oz to 10lb (2.5-4.36kg), averaging 7lb 8oz (3.4kg). They spanned 6ft 3in to 7ft 3in (1.9-2.2m), averaging 6ft 9in (2m). Females averaged larger than males, and individuals were recorded spanning up to 8ft 3in (2.5m). Another 127 averaged 7lb 15oz

(3.35kg), but reputedly still larger individuals, weighing up to 11lb (5kg) and spanning 10ft to 10ft 6in (3.05-3.2m), are more doubtful.

The Wedge-tailed Eagle, Martial Eagle, Verreaux's Eagle, Golden Eagle, Bald Eagle, Crowned Eagle and a few others form a group a little smaller than the very largest. Female Martial Eagles, weighing 14lb (6.5kg) or more, may be the largest; but large Golden Eagles are nearly as big. Male European Golden Eagles span 6ft 2½in to 7ft (1.89-2.13m), averaging 6ft 7in (2.02m). They weigh 6lb 11oz to 9lb 11oz (3.1-4.4kg), averaging 8lb 6½oz (3.86kg). Females normally span 7ft to 7ft 5in (2.15-2.17m), averaging 7ft 2½in (2.2m), and weigh 8lb 11oz to 12lb 13oz (4-5.85kg), averaging 10lb 13oz (4.9kg). Exceptionally, they may span 8ft 3½in (2.55m) and weigh 14lb 7oz (6.6kg). American Golden Eagles are about the same size; but the Asian race, the celebrated Berkut, trained to catch foxes or even wolves, is larger though not, on published data, much heavier.

The weight to wingspan ratio of Golden Eagles is about 1.9g/mm in males and 2.2g/mm in females; male Golden Eagles are markedly lighter and slighter than females. A male Crowned Eagle weighed 9lb (4.08kg) and spanned just over 6ft (1.85m); his weight to span ratio was 2.2g/cm, suggesting he was less agile than a male Golden Eagle. However, the Crowned Eagle's wings are very broad; and this male had a wing-loading of 0.67g/sq cm, slightly more than that of a Golden Eagle, which has narrower wings. The wing-loading of Golden Eagles (on somewhat doubtful data) is about 0.65g/sq cm; that of the European Sea Eagle about 0.68g/sq cm; and that of Tawny and Steppe Eagles 0.53-0.57g/sq cm, according to race. The forest-loving Crowned Eagle must often lift heavy prey from the ground into a tree, without the aid of wind, whereas Golden Eagles which live in open country can normally increase lift by taking off into wind.

The largest eagles are not necessarily the most powerful. The favourite prey of Golden Eagles throughout their range is rabbits and hares, weighing 3-8lb (1.36-3.63kg); but they often kill smaller prey, such as grouse weighing 1lb to 1lb 5oz (500-600g). The staple prey of the slightly lighter Crowned Eagle is a small forest antelope, the Suni, or monkeys, weighing 5-11lb (2.27-4.99kg). Crowned Eagles often kill still larger prey weighing 20lb (9.07kg) or even more, up to 40lb or more (18-20kg). Thus the Crowned Eagle habitually kills prey of its own weight or more, whereas the heavier Golden Eagle habitually kills prey of about half its own weight. The African Martial Eagle, larger and heavier than a Crowned or a Golden Eagle, normally feeds on game birds such as guineafowl and francolins, weighing 1-4lb (0.45-1.81kg), one-tenth to one-third of its own weight, and rarely kills such heavier prey as antelope calves.

Any of these big sea eagles, Harpies or booted eagles could theoretically kill a young human baby, weighing 8-10lb (3.63-4.54kg), particularly as a baby is an extremely helpless animal. However, an eagle normally could not approach a baby because it would be carried, watched or guarded by its mother; and could only carry it away if aided by wind to increase lift. There are no credible instances of baby-snatching within historical times; and it is probably physically impossible for an eagle to lift such weights entire. The fear that it might happen, which still persists among civilised educated people is not, oddly enough, common among primitive African or South American tribes.

At the other end of the size-scale, perhaps the smallest eagle is the Nias Island Serpent Eagle, which could span only a little over 3ft (1m); but it has not been weighed. A male European Booted Eagle weighed 1lb 5oz (595g) and two males spanned 3ft 10in and 3ft 11in (1.16m and 1.21m). Still smaller, an immature of the New Guinea race of the Australian Little Eagle weighed 483g, just over 1lb. Male Ayres' Hawk Eagles, still among the smallest, weigh 1lb 7oz to 1lb 15oz (714-879g) and a female 2lb (940g), or 1½-2lb for the species. Such eagles are smaller, lighter and swifter than European Goshawks. Ayres' Eagle normally feeds on birds much lighter than itself, but can kill guineafowl up to twice its own weight.

Between these extremes there is every gradation from large to small, but although the wing, tarsus and tail measurements are recorded for most species and races one cannot obtain a good idea of weights, wingspans or wing-loading, and consequently performance, for many species. One of the few people ever to record such data was the late Col Richard Meinertzhagen. His records reveal that the Steppe Eagle can be almost as big as a Golden Eagle; females of the most eastern race, *A. r. nipalensis,* weigh 5lb to 10lb 8oz (2.3-4.85kg), and span 2-2.6m or up to 8ft 6in. The African Tawny Eagle weighs 4lb 8oz to 5lb 9oz (1.95-2.5kg) and spans 5ft 8in to 6ft (1.72-1.85m). The weight to span ratio in the eastern Steppe Eagle would thus be about 2.8g/mm but in the Tawny Eagle only 1.25g/mm. Wing-loading in the Steppe Eagle is given as 0.57g/sq cm and in the Tawny Eagle as 0.53. Lower wing-loading and relatively longer wings should make the Tawny Eagle more active, less sluggish, than the Steppe Eagle; and this surmise is borne out by field observations and recorded prey. It is especially regrettable that recent field workers in Rhodesia, who deliberately killed a number of Steppe Eagles to take certain measurements, weighed their birds but did not ascertain the span and wing-loading.

To sum up, the very largest eagles weigh 15lb (6.7kg) or more, and may span over 8ft (2.4m); those of open country have relatively longer wings for their weight than forest species. The smallest eagles weigh about 1lb (454g), and span only about 3ft (0.92m). Wing-loading automatically increases with bodily size, since the weight of a bird increases as the cube or volume, and the wing surface as the square or area. Study of such dimensions suggests that the smaller eagles, weighing less in relation to their wingspan and wing area must automatically be more agile and swift than larger eagles; and this is what we find in the wild state. A Verreaux's Eagle is a magnificent flier, as anyone will admit; but it cannot match the quicksilver agility of the little Ayres' Hawk Eagle that may live in the forest on the same hill.

7 Senses: Sight, Hearing, Smell

The eagle eye is proverbially acute. At close quarters that piercing stare has no equal in the bird world. Eyeball to eyeball with an eagle, perhaps perched on a branch near his hide, a watcher feels that he must be detected; and perhaps he sometimes is.

The general form of an eagle's eye, and a general idea of how and what they can see, is known. However, strangely, so far as I know, no good modern comparative study is available from which the actual visual acuity of different species can be estimated. Modern equipment should make such a study far easier than it was for earlier researchers.

Visual acuity, definition or resolving power depends on the structure of the eye itself and of the retina within it. The retina of all birds' eyes is thick and served by very sensitive nervous connections. The type of vision is controlled by the relative numbers of two specialised types of visual cells, rods and cones. Rods are sensitive to poor light, and are best developed in nocturnal birds. Cones are associated with visual acuity and permit colour vision. The greater the number of cones in a given area of the retina, the greater the visual acuity. In eagles' and other diurnal birds' eyes, large or small areas contain nothing but cones, indicating that acute sight and high resolving power is more important than sensitivity to movement in poor light.

Eagles' eyes, like those of other diurnal birds of prey, are

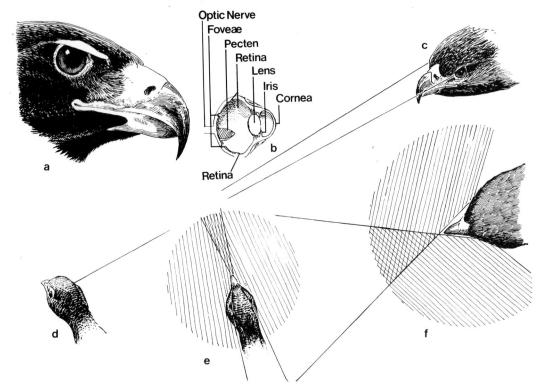

Optic Nerve
Foveæ
Pecten
Retina
Lens
Iris
Cornea

a

b

Retina

c

d

e

f

A Verreaux's Eagle showing protective supraorbital process; b. section of eye to same scale; c. the forward binocular vision of the eagle; d. the lateral monocular vision of the grouse; e. the field of vision of the grouse; f. the field of vision of the eagle

round or globose, relatively very large, sometimes even larger than a human eye, and fit tightly into the eye socket. An eagle cannot glance up and down or right and left by moving its eye easily within the socket, as we can. To see behind or above it must move the whole head on its flexible neck. An alert eagle therefore constantly turns its head this way and that, sometimes even upside down.

The outermost part of the eye, the clear cornea, is protected and cleaned by the nictitating membrane, or third eyelid, which is repeatedly drawn to and fro across the surface without blinking the eyelids themselves. The nictitating membrane is often drawn across the eye when feeding young; otherwise, the young bird, snatching at food, could damage its parent's eye and so endanger its own survival.

The cornea deflects incoming light and is separated from the lens and the iris by a watery substance. The iris acts like the diaphragm of a camera lens, opening and closing the circular pupil. For reasons unknown it is often brilliantly coloured, especially in the snake eagles, when it is usually bright yellow or whitish. Some young eagles have a brown iris which, in the adult, becomes yellow; and in some eagles, for instance Ayres' Hawk Eagle, the colour of the iris darkens

Close-up of head of juvenile Black-breasted Snake Eagle showing large eye and loose feathering at back of head *(Peter Steyn)*

with age from pale yellow to a more intense yellow-orange.

The size of the pupil can be controlled by muscles according to light intensity, contracting in bright light and opening in poor light. Birds' pupils do not, however, respond so much to changes in light intensity as some other vertebrates'. This may be connected with dark pigments in the retina, which move forward in intense light to protect the sensitive visual cells. At close quarters the size of an eagle's pupil apparently varies little. Light entering the eye through a small pupil passes only through the gently curved centre of the lens, so minimising visual distortion.

The lens of an eagle's eye is large, oval in section and, because of the globose structure of the eye, is far enough from the retina to cast a larger image, relatively, than in the commonest type of somewhat flattened avian eye. The retina itself, rich in cones which increase visual acuity, perhaps gives an eagle resolving power four times as great as that of a human eye. Moreover, in the eyes of eagles and of other diurnal birds of prey there are curved pits in the retina, known as foveas, in which the density and nerve supply of the cones is still greater; they are therefore centres of unusually acute vision, perhaps eight times as acute as our own. The two foveas in eagles' eyes, one (lateral) directed sideways, the other (temporal) forward, are used together. The temporal foveas give binocular vision through about forty degrees of arc, which could be increased by small lateral adjustments of the eye itself. Forward directed temporal foveas seem important to predatory species; vultures, for instance, which can find a stationary carcase at leisure, lack temporal foveas. Foveas also assist distance perception, evidently important to eagles hurtling to prey, when they must judge distance to a nicety.

In all birds' eyes a peculiar structure called the pecten, a pigmented, highly vascular, pleated or vaned body, stands up in the centre of the eye near the optic nerve, supported by the gelatinous vitreous humour. Composed almost entirely of blood vessels on a fine fibrous base, its function is still not clear. It is smallest in nocturnal birds but largest in diurnal predators, such as eagles. It thus appears to be most developed in birds with very acute sight, catching active prey. It may be a structure to provide nutrition and oxygen for the retina, which itself lacks any blood vessels.

To sum up, eagles cannot, as we can, move their eyes in their sockets, but compensate for this by a very flexible neck. They can look both forwards and sideways in a manner we cannot, but have forward binocular vision only through a much narrower arc. Attacking their prey at speed, they can nicely adjust focus and distance perception to avoid damage, whereas if we travelled at such a speed we should smash incapably into the ground and burst. Finally, because of the superior resolving power of their retina and foveas they can see detail from four to eight times as fine as we can; their eyesight is certainly much more acute than ours.

One can judge one's own visual acuity by placing an inch-long object on top of a post of similar colour, backing away till it disappears, and approaching again till it reappears. One can then calculate the range at which the object could be seen with four to eight times one's own visual acuity. I myself can see such an object at about 33yd (30m). With four times my visual acuity, an eagle could perceive the same object at about 130yd (119m) and, using its foveas, at 260yd (238m). A foot-long (30cm) rabbit could theoretically be seen by the same eagle at 1,580yd (1.45km) without the foveas, and at 3,160yd (2.9km)—over 1¾ miles—with the foveas. Strong contrast between prey and surroundings would increase visual efficiency; but haze, or poor light, would reduce it. The eagle's vision is extraordinary, but not miraculous. Such calculations help to explain just how an eagle can detect well-camouflaged prey at seemingly remarkable range; and why odd-coloured animals, such as albinos or black variants, would be more liable to predation and elimination in the wild state.

I have watched eagles stoop at or kill objects which I could not see at the same range. One Martial Eagle launched a long slanting stoop at a guineafowl feeding in a patch of farmland, starting from near the summit of a hill perhaps 4 miles (6.4km) from the guineafowl. I did not see what the eagle was after till it disappeared, to rise again with the stricken guineafowl in its talons. Theoretically, I could see a guineafowl, about 15in (38cm) long at about a mile (1.6km) in good light. This Martial Eagle may not even have used its foveas to perceive its prey, though they no doubt came into play as it was hurtling towards its quarry.

Sight is also important for eagles in their territorial relations. Actual fighting is normally avoided or ritualised by well-armed carnivores, mammalian or avian. Verreaux's Eagles in the Matopos Hills establish their territories simply by perching where their neighbours can easily see them; or by aerial display over and near the boundaries. Scottish Golden Eagles, nesting 3-4 miles (4.8-6.4km) apart, can easily see each other perched on ridges or soaring high in the air. Even Martial Eagles with nests about 8 miles (12.9km) apart can see each other soaring somewhere around the centre of their territories, if their visual acuity is four to eight times as good as mine.

Sight is by far the most important of eagles' senses. They also have good hearing; but it is seldom used to locate prey, though it may help. Thus I have known Tawny Eagles in northern Kenya come to the sound of gunshots and perch, waiting for wounded sandgrouse. Probably, hearing is more important for species which hunt in thick cover than in the open.

Hearing is also important in nuptial or advertisement display. Some eagles such as the Golden Eagle are relatively silent; others are very vocal, for instance the African Fish Eagle, which is constantly calling, often in duet. Visual and auditory acuity may be strikingly combined. I once watched a female African Fish Eagle look up into the sky and call; an answering call enabled me, with x12 binoculars, to locate her mate, returning after four hours' absence. Not only had she seen him at a range beyond my own naked-eye vision, but she had presumably *recognised* him—since she did not call to several other Fish Eagles soaring nearer at the same time. He could hear her, and answered; he was perhaps 1¾ miles (2km) away.

The male of a pair of Crowned Eagles displays, uttering his loud 'kewee-kewee' call, nearly every fine morning. Beyond the range of my naked eye, I can pinpoint the sound by ear and locate him with binoculars. Such loud vocal displays would enable other Crowned Eagles, perched within the forest canopy and unable to see the displaying bird, to know that he is there. Noisy vocal aerial displays are used more by species of thick woodland or forest than those of open country. The Martial Eagle, which lives in open savanna, is much less vocal than the Crowned Eagle. Similarly, the Brown, Smaller Banded and Southern Banded Snake Eagles all have deep, crowing voices, used both in aerial display and when perched. All live in thick woodland, whereas the Black-breasted Snake Eagle, inhabiting open plains and light savanna, calls seldom, while its voice is a rather weak, melodious whistle.

Voice and hearing also aid communication between adults and young. Young in the nest often emit loud or piercing hunger calls. The adult Crowned Eagle, after the young has flown but is still dependent, and may be perched invisible in the forest up to a mile from the nest, calls loudly when it brings prey. In due course the young one hears, responds with loud calls, flies into the nest and is fed. Lack of the right auditory response in this case is the final indication to the adults that the eaglet is independent.

Both sight and hearing are thus important, not only in detecting and killing prey, but also in communication and signalling. Other senses are unimportant. Eagles apparently lack any sense of smell. Any eagle that eats carrion finds it by sight, either directly, or through the movements of other carrion-eating birds. Although they lack any sense of smell, eagles may have some sense of taste. Certain animals, such as mongooses, which have a very pungent, musky odour, sometimes appear to taste repulsive. The eagle shakes its head, as if in disgust. I have, however, seen a Golden Eagle select a weasel, also a strong-smelling carnivore, from among several fresh grouse, and feed herself and two eaglets on it with no apparent distaste.

An eagle could probably experience a sense of touch mainly through the bill and the feet. The bill apparently cannot be very sensitive; but is delicately used in preening. Although eagles seldom bill or preen each other or their young, some eagles, notably the Bateleur, plainly enjoy being fondled or stroked, so are presumably sensitive to touch on the skin or feathers.

It is hard to credit that an eagle's immensely powerful foot can also be sensitive. Yet it may have limited sensitivity, for when an eagle is feeding it shifts the foot continually to achieve the right position to hold down the prey. A half-grown bushbuck killed by a Crowned Eagle had many deep talon wounds on its neck, suggesting that the eagle, in the act of killing, might repeatedly have shifted its grasp during the struggle, until the huge, dagger-like hind toe found a vital spot, perhaps between two vertebrae, where it was able to pierce the spinal column and immobilise its very powerful struggling victim. Such a point would be extremely difficult to prove; but as in many cases in the study of eagles, incomplete evidence forces one to take refuge in conjecture.

8 Adaptation for Predation

Without exception, eagles locate their prey by sight, sometimes aided by hearing, and kill it with their feet. It is no light matter to be bitten by a big eagle but the bill is not primarily used for killing, although in the act of starting to feed an eagle may use its bill finally to dispatch still living but disabled prey such as snakes or fish.

Steller's Sea Eagle and the Philippine Monkey-eating Eagle have exceptionally deep, laterally flattened, arched bills. Their purpose is obscure, for their nearest relatives, the European Sea Eagle and the still more powerful Harpy Eagle, lack such exaggerated bills. These great beaks may not be an adaptation for feeding, but may serve some other purpose—perhaps display. The lateral flattening of the beak may also permit the eagle to see beyond its own nose, so to speak, when using binocular vision; but why this should be necessary in these two species alone is obscure.

Since the feet are the most important killing instruments they are the most specialised members. The feet can accommodate themselves to the size and shape of the prey taken, a small animal being crushed in the grip of overlapping talons; while a wide spread of the foot, enabling the bird to seize a large animal, also places the talon points in a position to pierce when the grip of the foot is exerted. The feet of eagles are specialised according to the preferred type of prey taken, so much so in some cases that they could hardly adapt to killing other prey.

Sea and fish eagles, which eat fish, have rough spicules on the soles of their toes, to help in gripping slippery prey. Their feet are less highly specialised than those of the Osprey, which has more pronounced spicules, and also more powerful

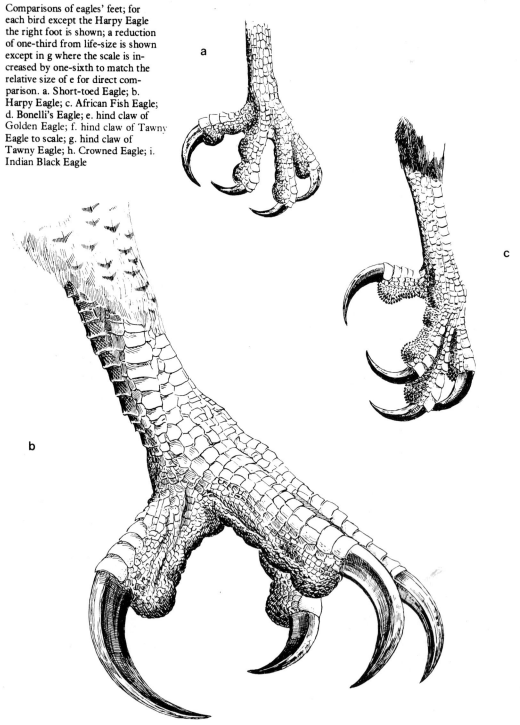

Comparisons of eagles' feet; for each bird except the Harpy Eagle the right foot is shown; a reduction of one-third from life-size is shown except in g where the scale is increased by one-sixth to match the relative size of e for direct comparison. a. Short-toed Eagle; b. Harpy Eagle; c. African Fish Eagle; d. Bonelli's Eagle; e. hind claw of Golden Eagle; f. hind claw of Tawny Eagle to scale; g. hind claw of Tawny Eagle; h. Crowned Eagle; i. Indian Black Eagle

a

c

b

CJFC.

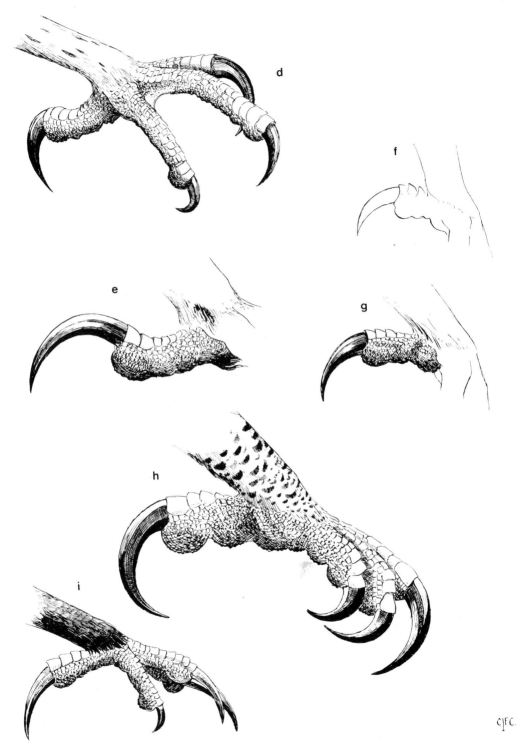

d

f

e

g

h

i

CJFC.

legs relative to its size. This difference perhaps reflects the preferred mode of killing fish, for Ospreys plunge right in with a heavy impact, while fish eagles normally snatch fish in passing on the surface, or descend on them gently, like a parachute. The large sea and fish eagles, more inclined to kill mammals such as hares or seal calves, have more powerful feet than the smaller tropical species. The vegetarian Vulturine Fish Eagle should apparently need neither spicules nor powerful feet; but it has not lost the powerful grip of a true predator, nor has it, like vultures, abandoned sharp talons. It has preserved versatility; and if it cannot find oil palms, it can catch small fish or mammals instead.

All well-known snake eagles have short-toed, relatively stout feet and legs. The otherwise aberrant Bateleur has a typical snake eagle's foot; but the eastern Crested Serpent Eagles apparently have proportionately longer toes. These short stout toes are clearly more suited to grasping and killing thin, wriggling snakes than long thin toes, ending in long curved talons. I have not experienced the grip of a true snake eagle; but the power of a Bateleur is tremendous. A sick adult drove one talon into the top joint of my middle finger, forcing me to tear it out, for the bird would not release me.

Since snakes are fragile animals, with very easily broken backbones, the mere impact and clutch of a snake eagle should disable a large venomous snake so that it could not strike effectively. The hinder half of a 6ft cobra, gripped by the middle, would be effectively paralysed; its fore-part could probably still writhe and wriggle, but could not strike effectively from a solid base. It could only lunge feebly with its head at the eagle gripping it. Stronger, thick-bodied snakes, such as puff-adders, must present more of a problem; and the still stronger-bodied constricting snakes are apparently never taken; they are usually too large.

Most of the harpy group are forest or woodland birds, and are believed to eat mainly mammals. The feet of the Harpy are much the most powerful of any bird of prey. The 1in (2 cm) thick tarsus of a female ends in a foot spanning 9-10in (22.9-25.4cm), equipped with massive dagger-like talons more than 1½in (3.8cm) long. Such a foot is clearly adapted to dispatch large and powerful mammals, while the talons could be driven through and through the body of a young monkey to kill it almost instantly. Other members of this group lack such enormously powerful feet. Perhaps they do not need them, even if they live on arboreal monkeys. Monkeys are, for their size, relatively frail, nervous, and much more easily killed than antelopes or pigs of equivalent weight. The eagle

Crowned Eagle on its kill (*L. C. Parker*)

may also strike a monkey with such force that it dies by falling to the ground. The enormously powerful feet of the Harpy are therefore a mystery at present.

The true or booted eagles vary in size and habits more than any other group; consequently they show greater variation and specialisation in their feet. The most peculiar are the feet of the Indian Black Eagle, with long toes and thin, rather gently curving talons. Such a foot is not well suited to dispatching large and powerful prey, but would apparently be ideal for snatching up birds' nests full of eggs or young.

In other booted eagles, the power and shape of the leg, foot and talons varies according to the preferred prey. Mammal-eaters tend to have relatively thicker, shorter toes, with heavy curved talons, and bird-eaters relatively longer, slimmer legs, ending in long toes with long sharp talons. The African Crowned Eagle, with very stout powerful legs and feet, habitually kills mammals of up to four times its own weight; but its near relative, the larger and heavier Martial Eagle, with longer slimmer legs and less powerful, wider-spreading feet, habitually kills game birds or medium-sized or weak mammals of its own weight or much less. The feet and legs of Martial Eagles are well-adapted for catching fast-moving, dodging game birds, whereas the thick-toed and immensely powerful feet of Crowned Eagles are adapted for a paralysing grip on large, strong mammals such as adult forest duiker.

The size of prey taken also affects the span and size of the foot, especially of the long hind claw and talon. Bonelli's and the African Hawk Eagle have relatively very large feet, with a very powerful hind toe and a long stiff talon. Weight for weight, these eagles are among the most potent of avian predators. African Hawk Eagles often kill adult guineafowl and African hares two to four times their own weight. However, they retain the long leg, well adapted to killing the smaller, more agile game birds which are their favourite food.

Golden and Verreaux's Eagles have relatively powerful feet, with a long strong hind claw and talon. A mere glance suggests that these birds should be able to kill larger mammals, in proportion to their own weight, than Tawny or Steppe Eagles which habitually kill easily-caught rodents much smaller than themselves. In these nearly related species the power of the foot and the length of the hind claw apparently relates to the preferred prey. No very powerful foot is needed to despatch rodents, but in Golden and Verreaux's Eagles the regular need to kill large mammals necessitates a powerful hind claw. However, one can carry this too far, for recent research in Tsavo Park and elsewhere shows that Tawny Eagles can and do regularly kill large gamebirds, hares, and even dikdik—small antelopes weighing eight pounds or more.

Some small booted eagles such as Ayres' Hawk Eagle feed on small active birds caught in the treetops with extraordinary agility, or perhaps in flight in the open. Such eagles have developed long slim legs and feet with long thin talons resembling those of bird-catching Accipiters. However, some of the smaller forest members of the genus *Spizaetus* have shorter legs and relatively short, stubby, powerful toes. Such feet suggest that they may feed more on small forest animals and reptiles than on birds; but the facts are unknown. Examination of feet can suggest the favourite or normal prey;

but conclusions drawn without supporting facts can be misleading, as in the Tawny Eagle.

With a few specialised exceptions, the relative proportions of eagles' wings and tails are primarily adapted to free movement in the habitat. Forest eagles all tend to have rather short, broad, rounded wings, and long tails, useful for manoeuvring among branches. Eagles living exclusively in open, mountainous country have long wings and rather long tails. Fish and sea eagles, which normally catch easily killed but often heavy prey on open watersides, usually have very broad wings and rather short tails. They need not manoeuvre very rapidly; but may have to lift very heavy weights relative to their own.

Different groups of eagles show parallel evolution according to habitat. For instance, the Congo Serpent Eagle, Cassin's Hawk Eagle and Crowned Eagle of African forests; and the Harpy, Guiana Crested Eagle, and several eastern forest hawk eagles all have the short wings and long tails characteristic of the forest habitat. The folded wings fall far short of the tail tip; and the ratio of tail to standard wing length (from carpal joint to tip of primaries) is 68-85:100. Other forest raptors, notably the bird-eating Accipiters and the aberrant, crepuscular forest falcons, *Micrastur* spp, have similar broad wings and long tails.

In the Brown and Banded Snake Eagles, Bonelli's and the African Hawk Eagle, inhabiting woodland, the wings are moderately long and the tail relatively shorter than in forest species; the tail to wing-length ratio may be 54-69:100. In the Golden, Tawny and Martial Eagles, all hunting in open country, the tail is still shorter, 47-51 per cent of the wing. However, the European Snake Eagle, with its two African races, also hunts in open country and has a tail 54-57 per cent of the wing; but it regularly uses its relatively long tail to increase lift when hovering, like a Kestrel.

Extreme specialisation in the wings and tail are shown by the Indian Black Eagle and the Bateleur. The Indian Black Eagle is apparently a slow-soaring searcher, perhaps with low wing-loading. Its rather long, soft and flexible primaries, relatively less emarginated than, for instance, those of the Golden Eagle, may assist slow flight, useful in methodical searching of dense cover. They resemble the primaries of the unrelated African Harrier Hawk, also a slow methodical searcher, with low wing-loading for its weight.

At the other extreme of specialisation the Bateleur probably cannot fly slowly at all and spends much of the day gliding swiftly at 35-55mph airspeed. Its extremely long,

Wing forms: a. European Sea Eagle;
b. Bateleur Eagle; c. Golden Eagle;
d. Bonelli's Eagle; e. Tyrant Hawk
Eagle

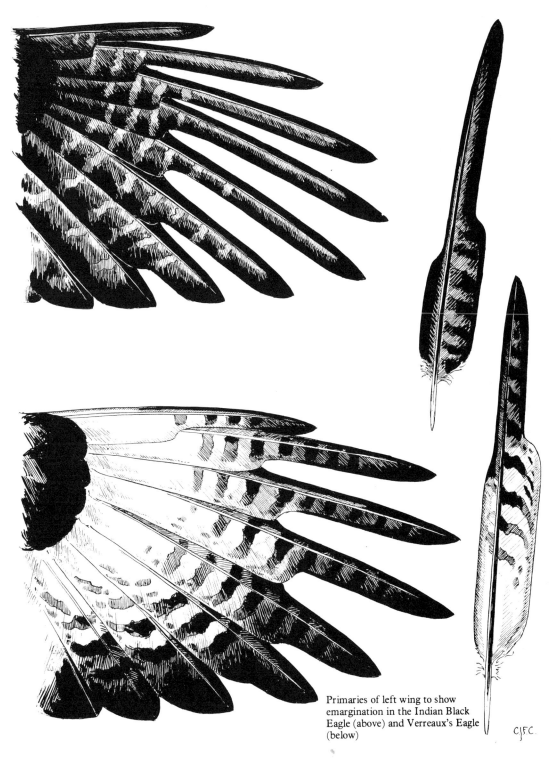

Primaries of left wing to show
emargination in the Indian Black
Eagle (above) and Verreaux's Eagle
(below)

CJFC.

65

pointed wings contain more secondaries than those of any other raptors except some of the larger vultures. When adult, its tail is so short that the feet project beyond it, and it is almost useless in aerial manoeuvres; immatures have longer, but still relatively short tails.

The Bateleur compensates for its lack of a steering tail by canting from side to side in flight. It feeds upon snakes, carrion and a surprising number of birds, especially in the breeding season; is a pirate of prey from other raptors; and is, structurally, perhaps the most aberrant of all eagles. Though its very long wings fit it for effortless gliding at speed, they do not seem to prevent it from performing astonishing aerial manoeuvres, such as occasional 360 degree rolls; and in a vertical stoop it could apparently catch flying birds or strike dead quite a large animal. However, I believe the Bateleur normally kills rather small or weak animals or snakes; and readily picks up small carrion such as road kills. If it can kill in a more spectacular fashion, its power is seldom utilised.

Adaptations of the wing and tail are not necessarily closely adapted to the act of killing. To kill agile prey, an eagle must be able to fly swiftly and manoeuvre rapidly, but killing mice or rats, habitual in several eagles, requires no great powers of flight or manoeuvrability. Few eagles ever kill flying prey; they usually kill their prey on the ground, taking it by surprise. They need their flying powers as much to reach a favourable position as for killing itself.

Most eagles kill from perches when they can, but fly to hunt when necessary. When adequate perches are not available the eagle must soar or hover in order to be able to catch its prey. Eagles of open country normally soar or hover. The only eagle which regularly hovers like a kestrel or buzzard is the European Snake Eagle, with its two African races, all of which hover gracefully, with slowly fanning wings. Very rarely, Martial Eagles and Brown Snake Eagles also hover. A hover is, in effect, an aerial perch, in which the body and wings move in response to aerial currents, but the head is held rock steady. In kestrels, the tail is long and fanned to produce extra lift; but in the European Snake Eagle hovering habits have not resulted in a proportionately longer tail (tail: wing length=56:100).

For effortless soaring the larger eagles of mountainous country have long, rather broad wings, with six or seven emarginated primaries at the wingtip. The degree of emargination of the primaries affects the shape of the 'slots' formed when the feathers of the wingtip are fully spread. The primary is usually emarginated on both webs so that the wingtip slots are nearly square at their base; this is apparently more efficient than a sharply angled wing slot, and gives better control at the wingtip.

These wing slots are constantly adjusted by eagles soaring along a slope while hunting. Slight movements of the spread feathers at the wingtip apparently help to maintain the head and body steady while the wings adjust to the often buffeting air currents characteristic of mountain country. In relatively still conditions, small adjustments of these wingtip feathers may help the eagle to maintain a straight and level course.

The advantage of soaring steadily in a strong wind is easily appreciated by anyone who has tried to hold binoculars steady in a small, light, bucking aircraft. The broad wings and separated wing-tip primaries enable a hunting eagle to search intently for its prey almost regardless of weather conditions. Such separated primaries are characteristic of other non-predatory soaring birds such as storks and pelicans. They are thus primarily an adaptation for soaring, not for hunting; but in eagles the constant delicate adjustments of the wingtip feathers are also an aid to the hunting bird, necessary for its survival.

Part III Behaviour Away from the Nest and Outside the Breeding Season

9 Diurnal Behaviour

It is usually very difficult to find out how an eagle spends its day. One may locate them at a roost (where they sleep all night), reach there before dawn and watch them carefully; however, in most cases they take flight after an hour or two, fly out of sight in a few minutes and usually cannot again be located. In forest, particularly, this is an acute problem, but it also applies to open mountainous country or woodland.

A composite picture can be built up by noting what a particular eagle is doing whenever it is seen. Although I have never been able to follow a Crowned Eagle far through the forest, repeated observations over many years give me a fair idea of their way of life. I can plot on a map where I have seen either the male or the female perched; where I know they have killed prey; and where I have seen them displaying or soaring. Through successive years I can recognise individuals by their plumage characters; and on successive days, by the state of their wing moult. Thus, I can recognise any strange adult visitor, as the odds against seeing two different males or females in exactly the same stage of moult on the same day are enormous.

Even so, after fifteen years I know little good detail of these Crowned Eagles' lives. I know they kill once every two to three days, but I have never *seen* one kill—though several times I have just missed it. Likewise, the observers who have been watching the Verreaux's Eagles in the Matopos hills with extraordinary diligence in recent years have only seen two kills, though this eagle feeds almost entirely (99.9 per cent) on hyrax, caught in the open.

The modern science of radio-telemetry has so far told us little about diurnal behaviour in eagles. It has proved extremely useful in the case of smaller predators, mammalian or avian, especially nocturnal owls and smaller raptors. However, at the moment, transmitters powerful enough to send a signal detectable far from the receiver, perhaps obstructed by mountains or forest, are not small enough to attach to an eagle without impeding its flight. Very small transmitters can be attached to individual feathers; but they have a limited range, and forest interferes with their efficiency. Such small transmitters should soon be specially useful for forest species, which probably move less than soaring species of open country but are hard to locate; or, if waterproof, for sea and fish eagles which can often be followed in a boat.

Radio telemetry has recently been used on American Golden and Bald Eagles, and the results in the latter case confirmed by direct observation. The Bald Eagles in winter left their roosts soon after dawn and flew direct to favourite feeding perches, alternately flapping and gliding. They then made short flights out over the water and attempted to catch fish by swooping—each varied action detected by differences in the transmitted signals. Those that caught fish and fed had normally done so within two hours of first flight, by 10am. If the day was dull and cold, they then spent most of it sitting on other perches, returning to roost in the evening. If it was fine, however, they were stimulated to soar; and would soar much of the late morning and afternoon, returning to their roosts by degrees. All were on their roosts well before dark. In Australia Wedge-tailed Eagles were observed for 480 hours from a tower. An active period of low-level flying began soon after dawn and continued for 1-2 hours, in which time the eagles often found carrion or observed prey. As soon as the heat of the day produced thermals, soaring began; the pair often soared together, and strong winds and rain reduced soaring. High aerial flights lasted 6-90 minutes, and some were followed by radar. In one of these, the bird flew for 38 minutes only, but in that time rose to a maximum height of 780m (2420ft) above ground, and the ground plan of the flight showed that it covered a huge area, 2000 by 6000m (2100 by 6100yd) or about 12sq km (4.6sq miles). Thus, with its keen eyesight, that eagle could in one flight survey most of its home range. These limited observations suggest that eagles may spend very little time actually hunting for their prey.

The African Fish Eagle is common, conspicuous and often very tame, so is an ideal species for such study. At Lake Naivasha in Kenya the eagles remain year-round in their breeding territory extending over only 200-300yd (m) of shoreline. I can anchor my boat offshore on the evening of one day, watch the fish eagles go to roost, sleep in the boat, and at dawn begin watching. I have thus been able to watch two to three pairs continuously from dawn to dark. One full

DIURNAL BEHAVIOUR OF FISH EAGLES FROM PAIR WATCHED FROM 05.45 to 18.30 on 5.10.71 (765 minutes)

(A) MALE

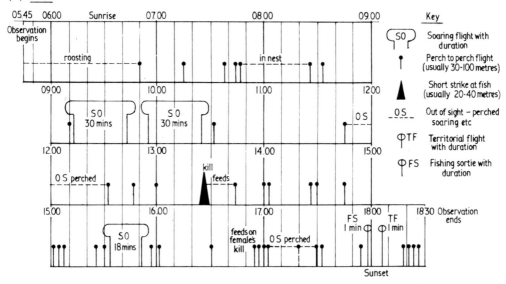

Male was active most of day. Spent 1hr 18min soaring; made 38 perch to perch flights; 1 short strike (successful), 1 fishing sortie, 1 territorial flight. Total flying time 99·5/765 min = 13% of observed time. Made 1 kill in 2 attacks (small fish), also fed on part of female's kill. Spent about 40 min in nest, although not breeding. Copulated with female once at 15.25.

(B) FEMALE

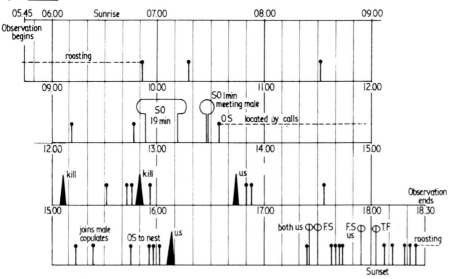

Female was inactive most of forenoon, making only 6 perch-perch flights and soaring with male for 20 min. In afternoon and evening she made 23 p-p flights, 4 short strikes, 3 fishing sorties (7 attacks), and 1 territorial flight. Total flying time estimated 42/765 (5·5%). In 7 attacks, made 2 kills (of small fish), but left part of first (taken at 15.06) on feeding perch where male ate remains between 16.54–17.00. Despite this, she apparently was still hungry and made 5 unsuccessful attacks after her second kill. Did not visit nest with male from 07.45–08.27, but joined him on perch at 15.25, copulated, and later spent about 20 min in and near nest. Her inactive morning is perhaps explained by a good feed on the previous day (inferred).

day provides between forty-eight and seventy-two eagle-hours for analysis, and I can now reliably say how these eagles spend their day.

Pairs roost close together, often side by side on the same branch. They leave their roosts a few minutes after dawn and fly to lake-shore perches. They may make a short territorial flight or two, and almost invariably advertise their whereabouts by a bout of loud calling, answered by their neighbours. Thereafter they spend 75-90 per cent of the day perched; the lighter male is more inclined to fly about and soar for longer periods than the larger heavier female. Either sex may kill a fish or pirate one from a pelican or heron, in a few seconds, at almost any time from early morning to late evening. If they are not hungry, they may make no serious attempt to fish and do not kill every day. Whichever obtains a fish normally feeds itself first; and its partner usually eats the rest. However, if one member of the pair only kills something small its mate often goes hungry. Alternatively, one of the pair may kill when it is not itself hungry, so that its mate obtains food without itself making any effort.

Sometimes the fish eagles fly out of sight; but then often perch in trees behind the water's edge, where they can be located, or re-located by their frequent calls. Sometimes one or both of a pair soar to great heights and depart from view, perhaps to fishing areas 5-6 miles (8-9.5km) away, and are then temporarily out of my ken. However, more often they descend from high soaring after half an hour or less, and I can reasonably assume they have been soaring since they disappeared. If one returns with a part-eaten fish, or with an obviously full crop, then it has been fishing while away. When continuously watching two to three pairs I seldom miss an actual kill, though it takes only a few seconds.

A very good idea of the amount of time and effort spent hunting and in other activities can thus be built up. This can be expressed either quantitatively in tables, or in graphic form, for either sex of a pair. Results broadly confirm the composite picture gathered by noting what any fish eagle was doing whenever seen. Scattered observations made on hunting methods and the times and methods of killing are also broadly confirmed by direct daily observations. The good correlation between these two ways of gathering data suggests that, even in species not as easily watched as African Fish Eagles, a composite picture built up from enough scattered observations is near the truth. If observers of eagles record every single sighting, what it was doing, and for how long, they will gain a good idea of how an eagle spends its day.

In Cheylan's observations on the annual activity of Bonelli's Eagle the hours of daylight varied from a maximum of 16 hours in summer to $9\frac{1}{4}$ in winter. The eagles were not on the move or hunting for all this time. In autumn they normally left their roost, after preening, about two hours after first light, and would make short flights before leaving for the hunting range to the north. They were back about $1\frac{1}{2}$-2 hours before dark. It was impossible to determine what they were doing when out of sight; but one may safely assume that they were not hunting the whole time they were away from the nesting and roosting area. The pair usually left together, probably hunted together and shared kills. During autumn and winter display periods and during the breeding season, they were more active, but still perched much more than they flew about. Even then, much of their flying was in display, not hunting.

Available evidence shows that eagles spend very little time actually hunting, but easily catch the food they need when they need it; they need not hunt constantly, though they must sometimes work hard for their food. Species such as the African Long-crested Eagle, which feed upon smaller animals, and usually catch more than one per day, are many times more likely to be seen killing than those which kill large mammals every two or three days. A hyrax weighing 8lb (3.6kg) equals about forty field rats.

Several recent studies of large mammalian predators, such as the lion and cheetah, have also shown that these animals spend most of their time loafing around, even by night, and only a fraction of the twenty-four hours actually hunting. Like the larger eagles, lions may then kill prey sufficiently large to gorge, and thereafter go without food for several days; cheetahs, on the other hand, kill almost every day, practically at will.

Most who have watched eagles for long periods would agree that they spend very little time actually hunting; it follows that when they do kill they can often do so quickly and easily. In well over 2,000 hours spent in eagle haunts in Scotland, I have seen Golden Eagles kill twice. In Africa, I have seen Martial Eagles kill three times; Wahlberg's Eagle less than ten times; Ayres' Hawk Eagle once; Verreaux's Eagle once; and the African Hawk Eagle and Crowned Eagle never. I have many times seen Tawny Eagles feeding on carrion, pirating prey from other species, or picking up locusts or termites from the ground; but have seen them kill their own larger prey only four or five times. I have seen African Fish Eagles kill at least a hundred times, chiefly

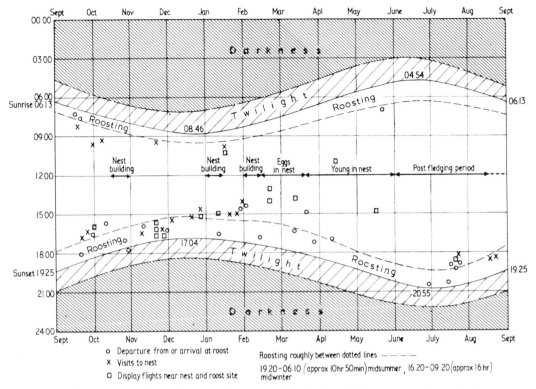

because I have spent many days watching specifically for this. If observers spent more time actually watching hunting or resting eagles they would probably see kills more often, but to see an eagle kill in casual watching is rare.

To sum up, eagles roost, according to species, from an hour before dark to an hour or two after dawn, on trees, rock cliffs or sometimes on the ground. At the Equator, with more or less equal day and night length, this accounts for fourteen to sixteen out of twenty-four hours. In the fish eagle activity may begin before sunrise, and the roosting time may be less than twelve of the twenty-four hours. In northern summers, with long light nights, an eagle may actually roost for two to four hours; but in winter in the same areas may roost for up to twenty hours; it can then only search for food for a few hours daily. These figures indicate that, for European and North American eagles which remain resident in their ranges year round, winter could be a time of severe difficulty if they could not find carrion.

Having left the roost, a few aberrant species such as the Bateleur may fly about all day. More often an eagle flies to some favoured hunting perch or area and, if hungry, hunts until it has caught prey. In Utah, Golden Eagles in summer

Variation in hunting times of Bonelli's Eagle (*adapted from C. Cheylan*)

hunted mainly between 9 and 11am and 4 and 6pm, perching or resting for fifteen to sixteen out of twenty daylight hours. In many species a kill made by either of the sexes, if large enough, suffices for both, perhaps with some surplus. Having killed and eaten, the eagle perches on a ridge or tree; or if conditions are suitable, soars high up, or performs brilliant feats of flight, playing in the powerful air currents about the summit of some hill. Forest eagles probably spend most of their time perched within the canopy, and soar only or mainly in order to display.

The actual time spent in flight is likely to be only a small part of the active time; and the time spent actually hunting may be only a small part of the total flying time, or the eagle may hunt only from perches. Some time before dark, near the Equator normally one to two hours before, the eagle flies to its roost, which may or may not be the same place as it roosted the night before, but very often is, at least for several days. Once it has roosted, its day, which is not normally a continuous, exhausting struggle to obtain enough to eat, is over.

10 Powers of Flight and Speed; Migration

Some eagles are magnificent fliers but, since they are often large, heavy birds, they may seem ponderous and magnificent rather than swift or agile. They never quite attain the lightning dexterity of some of the small Accipiters, or the sheer style and grace of a big falcon. However, at least some species, for instance the coal black and white Verreaux's Eagle, combine grandeur, grace and speed in surpassing magnificence; while the ease with which any eagle covers country must leave an earthbound observer envious.

The celebrated ethologist Konrad Lorenz has implied that eagles fly only to hunt; and that an aviary cage is quite adequate for the exercise of their flying powers. In my opinion this is quite untrue, for many eagles do not use their finest powers when hunting, but reserve their more magnificent feats of flight for nuptial display, or when soaring, for no very obvious reason. My studies of the diurnal behaviour of African Fish Eagles show conclusively that they use ten times as much energy in vigorous soaring or nuptial displays as in hunting prey. One cannot certainly say that when performing vigorous aerial evolutions on high they are never hunting; but certainly they do not soar primarily to hunt. Nor is soaring exclusively concerned with territorial behaviour or nuptial display, though it is frequently part of such activities.

Eagles' wings are adapted for soaring and gliding rather

than the swift attacking dives of falcons or the lightning manoeuvres of a sparrowhawk. With few exceptions eagles' wings are rather long and fairly broad, with a low aspect ratio (length:breadth). No eagle has the long, sharply-pointed wing of the true swift falcons, but forest eagles have relatively shorter, broader wings than those of open country, often resembling in silhouette gigantic Accipiters.

The Indian Black Eagle and the African Bateleur have wings specialised, respectively, for slow searching and swift effortless gliding over long distances. More than others, these two might repay careful study by aerodynamic experts. Bateleurs have also dispensed almost entirely with the normal long tail, used for steering. Heavy-bodied, very long-winged birds, they glide constantly over the terrain 100-300ft (30-100m) above ground, canting from side to side to steer, and moving at an airspeed of 35-55mph (56-88kph). They flap their wings mainly at take-off and to accelerate in pursuit of prey, or of another Bateleur. In gliding flight the long wings are often curved back, almost achieving the silhouette of a delta-wing aircraft. The Bateleur probably must maintain a fairly high speed to glide as it does, and cannot fly slowly. On the wing for about eight hours in twenty-four, it possibly covers 200-250m (320-400km) every day of its life with little effort. The most specialised in flight design of any eagle, and one of the most specialised in the world of birds, there is no other bird quite like it.

Some eagles living in open or mountainous country, including several not very closely related species such as the Golden Eagle, Martial Eagle and European Snake Eagle, have long wings of higher aspect ratio than those living in forests. Verreaux's Eagle also has very short inner secondaries, resulting in a deep notch in flight between the inner secondaries and the spread tail. The wingtip primaries are also often flexed back when soaring or gliding, so that the shape of the wing is a long pointed oval like a simple leaf. Perhaps such a silhouette is adapted to hunting close to cliffs, for Golden Eagles, especially the lighter, smaller males also, less markedly, show this silhouette.

Such eagles of open country can probably fly faster than the broad-winged forest eagles. Unfortunately few accurate timed records of speed exist; a stopwatch is seldom handy. However, although eagles may often appear to be travelling rather slowly they are moving faster than it appears. Their large size makes them seem much slower than, say, a swift; but they may actually outpace swifts.

A much-quoted record of actual speed is Fraser Darling's,

of a Golden Eagle, which left one known point, gained some height, and alighted on another; but despite travelling generally uphill, made the traverse at an average of 120mph (195kmph). At some stage during that short flight it must have exceeded 150mph (240kph); but since it never appeared to fly unusually fast one wonders what speed any similar eagle can attain when really trying.

Eagles occasionally do dive at electrifying speed, but probably do not often approach the theoretical maximum attainable in a vertical dive aided by gravity. A falling body accelerates at the rate of 32ft/sec/sec (9.76m/sec/sec) until at 'terminal velocity' the increasing resistance of the air and friction prevent further acceleration. Since weight increases as the cube, and surface area as the square of any body measurement, the heavier the bird the faster it theoretically can fall in a vertical stoop. A Golden Eagle, weighing $7\frac{1}{2}$-$8\frac{1}{2}$lb (3.5-4kg), should theoretically be able to dive much faster than a Peregrine Falcon weighing $1\frac{1}{4}$-$1\frac{3}{4}$lb (600-800g). However, allowance must be made for the aerodynamic efficiency of body-shape and tight or looser plumage.

A diving Peregrine Falcon resembles an efficient, blunt-ended, sharp-tailed projectile; an eagle probably is less efficient because of its big broad wings, even when folded or flexed. A Peregrine Falcon in a vertical dive is estimated to move at from 200mph (320kph) to less than 100mph (160kph), with one reckoning of 275mph (440kph). However, Philip Glasier, using calibrated speedometers on trained falcons, claims that a stooping Peregrine does not exceed 85mph (136kph). Few who have watched wild falcons or eagles stooping at speed will believe that this is their peak performance. The theoretical terminal velocity of a Peregrine Falcon is about 180mph (290kph); and most would believe a Peregrine capable of such a speed. A big heavy eagle, given similar aerodynamic efficiency, should theoretically be able to reach or exceed 200mph (320kmph).

I have twice been able to compare a Peregrine with an eagle, at close quarters, the comparison on the first occasion favouring the eagle, on the second the Peregrine. A recently fledged Martial Eagle was gliding past the nesting cliff of a Peregrine in Kenya, and was at once attacked by the tiercel, which dived in pursuit, screaming. The eagle merely tilted a little downward, partly flexed its great wings and, without appearing to accelerate greatly, drew easily away from the falcon. Perhaps neither was going full out.

On the second occasion a male Ayres' Hawk Eagle, among the swiftest of all eagles, stooped at his mate in display. Wings closed, he fell 1,000ft (300m) or more, and appeared to be travelling like a bullet as he approached her. However, as we watched, an immature Peregrine flashed into the field of the binoculars and overhauled and passed the eagle, travelling perhaps 20-30mph (32-48kph) faster than he. This Peregrine probably was travelling nearly full out as it had dived from some high pitch above the eagle's starting point, and its superior speed was probably due to the greater distance it had fallen.

Although they may appear to be flying faster, smaller lighter eagles are probably slower than big species. Fast vertical dives are more often used in display, or even in play, than in hunting. When hunting, eagles are usually stationary on a perch, or flying rather slowly, often close to the ground, searching it intently. When possible a hunting eagle uses updraughts along ridges to enable it to poise on set wings, or, like the European Snake Eagle, may actually hover with slowly fanning wings. Such soaring and hovering also necessitate fine control and mastery of flight.

The long-tailed, broad-winged Crowned Eagle of African forests, sometimes called a clumsy flier, can exercise beautiful control over the speed of its descent from a height. When descending nearly vertically, the eagle 'slips' air at intervals by raising or lowering the tail. To fall almost vertically at rather high speed, the eagle raises its tail and furls its wings; and when it wishes to reduce speed it lowers and spreads the tail and partly spreads the wings. Although such manoeuvres could be useful when attacking unsuspecting monkeys feeding in the forest canopy this exquisite control is more often used simply to alight with precision. The huge Harpy Eagle, also a forest species, can apparently fly among the branches of huge trees with astonishing dexterity.

Fish and sea eagles are less agile, more ponderous fliers than are the larger booted eagles of open country. Their wings are often broad as well as rather long in relation to their body-weight, and their tails relatively short, and for some reason wedge-shaped rather than square or rounded. In silhouette, a soaring European Sea Eagle shows very large broad wings with widely separated primaries at the tips, and a short tail widely spread almost to overlap the inner secondaries, so that the spread wings and tail form one continuous flying surface, quite unlike that of, for instance, Verreaux's or the Golden Eagle. Some sea eagles, for instance the American Bald Eagle and the eastern White-bellied Sea Eagle seem to have relatively longer, narrower wings and longer tails than their close relatives the European Sea Eagle and the African

Juvenile African Fish Eagle in flight
(*Su Gooders, Ardea Photographics*)

Fish Eagle. The reasons for the varied proportions of related species with similar habits deserve fresh study, which could soon be started by careful measurements of all living specimens in zoos or in falconers' hands.

Eagles of all sorts are seen at their best when soaring; the mastery and control they can then exhibit is superb. Two Scottish Golden Eagles seen under almost completely opposing conditions illustrate this well. The first was soaring below me along the southern face of Ben a Chlachair near Loch Laggan on a day so warm and still that I lit my pipe on the summit without shielding the match. The smoke rose practically without wavering; yet in air so still that neither I nor the smoke of my pipe could detect appreciable currents, the eagle moved easily along from pitch to pitch, the spread primaries at the wingtip gently opening and closing as if delicately fingering the light air currents of that summer's day. His body seemed rock-steady; only his wingtips moved in relation to the plane of flight.

In contrast, on Sgurr na Ciche in West Invernesshire, on a day of hurricane-force wind that tore great slabs of turf off rockfaces and hurled them away like dry leaves, a Golden Eagle soared above a pass, as rock-steady as the bird on Ben a Chlachair, but with his wings three-quarters furled to his sides. He was actually shooting through the airstream at perhaps a hundred air miles per hour, yet appeared to be nailed motionless against the sky. The eagle on Ben a Chlachair was probably hunting; that on Sgurr na Ciche probably merely playing in the wind. Both gave unforgettable exhibitions of mastery and grace.

When soaring in nuptial display, and performing the vigorous aerial evolutions of display, even big eagles may show lightning agility that would be admired in smaller birds. A displaying male Crowned Eagle hurls himself about in the sky in vigorous, spectacular, steeply undulating dives and upward swoops, accompanied by loud calling. Even more spectacular aerial displays may be performed by Golden Eagles or Verreaux's Eagles. On Mull in 1972 I watched four Golden Eagles displaying together for twenty minutes. Each bird attacked another in turn, the one attacked flipping over at the last minute and presenting claws in a lightning roll. Yet not one feather was lost by these powerfully armed birds. Verreaux's Eagles perform tremendous undulating displays, falling a thousand feet or more, swinging up to an equal height like the arm of a pendulum, sometimes rolling or somersaulting at the top of the upward swoop. It then appears that not even a falcon can perform better; and one is staggered by the agility and grace of these great birds.

Such spectacular feats are mainly used in play or display. Regular daily movement, whether within the eagle's territory or on migration, is usually achieved with the minimum of effort, little wing flapping, and by using thermals and mountain updraughts. In any windy mountainous area, powerful standing waves of air swiftly lift an eagle to any desired height with little effort. In the tropics, and on still hot days elsewhere, eagles climb to height on thermal bubbles, or on dust devils—twisting columns of air which carry dust and debris up to several thousand feet. I have seen a Tawny Eagle deliberately fly into the base of a dust devil, whirl round and round in tight circles within the column, and in a few seconds gain 800ft (250m). Eagles regularly make full use of such aerial aids to reduce the effort of moving from place to place.

Some eagles are regularly migratory; and several others, notably those inhabiting semi-arid tropical areas, are nomadic, making more or less irregular movements from area to area, possibly in response to prevailing climatic conditions. Tawny Eagles in Africa, and Wedge-tailed Eagles in Australia are apparently nomadic; and even the Bateleur, usually considered a resident in its breeding quarters, may also be nomadic, since it is seldom seen where continuous heavy rains are falling. Like many other eagles, Bateleurs are grounded in wet conditions and almost unable to fly in their normal swift, aerial gliding way.

Eleven species of eagles (three sea eagles, one snake eagle and seven booted eagles) perform more regular migratory movements. Of these, Wahlberg's Eagle migrates entirely within the African tropics. It breeds mainly in southern Africa from September to January, arriving in late August and departing again in about March. There are only a few, some doubtful, records of its breeding north of the Equator. However, its off-season or 'wintering' area (of course it suffers no winter in the tropics) is still largely unknown, though it may be in southern Sudanese savannas.

All ten other migratory eagles migrate to avoid the northern winter. In several, for instance the very widespread Golden Eagle, the northern populations, breeding in Alaska or Siberia, may migrate, while the southern populations, in California, Scotland, Spain or the Caucasus, remain in their breeding areas all winter, perhaps shifting to lower ground. Two subtropical eagles, the European Snake Eagle and the Booted Eagle, leave their relatively warm breeding areas and migrate to Africa or India in winter. Since different populations of Golden Eagles may migrate or not, the migratory habit is not a good reason for specific rank in the Steppe Eagle, as compared to tropical Tawny Eagles.

Some immature eagles are more likely to migrate than adults; and immatures, even in species permanently resident within the tropics, may be forced to leave breeding areas and move some distance to escape persecution by their elders. In Africa, immature Steppe Eagles migrate farther south than most of the adults, dominating the migrant populations in Rhodesia and South Africa. Again this is not a good reason for regarding them as a separate species, for most Golden Eagles wintering in the southern United States are also immatures.

Migrating eagles almost always travel overland and by day, chiefly because thermals are generated mainly or entirely over heated land. Over the sea there may be winds but no or few thermals; and an eagle that mistakes the distance and descends into the sea is doomed. Migrating eagles use thermals, or mountain air currents along ridges, to soar or gain height. They often follow long lines of escarpments, such as the Rift Valley in Africa. Having risen on a thermal to several thousand feet above flat country the eagle then sets its wings to a gentle downward glide and shoots off in the desired direction. Its glide may carry it many miles without interruption; or it may use another good thermal to regain height before its first momentum is fully spent. In either case it rarely flaps its wings, but conserves energy by using currents to rise by soaring or circling, and then gliding without effort.

Time of day, weather and physical proportions affect the efficiency of this process. Thermals seldom develop much before 9am on a sunny day in the tropics. The bigger and heavier the eagle, the wider its turning circle when mounting, so that a large Steppe Eagle needs a bigger thermal, developing later in the day, than a small Booted Eagle. Likewise a light eagle will rise faster than a heavy one; lighter males rise faster than heavier females. Weather phenomena such as thunderclouds, producing strong upcurrents, may be actively sought. Equally, migrant eagles may be caught by adverse weather conditions and grounded for some time; in Kenya bedraggled Steppe and Tawny Eagles are often seen sitting on trees or posts, unable to fly well as long as their feathers are wet. Migrant eagles may even be killed, as has happened with Black-breasted Snake Eagles caught roosting by a hailstorm in Rhodesia; or the Steppe Eagles found dead at 26,000ft (7,924m) on the South Col of Mount Everest. We assume that these were migrating normally, but were unluckily forced by bad weather to settle and die in that forbidding spot.

This normal mode of travel by diurnal soaring overland is both effortless and fairly fast, but results in concentrations of eagles at certain points, such as the land bridges into Africa, at the Bosphorus and Suez, and Gibraltar. In America no such concentrations occur because no American eagle migrates farther south than north Mexico; they do not pass over Panama. Eagles migrating into India or Burma from Siberia or north China probably travel through many Himalayan passes. Other eagles, such as the three migrant sea eagles (European, Pallas' and the Bald Eagle) follow flight paths along sea coasts, big rivers or via chains of lakes separated by dry country, as in Utah.

Even the best-observed concentrations at the Bosphorus and Suez raise knotty problems. By far the commonest winter migrant eagle in most of Africa is the Steppe Eagle; yet it is seldom recorded at Suez, and it is not clear how it enters Africa unseen in such numbers. Lesser and Greater Spotted Eagles, with some Imperial and other, rarer, species, are regularly observed at the Bosphorus and Suez; but thereafter the Spotted Eagles practically disappear. The Lesser Spotted Eagle apparently winters in southern African woodlands; but its route to these areas is obscure. It has seldom been recorded in any numbers en route; but why it should soar willingly within easy sight of observers at Istanbul, yet pass over Africa unseen, perhaps travelling by night, is a real conundrum. Again, why should the common and easily seen Steppe Eagle *not* be seen at Suez or the Bosphorus? Although the Greater Spotted Eagle was believed to winter in northern Ethiopia and the Sudan, I have lately examined thousands of large brown migrant eagles in Ethiopia without seeing a convincing Greater Spotted Eagle.

Migrating eagles need little energy, and many apparently migrate fasting, though this certainly does not always apply to Steppe Eagles. Any large eagle in good condition can fast for weeks if need be; and fasting could theoretically be advantageous in reducing weight and wing-loading to permit more efficient soaring on thermals and longer glides out of them. Temporarily abundant food supplies found en route, for instance locust swarms, may halt eagles for a time. Once settled in their winter quarters, they feed voraciously on whatever is available. In Ethiopia and Kenya, Steppe Eagles feed mainly on mole rats, but immature Steppe Eagles in Rhodesia and South Africa feed mainly on abundant flying adults of harvester termites, swarming after seasonal rain. Steppe Eagles in Kenya and Ethiopia cannot normally find winged termites because of the dry conditions there in winter, so must eat rats.

Eagles are not among the farthest travelled migrants, nor the swiftest. Theoretically an eagle could travel 400-500 miles (640-800km) in an eight-hour soaring day, averaging about 50mph (80kmph); such a speed would enable the longest distance migrants, Lesser Spotted and Steppe Eagles wintering in southern Africa, to reach their winter destination in ten days to two weeks, even allowing for the devious route via Suez. However, they normally take six to eight weeks for the journey, averaging only about 100-150m (160-240km) per day. Clearly, such a migration rate is no problem at all for a bird with an eagle's powers of flight.

11 Hunting Methods

The hunting methods of eagles are adapted to the favourite type of food and its ease of capture. A Steppe Eagle feeding on termites requires no great agility or energy to be able to catch such nearly helpless creatures; the only difficulty for so large a bird is to catch enough. The same Steppe Eagle, in northern Africa, must expend more energy to catch a mole rat, and still more to catch a hare in the highlands of Arussi in Ethiopia; but in both cases it is rewarded by a much more substantial prey.

The hunting methods of many eagles, especially forest species, are not well-known. Six of the eleven fish eagles, nine of the fourteen snake eagles, five of the six harpy eagles and fourteen of the thirty-two booted eagles—ie thirty-four out of sixty-three forms, or more than half—are little or scarcely known in this respect; another fifteen are no better than well-known in general terms. I believe that only one, the African Fish Eagle, has been observed systematically for long enough to be able to state quantitatively the amount of time spent hunting daily, and its rate of success in killing its prey.

The African Fish Eagle has been observed more systematically than others, since it is far easier to watch than most. I have now seen African Fish Eagles kill more than a hundred times, but in the twenty-five years I have been watching forest-loving Crowned Eagles I have *never* seen one actually kill, though I have sometimes been able to reconstruct what has happened from signs. The African Fish Eagle, inhabiting a fairly small territory, and hunting mainly in plain view over open water is obviously more easily watched hunting than a species which traverses great tracts of mountains or lives in dense forest.

The frequency with which prey is brought to the nest has been observed much better than the frequency of killing away from the nest, chiefly because the need to feed mate or young forces the eagle to return repeatedly to one point. The prey brought to the nest may not be all that is killed in the same period. However, since, whether male or female, the bird that kills normally feeds first on the prey brought to the nest, this presumably represents what is killed in the breeding season. Sometimes it reflects an unusually high rate of killing, especially when a male is feeding himself, his mate and one or more large young.

Eagles most often obtain their prey by direct capture of living prey, which all eagles use, and most, so far as is known, exclusively. Of sixty-three forms, only sixteen, mainly sea eagles and *Aquila* species, are known to obtain food in any other way; and even among these most of the prey is obtained by direct capture of live animals.

Some eagles, especially *Aquila* and large sea eagles, scavenge carrion. The size of animal then utilised is unlimited, and includes the largest, whales and elephants, though usually smaller. A few habitual carrion feeders also regularly pirate prey from other birds, whether live prey or a piece of carrion. Some recent mammal observers do not make any distinction between picking up something dead (scavenging) and attacking another predator to take what it has, which is piracy, or robbery, but not mere scavenging. The clear practical distinction between the two is that scavenging requires little energy, while piracy frequently demands much more energy and risk than may be needed in direct capture of live prey.

Several of the sea eagles are known to be pirates; and the Bateleur and the Tawny and Steppe Eagles obtain much of their prey by piracy. Since all these are also carrion eaters it seems likely that the piratical habit derives from carrion feeding. Several other carrion-eating birds and mammals, for instance South American caracaras, several large vultures, jackals, hyenas and even lions, frequently pirate prey killed by other animals.

Piracy may sometimes seem almost a compulsive preferred method. African Fish Eagles rob a large variety of water birds, from Pied Kingfishers and Hammerkops to Great White Pelicans and Goliath Herons; also Ospreys and other fish eagles. Parents may rob their own young; even mates rob their partners. An incubating fish eagle may leave its nest to rob another fish eagle. Fish eagles intently watch pelicans fishing, and pursue them at once when they see a catch—which the pelican then obligingly regurgitates as an escape reaction. Ospreys, smaller but probably more efficient fishermen than any fish or sea eagle, are regularly robbed by several fish eagle species. Fish eagles may even futilely pursue a possible victim, sometimes expending much energy to obtain nothing. I have watched a pair fruitlessly pursue a Yellow-billed Stork for over a mile, and force it down, for no reward—presumably because the stork had nothing.

The other habitual pirates are Tawny and Steppe Eagles, which take prey from their own kind and from any other raptor, a kestrel, a kite, a snake eagle, even the much larger Martial Eagle or Lammergeier. They have taken to watching European and Marabou Storks following the plough for mole rats on Kenya highland farms. No sooner does a stork collect a rat than a waiting Tawny Eagle is after it to pirate the prey. Tawny Eagles and Bateleurs bark aggressively during piratical attacks, so attracting attention; but fish eagles are normally silent pirates. The Bateleur is less compulsive, but a very vigorous and noisy pirate. Other eagles may occasionally commit acts of piracy; I have seen a Brown Snake Eagle pirate a snake from a Tawny Eagle; and a Verreaux's Eagle pirate a probable hyrax from a Martial Eagle. Except for fish eagles and the Tawny-Steppe Eagle group, piracy is rare.

Carrion is particularly important to northern species which winter in cold climates. Usually a large or very large animal, a sheep, deer or even a whale, in freezing conditions, may have to be thawed by the sun before becoming edible; but it lasts for weeks, is easily found and can be visited repeatedly. In less severe climates, carrion will do when preferred live prey is scarce. Although it has been suggested that readily available carrion is one reason for unusually dense populations of Golden Eagles in north-west Scotland, in these areas eagles kill the scarce grouse and hares when they can, at least for their young. The only carrion actually taken to the nest is an occasional dead lamb. Some other habitual carrion feeders, such as the Tawny Eagle, do sometimes take old and putrid carrion to the nest for the young. The abundant carrion often available in the range during winter and spring, even summer and autumn, means that these northern eagles will not starve for lack of food.

Most eagles prefer, and most often kill, natural prey of fish, snakes, birds or mammals. Interest therefore centres on how they manage to kill such prey, varying from a termite or a beetle to a guineafowl, bustard, hare, hyrax or rarely a duiker, bushbuck or roe deer. No healthy animal weighing more than 40lb (18kg) is normally killed by any eagle; but there have been occasional reports of Golden Eagles killing still larger animals in snow, or when weakened. If an eagle stoops at a grizzly bear or a leopard it is not for food. Siberian Golden Eagles trained to fly at wolves are trained to behave unnaturally, for no wild eagle would attack a wolf for food.

The mode of hunting live prey depends mainly on the prey concerned and how it is most easily captured. Little skill or effort is needed to catch small, weak prey, such as termites or small frogs. Tawny Eagles may locate swarming termites by watching other birds circling to catch the flying insects, descend to the opening of the termitarium, perhaps driving away any lesser species found there, and feed avidly on the emerging insects until gorged. In southern Africa many Steppe Eagles live almost exclusively on alate harvester termites which, although small, are very fat and can be gobbled as fast as the eagle can pick them up. Larger eagles, even the lordly Verreaux's, also feed on termites when they can. In Europe, Lesser and Greater Spotted Eagles are said to walk about on the ground in marshy places hunting frogs and even grasshoppers; so such small fare is not to be despised.

Small rodents, often abundant and easy to catch, are the next size upwards in the range of prey. Many eagles eat them in numbers. The African Long-crested Eagle, for instance, is a habitual rodent-eater, catching grass rats from perches on telephone poles, electric pylons or trees. From here it simply falls on the prey, in a short gliding stoop, accelerating at the last moment as it finally raises its wings above its back to drop on the unsuspecting rodent. During a rodent plague gorged Long-crested Eagles may perch in trees while dozens of grass rats run about on nearly bare ground 30ft (9m) below, unaware that the eagle is there.

If common enough, such prey also suffices several larger eagles, notably the Steppe Eagles of eastern Europe. A meal weighing up to 3oz (100g) can be obtained in a few short easy attacks; little energy is needed here, either. However, none of the largest mammal-eating eagles, such as Verreaux's or the Golden Eagle, can wholly depend on rodents; they must regularly catch larger prey to survive.

Steppe Eagles, feeding on abundant rodents in summer on the steppes, feed largely upon mole rats in the highlands of Ethiopia and East Africa. Mole rats can weigh 8-12oz (225-300g) but are usually blind or semi-blind, and can easily be located, like European moles, by their movements near the surface. The Steppe Eagle need only to settle quietly on a hummock close to the heaving earth and bide its time. The mole rat is easily caught in a short flight of, at most, a few yards, ending in a pounce with outspread talons buried in the ground. The eagle's main problem may then be to retain possession of the mole rat in the face of probable piratical attack from others of its kind.

The Steppe Eagle seems rather more sluggish, more inclined to perch on the ground, and less likely to hunt active prey than the smaller and more versatile African Tawny Eagle. Tawny Eagles hunt termites or mole rats too; but also take many game birds, scavenge camp-ground or village scraps, pirate other birds' prey, kill for themselves animals as large as a jackal cub or a hare and even kill some large birds in flight. Kenya Tawny Eagles near Lake Elmenteita frequently kill adult flamingoes, apparently by a swift stoop at a flying flock. The Tawny Eagle's versatility is probably one reason for its success; and certainly there is no good reason for despising it, as some do.

Rabbits, hares and other mammals of similar size (3-8lb, 1.5-3.7kg) form the staple diet of several large eagles, such as the Golden, Verreaux's and the Wedge-tailed. In the Golden and Wedge-tailed Eagles, all investigations have shown that where they can catch them in numbers rabbits and hares are preferred prey. Verreaux's Eagle feeds almost exclusively on rock hyrax, taking also occasional guineafowl or dikdik; it really thrives only where hyrax are abundant.

Although such animals are normally caught by a short, swift, surprise attack, they are very much more alert and difficult to surprise in the open than are small rodents or burrowing mole rats. The eagle may have seen the prey from some distance and may approach at speed, knowing the ground; or it may seize a sudden chance while soaring. For example, in Scotland I watched a soaring Golden Eagle suddenly dive on and surprise a mountain hare sitting near its form. In Utah, I watched a Golden Eagle flying low over the ground at speed, apparently making purposefully for some point. Suddenly it dropped behind a sage bush; and a few moments later rose with a ground squirrel in its talons. It probably knew that the ground squirrel was sitting in the open behind that bush and came at it low, using the cover, to snatch the agile animal unawares. Ground squirrels, which are heavier than one would think, are the staple prey of Alaskan Golden Eagles. African ground squirrels of the genus *Xerus* are common, but may be too alert to be caught often.

Where they cannot catch medium-sized mammals, such eagles as Golden Eagles will eat game birds. Scottish Golden Eagles regrettably often kill grouse and ptarmigan, and are therefore persecuted, despite legal protection. In wooded Estonia, Golden Eagles feed largely on game birds. Tawny Eagles, Bateleurs and some of the eastern eagles of the genus *Spizaetus* also eat many game birds. However, if medium-sized mammals are available, they will be taken in preference, presumably because easier to catch. Most game birds are caught on the ground; but authentic records prove that Golden Eagles can catch grouse in full flight.

Some eagles, such as the Martial, Bonelli's and African Hawk Eagle make a staple of game birds. In some cases I have watched the eagle come on its prey at speed, low among trees, and because of its speed has probably launched its attack from some distance. Others have described game birds taken by a quick twist and pounce from flight, almost as if they were mammals.

Such attacks are not always successful, even if launched at high speed. Spectacular failures I have seen include one by a Booted Eagle in Spain, which essayed to catch a Red-legged Partridge. It came down out of the sky like a shell; but the partridge dodged it and got away, leaving the eagle standing on the ground. Another was a Red-eyed Dove perched on a dead tree, attacked by a Wahlberg's Eagle in a long, nearly vertical stoop; it literally flew out of the eagle's outstretched foot at the very last minute; however, some such attacks doubtless succeed.

Occasionally, eagles may kill birds in flight, as reliable eyewitness accounts prove, though they do not necessarily reflect normal hunting methods, but only the most spectacular. Golden Eagles have been seen to turn over and snatch in flight a Red-tailed Hawk that was mobbing one; and to kill ducks and geese flying across mountain passes. Bonelli's Eagle, one of the swiftest and most agile eagles, has been seen to dive at a jackdaw, pass below it, and turn upwards to catch the jackdaw from below. Another Bonelli's Eagle stooped at a pigeon behind rock columns, and caught it as it took off. However, even the most agile eagles seldom catch birds in flight, and most avian prey is taken on the ground.

I have only once seen a kill in flight, by that versatile bird the Tawny Eagle. The victim was a Speckled Pigeon perched in a tree in Ethiopia. The eagle stooped at it at great speed, shooting over my head from long range in a steeply slanting dive. The pigeon saw it coming and took flight; but the eagle made an acute-angled turn behind it, a few feet above the ground. In 200yd (183m) it struck at the pigeon twice, and the second time disabled the quarry, dispatching it when it dropped into a field. The eagle finally killed its prey on the ground, but it had caught it in fair level flight, after an unsuccessful attempt to surprise it by a swift stoop.

Ayres' Hawk Eagle and probably some of the small eastern hawk eagles live on forest birds. Most prey brought to an Ayres' Eagle's nest is thrush- or starling-sized birds or doves; rarely a large game bird. Such kills are seldom seen, but are at least sometimes achieved by extraordinary agility, combining the powers of a falcon and a goshawk. An Ayres' Eagle once stooped past me as I sat on a cliff-top near her nest, shot through the branches of a tree, and emerged beyond carrying a bird, perhaps a bulbul, in her foot. She probably saw the prey before diving at it, for I have also seen an Ayres' Eagle suddenly hurtle into a baobab tree and just fail to catch one of a flock of Superb Starlings, despite twirling feats of agility that would have been creditable in a small sparrowhawk. Such small eagles are the most agile of any; probably they kill flying birds regularly.

The large mammals sometimes killed by forest eagles such as the Crowned Eagle are normally surprised on the ground or in trees. In many areas the Crowned Eagle is said to feed mainly on monkeys; but in all areas where I have studied them, their chief prey is small forest antelopes, with tree hyrax as a variant, and only an occasional monkey. They scarcely ever take birds; and where rock hyrax are abundant they feed mainly on these.

I have never actually seen a Crowned Eagle kill; but from observation of unsuccessful attacks, and reconstruction of the signs when I have come on them with fresh kills, I think I understand the methods used. All the signs suggest that the eagle merely drops on its prey from a branch, at close range, much as a Long-crested Eagle kills a small grass rat from a telegraph pole. The difference lies in the size and weight of the prey killed; the Long-crested Eagle's rat is a tenth of its own weight, and weak; but the large animals killed by Crowned Eagles may be up to four times the eagle's weight, and capable of violent struggles.

I have twice found bushbuck recently killed by Crowned Eagles. In the second case, a half-grown male, I was able to weigh a back leg, and calculate that the live animal must have weighed at least 40lb (18kg) and perhaps 50lb (22kg). It had apparently been attacked when crossing an open space and, judging by the talon wounds, had fled into a forest of Eucalyptus with the eagle riding on its back. It had then been downed and dispatched, apparently by talon clutch of the neck, without a very long struggle. In the other case, a rather smaller bushbuck, the struggle had been severe. The eagle had dropped on its prey from a perch, as the buck was walking along a trail in shrubs. The startled animal had leaped some yards to the right, where it had been downed, and its flailing legs had flattened a large patch of bushes. The eagle had eventually killed it, losing only one feather in the process. It had then dismembered the buck (too heavy to move entire), and dragged the portions down a passage through thick shrubs to the shade of the tree from which the attack had been launched. Here I found the female on the remnants, probably the day after the buck had been killed. However, even in these big powerful eagles, such epic encounters are rare. Most of the prey taken is smaller and lighter than the eagle itself.

Most of the eagles that feed on fish or snakes catch their prey from perches. Sometimes it requires no effort, as when Bald and Steller's Sea Eagles feed on dead and dying Pacific salmon kelts. African Fish Eagles catch most of their prey with little effort, by what I call a short strike from a perch, a flight of 30-50yd (27-46m), ending in a kill, the whole action taking ten to thirty seconds. Less often, the eagle makes a brief fishing sortie, circling over the water for some minutes before returning to a perch. Still less often it kills a fish from

Young snake eagle swallowing
snake *(author)*

high soaring flight, usually by descending gently to make the kill, but occasionally plunging right in with a heavy splash. Wind stimulates soaring; and fish eagles often hunt in rough water from soaring flight.

In one short strike, exemplifying the usual method, the eagle was perched on a coral block at low tide, while I was snorkeling nearby. Suddenly it flew out, nearly level, for ten yards or so, seized a large fish, and returned in thirty seconds to another perch. If I had not been watching I should have missed it. Owing to my aquatic posture, I was able to creep up to within 20ft (6½m) of the eagle, watch it feed and identify the prey; a large, colourful wrasse, *Cheilinus trilobatus*, stranded by the tide in a coral pool. I later examined the remains and estimated the weight of the wrasse at nearly 2lb (900g).

I have never seen the moment of kill by a snake eagle; but have often seen them just after they have lifted a snake into the air. The wriggling serpent tries to wrap itself around the eagle's feet and escape, but is soon killed by mangling the head; thereafter it hangs limp. Most snake eagles, including the eastern Crested Serpent Eagles, hunt from perches; but the European Snake Eagle and its African races hunt mainly from soaring or by hovering, a form of aerial perch; and the aberrant Bateleur constantly seeks prey with head turned earthward as it glides swiftly across the plains.

Whatever the method adopted, I believe that eagles spend comparatively little time actually hunting, and are normally able to obtain their food requirements with little difficulty. This view is supported by the fact that all experienced observers of eagles see very few kills. If eagles were constantly hunting with intent to kill, but without success, they would more often be seen trying. Both European Sea Eagles and Verreaux's Eagles have been known to leave the nest and return with a large kill in a few minutes.

In the African Fish Eagle the total time spent fishing varied from 0.05 to 8.1 per cent of the time the eagles were in view. The highest figure, 8.1 per cent, was by a male with young in the nest and the female brooding. The least time spent hunting was by a pair which caught a fish at 8am, with their second short strike of the day. Although the eagles sat on perches ready to strike for perhaps two hours, less than two minutes was actually spent hunting. They spent the rest of the day loafing, for the fish, a large *Tilapia*, sufficed both. Some observed pairs, perhaps sated the day before, do not even make any serious attempts to kill during a day. The short time spent hunting, however, includes from two to ten attacks per kill made.

Even if such a life of ease and loafing is not normal for other eagles, it seems certain that they spend far less time hunting than is generally believed; if seen soaring high, they are probably not hunting. In Utah, Golden Eagles spend not more than six and usually only three or four hours hunting in a fifteen-hour summer day. Bonelli's Eagle in France in winter is only absent from the roosting area, not all that time hunting, for about six hours in a nine-hour winter day. Verreaux's Eagles in Rhodesia spend much of their time either perching or soaring high in display, in neither case actively hunting.

More quantitative data are needed; but all evidence at present suggests that only short periods are spent hunting and that prey is not difficult to catch. This conclusion is hard to reconcile with the orthodox view that populations of predators are limited by the amount and availability of prey. However, many more direct observations on the hunting behaviour of all sorts of eagles are needed. Even ten carefully recorded kills for any species (far more than at present available for most) would give a fair idea of preferred methods, while fifty or more records are suitable for quantitative analysis. Until such accurate data is collected, the mode of hunting of most eagles will remain largely a matter of anecdote and fable.

12 Appetite: Food Requirements, Digestion

Eagles, like other predators, hunt mainly when they are hungry, and do not wantonly kill large numbers of prey they do not need, as some allege. However, they may seize a good chance to kill, even if not very hungry. A male African Fish Eagle which pirated a fish from a pelican took it to a perch, but then ignored it for hours while his mate came to the perch and fed on it; later he ate the remains. He must have robbed the pelican only because the chance was too good to miss. Male eagles, with mate and young to feed, also kill more than they need for themselves alone; their rate of killing does not then wholly depend on their own appetite or hunger. Some full-fed eagles can be attracted to a baited trap; apparently they simply cannot resist the seemingly easily captured live bait. Others, hungry or not, cannot be trapped in this way at all; these fortunately include the Golden Eagle, otherwise all too easy to exterminate.

With these exceptions, an eagle's food need depends first on its body-weight, combined with the effects of temperature and exercise, or the energy used when hunting. The basic requirement of an idle captive eagle in a warm climate is a simple function of its body-weight. The largest species can maintain condition with no more than 5 per cent of their body-weight per day, while smaller eagles such as Wahlberg's or Ayres' Hawk Eagle require more, 8-10 per cent. The relationship between body-weight and food intake may not be exact. Verreaux's Eagle, for instance, apparently needs relatively more food than the very similar-sized Golden Eagle. Their food need has been estimated at 13oz (350g) per day, almost a third more than a Golden Eagle of similar weight. However, this estimate is not based on detailed records from captive birds, available for the Golden Eagle.

Although well insulated with feathers, eagles do feel the effects of cold and the basic requirement of a captive Golden Eagle increases by about 10 per cent in winter; one weighing 8lb (3.7kg) needed just under 8oz (214g) in summer and just over 8oz (236g) in winter. In the tropics the effect of cold is negligible.

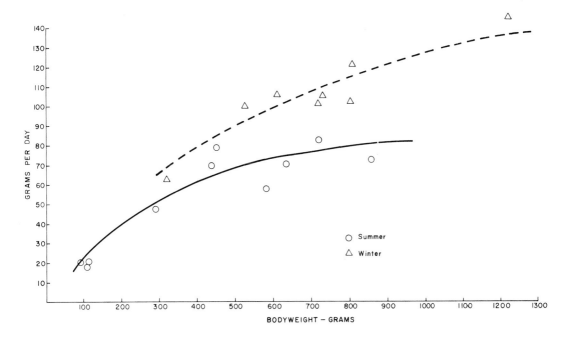

Exercise in normal flight also increases the food need. The same Golden Eagle, when exercised, ate another 17g, raising its total intake to 8 oz (231g) in summer and 9oz (253g) in winter. The effect of exercise is more difficult to assess in wild eagles because direct observations of some species prove that they use more energy in play and soaring than in actual hunting. However, eagles must sometimes fly longer and harder to catch their wild prey than in the flying exercises given by a falconer. Again, an African Fish Eagle, spending an average of 1.2 per cent of its day actually flying to hunt, suggests on the contrary that an eagle forced to flap its wings repeatedly when exercised by a falconer might even work harder than would always be necessary in the wild state.

The data available from captive birds (which is not nearly complete enough and could easily be greatly augmented by falconers or zoo keepers) permit a reliable estimate of the amount an eagle must eat daily. This varies slightly from place to place and season to season; but in the one really detailed study we have, the Golden Eagle ate 5.8-6.8 per cent of its body-weight—scarcely the gluttonous appetite of a wanton killer. This might also vary according to the type of prey taken; a weak, sickly, dead deer, for instance, probably provides less nourishment per unit weight than a solid fresh rabbit or hare.

Estimates of the amount eaten in the wild state are inevitably approximate, for even when watching a nest for long

Diurnal raptors—Food consumption and bodyweight

periods one can only estimate the weight of prey brought; the eagles may not have eaten all of prey left outside the nest, for instance portions of large mammals, which they must dismember to carry. I have twice been able to estimate what wild Crowned Eagles actually eat. In the first case, I gave the eagles a dead female vervet monkey weighing 5lb 14oz (2.65kg). To my surprise the incubating female eagle accepted it; and both she and the male fed on it for five days, leaving only a few fragments of large bones. I estimated that they ate an average of 4oz (110g) per day per eagle, about 3 per cent of body-weight for fourteen days during which they were not known to kill anything else.

This same female one day caught an adult female suni antelope weighing 9lb 11oz (4.52kg) opposite my house. I weighed the animal and replaced it; and that afternoon the female dismembered it and ate 2lb 6½oz. (1.1kg) in one meal, about a third of her body-weight! Unfortunately, some other mammalian predator found the remains during the night and ate some of it, so that I was unable to complete the experiment. However, these two cases with the same wild female indicate that eagles can eat a third of their body-weight at a sitting; but can subsist on less than 5 per cent of body-weight daily for two weeks in a warm climate.

A young Martial Eagle, weighing 12-13lb (5.5-6kg) ate all but the head, stomach and large bones of a suni it had killed in four days. Assuming that the suni weighed about 9 lb (4.3kg), the eagle ate about 8lb (3.7kg), averaging 2lb (925g) or 16 per cent of its body-weight per day. I could not know how long the eagle may have been hungry before it killed the suni, or how long it subsisted thereafter without killing again, but it would be fair to double the known feeding period, reducing the estimated daily consumption to about 8 per cent of body-weight. Thus, evidence from wild birds suggests that estimates of food requirements from careful records of captive eagles are a good approximation of the needs of wild individuals.

The amount an eagle must kill exceeds what it must eat, by a varying quantity, which I call the 'waste factor'. This depends on the size and type of the prey, and the ability of the eagle to digest bones, fur, scales or teeth. Some prey, such as snakes and frogs, is digested almost completely. Snake eagles cast up scarce pellets composed only of the indigestible scales, and excrete hard little lumps, resembling hyena droppings, quite unlike the normal white liquid spray of a typical eagle. Fish, except the scales, are likewise digested entire; and only the large bones of, for instance, catfish are rejected by

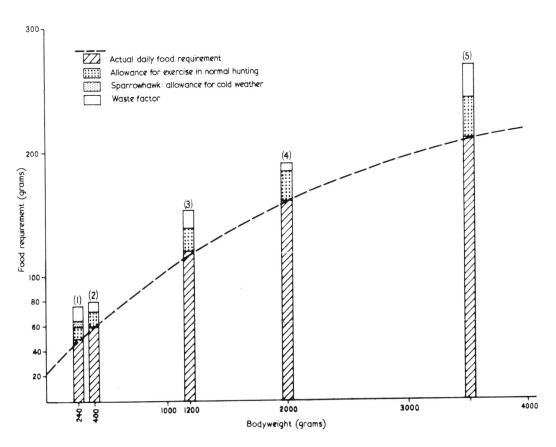

Estimated food requirements of some African raptors

African Fish Eagles. Birds are partially plucked first, then almost entirely eaten by eagles, their small bones presenting no problem; some feathers and beaks are later cast up in pellets. Those of puffins, eiders and other water birds make up most of the castings of European Sea Eagles, for the fish they eat is digested, all but the scales.

Large mammals which the eagle cannot normally carry entire are most likely to be partly wasted. Many animals the size of a hare are torn in half, and the eagle may or may not retrieve the half left lying; another scavenger may find it first. The stomach, packed with inedible vegetable matter, is normally rejected; some of the large bones cannot be eaten, and the head or skull may be left. However, sometimes most of even a very large mammal is utilised. Of two bushbuck killed by Crowned Eagles, the first was largely consumed. They dismembered it, and each brought a leg (which must meantime have been hidden in trees) to the nest next day. In the second case the over 40lb (18kg) bushbuck was killed one afternoon; by evening the eagle had dissected off and removed one foreleg. The body was found and largely eaten by a mammalian predator, probably a leopard, during the night. Next day the eagles took away parts of the remaining back leg (which I had cut off to weigh), leaving the remains. At least 60 per cent of the second bushbuck, but at most 30 per cent of the first, was wasted. The high waste factor, inevitable when an eagle kills prey it cannot possibly lift entire, may be one reason why eagles seldom kill animals much heavier than themselves. The struggle to overcome such an animal may be a risk which is, biologically speaking, not worth taking.

A Golden Eagle with a basic food need of just under 8oz (214g), increased to 9oz (253g) by exercise and cold weather, must kill $11\frac{1}{2}$ oz (316g) of prey per day to keep alive. This equals rather more than half a red grouse; an eighth of an adult mountain hare; or a tenth of an American jackrabbit. Since such eagles gorge heavily when they first feed, ingesting up to 3lb 4oz (1.5kg), a really hungry Golden Eagle would leave nothing of a grouse but need not then kill again for another day. It would, however, leave most of a hare or jackrabbit for its mate.

In most eagles both of a pair feed upon the remains of what either kills, the killer normally feeding first. I have personally observed this in twelve species; and suspect the habit is almost universal if one eagle can locate the other. This habit reduces wastage of large kills; and when surplus prey for the young accumulates in the nest it is usually removed by one or other parent, and not wasted.

Heavy gorging not only satisfies appetite and reduces the inclination to kill, normally stimulated by hunger, but must also affect flying performance. Eagles never, apparently, gorge to quite the same extent as vultures (which may eat so much carrion that they cannot take off); but a Golden Eagle which has eaten 2lb 3oz (1kg) automatically increases its wing-loading by about 25 per cent. It may then find it difficult to take wing, lifting what is left of the prey. The food eaten is normally first retained in the crop, creating a large and obvious bulge. Perhaps, by taking a heavy meal and thus weighting itself forward, an eagle may be better balanced to lift the rest of its prey with the feet, to carry it trailing beneath the tail.

Snake eagles when eating snakes are a remarkable exception to the normal rule of first storing food in the crop and later digesting it. When they eat meat they store it in the crop like other eagles; but if they swallow a snake whole it goes straight in and down into the intestine. A snake eagle which

has eaten a large snake has a palpable lump in its lower abdomen between the legs. This could be a useful adaptation to accommodate a long and awkward piece of prey which might be difficult to carry away in flight if it was all stored forward, in the crop.

A gorged Martial Eagle with bulging crop *(Clem Haagner, Ardea Photographics)*

Eagles digest most of what they eat, even the small bones, but they cast up pellets of indigestible matter, fur, scales, feathers, and some bones, teeth or beaks of prey. These pellets can sometimes provide valuable evidence of the eagle's food, for instance beneath a winter roost. However, since much prey is digested completely they are only indicative. A Golden Eagle feeding heavily and often on a skinned deer carcase would cast up nothing; but if it also ate a ptarmigan or two it would cast up a pellet of feathers, and might be thought to be feeding mainly on ptarmigan. Normally an eagle would ingest some deer hair or sheep's wool with the meat, which would appear in castings. An eagle eating plenty of such roughage may cast almost daily; but if it feeds on snakes or fish or frogs, or meat without fur, it must only cast occasionally. Accordingly, castings are nearly useless as a quantitative method of assessing what eagles eat.

Whatever remains after feeding and casting passes through the gut and is excreted. In snake eagles the droppings are hard and dry, consisting apparently of minutely fragmented bone; they resemble the droppings of that bone-eating avian hyena, the Lammergeier. Most eagles produce a white liquid spray, which they forcibly eject for several feet. To get a true idea of the amount of any prey wasted, the castings and the excreta should be subtracted from the amount actually eaten to estimate the true daily food requirement. Though these finer points of digestion have been studied in domestic animals, such work has yet to be done with captive eagles. We assume that what an eagle actually eats is its daily need; but actually what it must *kill* in order to eat that amount is the crucial figure in its biology.

13 The Effect of Eagles on their Prey

So far as I know, the full effect of any species of eagle on its prey has never been accurately calculated. It can be broadly estimated from a number of different factors, including: (i) the eagle's appetite, the amount it must kill, allowing for wastage; (ii) its prey preferences; (iii) the size of the home-range or territory in which it hunts; (iv) the numbers of the preferred prey in the home range; and (v) the vulnerability or otherwise of the prey—an eagle can only eat what it can see and catch in daylight, and usually eats what it can catch most easily.

Eagles eat 5-10 per cent of their body-weight daily, to which we add wastage of up to 25 per cent, varying with the type of prey killed. Given this, and accurate breeding and survival rates, the amount of food needed to support a pair of eagles and their young in their home-range year round can be estimated. Thus, the basic food requirement of an average adult Scottish Golden Eagle is about 8oz (230g) daily; a pair of adults, allowing for wastage, need about 380lb (174kg) of live prey and 88lb (40kg) of carrion—470lb (214kg) altogether; the requirement of an average of 0.8 young reared to the flying stage is about 119lb (54kg) of live prey; and that of the independent young and a small (20 per cent) proportion of flying immatures and surplus adults (which must exist) is 95lb (43kg) of live prey. An average range must therefore produce 600lb (271kg) *killed*, of which 546lb (249kg) is actually *eaten*, plus 110lb (50kg) of carrion *eaten* (660lb, 299kg eaten). The true total requirement might be rather less, since the young are normally forced to, or do, leave the parental home-range on independence to subsist elsewhere. However, the figure of 600lb (271kg) of live prey killed plus 110lb (50kg) of carrion is a good approximation of the needs of a resident pair of Golden Eagles and their descendants.

This can be converted into a known number of adult grouse, hares or rabbits, dead sheep or deer: 600lb (271kg) equals about 500 red grouse or ptarmigan, or 105 mountain hares, or combinations of both; 110lb (50kg) of carrion is provided by one dead deer and two or three dead sheep; evidently this is easily available. Recorded prey preferences mean that the 600lb (271kg) of live prey will normally include 400lb (181kg) of mammals and 200lb (90kg) of birds; equivalent to about 150 large birds including about 130 grouse or ptarmigan and 70 mountain hares. The effect on any single species of prey is less than when an eagle feeds exclusively on one species.

In most of the western United States, the Golden Eagle feeds more exclusively on rabbits and hares (jackrabbits) than in Scotland. About 99 per cent of the weight of prey brought to Utah nests was jackrabbits and cottontail rabbits; in winter much carrion is taken, but also includes many jackrabbits killed on roads. Since anything but the rabbits and hares can practically be ignored, it should here be easier to calculate the effect of eagles as predators.

Verreaux's Eagle in Rhodesia feeds almost exclusively on hyrax (about 99.9 per cent of all prey recorded). The average size of a home-range (in which a pair resides year round but which the young leave on independence) is 4.2 square miles (10.9sq km). However, the hyrax, living among jumbled rock piles and dense vegetation, are very difficult to count; nor is the average weight of hyrax killed known. In this seemingly simpler case an accurate estimate is at present impossible because of the habits of the prey. The apparently more complex effect of the Golden Eagle is actually easier to calculate.

The average total area of hill country available to a pair of Scottish Golden Eagles year-round varies from 8,000 to 18,000 acres (3,237-7,285ha), averaging about 11,500 acres (4,653ha). Although, in theory, all of this, and perhaps areas outside it, can be hunted by a pair, the whole available range is probably not utilised. In an 80 square mile (207sq km) study area in Utah with an average of 4.25 pairs of Golden Eagles, giving each pair a total available range of 18.8 square miles (27.7sq km), the actual area utilised during the breeding season averaged only about half, 9.03 square miles

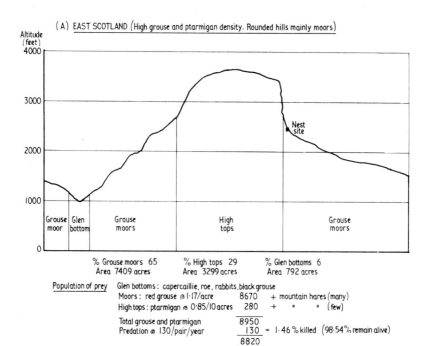

(A) EAST SCOTLAND (High grouse and ptarmigan density. Rounded hills mainly moors)

% Grouse moors 65
Area 7409 acres

% High tops 29
Area 3299 acres

% Glen bottoms 6
Area 792 acres

Population of prey   Glen bottoms : capercaillie, roe, rabbits, black grouse
Moors : red grouse @ 1·17/acre   8670   + mountain hares (many)
High tops : ptarmigan @ 0·85/10 acres   280   +   "   "   (few)

Total grouse and ptarmigan   8950
Predation @ 130/pair/year   130   = 1·46 % killed (98·54% remain alive)
                                        8820

Notes   Predation has negligible effect on grouse and ptarmigan populations. In such areas a larger proportion of prey would be hares, roe, capercaillie etc, so that the effect on grouse is even less than indicated. Eagles are nevertheless persecuted in such areas as killers of grouse.

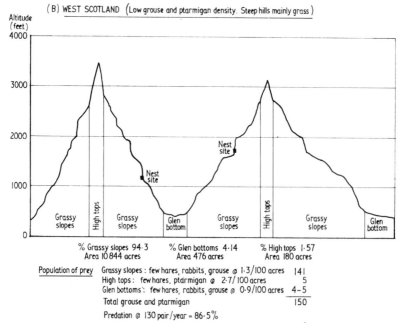

(B) WEST SCOTLAND (Low grouse and ptarmigan density. Steep hills mainly grass)

% Grassy slopes 94·3
Area 10.844 acres

% Glen bottoms 4·14
Area 476 acres

% High tops 1·57
Area 180 acres

Population of prey   Grassy slopes : few hares, rabbits, grouse @ 1·3/100 acres   141
High tops : few hares, ptarmigan @ 2·7/100 acres   5
Glen bottoms : few hares, rabbits, grouse @ 0·9/100 acres   4–5

Total grouse and ptarmigan   150

Predation @ 130 pair/year = 86·5%

Notes : Since, at that rate, predation would result in total extinction (which does not occur) it either (a) cannot be at that rate or (b) population figures available are too low. Since hares are also scarce, rabbits and sheep become important items of food, also such birds as curlews and crows. Eagles are not persecuted as killers of grouse in such areas, although their effect is potentially much more severe.

(23.4sq km), varying from 6.8 to 11.8 square miles (17.6-30.6sq km). In such cases one can calculate the total number of preferred prey in the home-range and estimate the possible effect of the eagles on them.

Histograms showing the effect of a pair of Golden Eagles on grouse in low and high populations

In eastern Scotland eagles often breed in areas abundantly stocked with grouse and hares; but in the grassy hills in the west hares, grouse or ptarmigan are scarce, though sheep and deer carrion is abundant year-round. Although eagles probably eat more carrion in the west, they still live largely on scarce live prey, chiefly grouse, ptarmigan and hares. An eagle territory can support from a maximum of about 11,000-12,000 grouse to as few as 150. If the eagles in each case kill 130 grouse per pair per year, the effect on a low population of 1,000 grouse is very much more marked than on a high population. This has been set out diagrammatically and amounts to 86.5 per cent of a low population of 150 grouse, but only 1.46 per cent of a typical high population.

Where grouse are numerous, Golden Eagles also catch more hares and rabbits, so that the overall effect on the grouse population is even less than 1.5 per cent. Where grouse are scarce, hares are also rare; and though the eagles can substitute carrion for live mammalian prey outside the breeding season, during the breeding season they prefer live prey. In Sutherland in 1967 I found that eagles were feeding their young mainly on scarce grouse and ptarmigan. Where the eagles are preying in spring on the small breeding grouse population, when its numbers are lowest, they obviously could have a relatively severe limiting effect, compared to eastern Scotland. Thus an apparently simple case can become complicated when examined more closely; and when one considers other factors the situation can become almost infinitely complex. For instance, in Scotland, grouse, hares and rabbits are also killed by foxes, wild cats and stoats; hooded crows and large gulls may eat the eggs of grouse and ptarmigan and compete for carrion. In a Golden Eagle territory of 11,500 acres there could be four or five fox dens. Foxes kill grouse if they can catch them, but eagles also kill fox cubs and hooded crows, the latter especially in areas where grouse are scarce. About 1.6 per cent by weight of the prey of Golden Eagles in Scotland is foxes, stoats and other carnivora; and another 0.3 per cent (2.5 per cent by number) is corvids, mainly hooded crows. By eating some foxes and crows the Golden Eagle appreciably reduces the effect of these other predators on the grouse population, so compensating to some extent for its own. Without much more detailed knowledge it is hard to calculate such varied effects exactly.

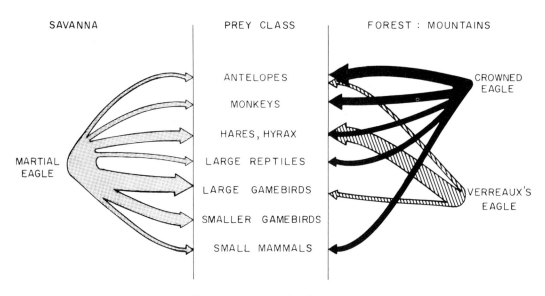

SAVANNA	PREY CLASS	FOREST : MOUNTAINS

ANTELOPES

MONKEYS

HARES, HYRAX

LARGE REPTILES

LARGE GAMEBIRDS

SMALLER GAMEBIRDS

SMALL MAMMALS

MARTIAL EAGLE

CROWNED EAGLE

VERREAUX'S EAGLE

Ecological separation—Martial, Crowned and Verreaux's Eagles

In the apparently simple but actually rather difficult case of the Verreaux's Eagle and rock hyrax, rock hyrax are eaten by at least ten other predators, including leopards, wild cats, large snakes and other avian predators such as the Crowned Eagle, African Hawk Eagle and Augur Buzzard. The number of some of these in the same area is accurately known; there are four pairs of Crowned Eagles which kill many hyrax, and fourteen of African Hawk Eagles which take only a few small hyrax. Among the mammalian predators not even the number of leopards is accurately known; and the numbers of wild cats, puff adders or cobras cannot even be guessed. What appears to be a simple case again proves to be very complicated.

In the Karroo of South Africa, human beings have controlled or eliminated jackals and some other predators; they also needlessly persecute Verreaux's Eagles. In this area, an average 25 sq ml (64.7sq km) range, supports about 150,000-410,000lb (68,000-185,000kg) of rock hyrax, which have multiplied because some of their other enemies have been reduced. Verreaux's Eagle is said to eat about 12oz (350g) per day, wasting about 30 per cent of a medium-sized mammal such as a hyrax. The total amount killed will thus be about 835lb (320kg), still only about half of 1 per cent of the *minimum* amount of hyrax available. It is obvious here that the Verreaux's Eagles could not possibly have any real limiting effect on the hyrax population.

Similarly the average area available for eleven pairs of Kenya Wahlberg's Eagles in 146 square miles (378sq km) of savanna and cultivation was about 13 square miles (33.7sq km) or 8,300 acres (3,350ha). Wahlberg's Eagle feeds upon small game birds (including young chickens), lizards and small mammals. Thirteen square miles of typical savanna could support a total of some 5,000 young poultry and small game birds; at least 150,000, perhaps 1,500,000, small rodents; and about 40,000-60,000 lizards. Clearly Wahlberg's Eagle which, allowing for wastage, needs only about 100 small game birds, 200 lizards and 120 grass rats, could not conceivably have any important limiting effect, especially on small rodents.

Again, Wahlberg's Eagle is not the only species concerned. The game birds in the same area are also eaten by African Hawk Eagles, Martial Eagles and large Accipiters; lizards especially by Chanting Goshawks and snake eagles, mongooses and some snakes; and the abundant grass rats by almost any predator up to a leopard. Wahlberg's Eagle alone may have little effect, but the cumulative effect of all predators in the area would be considerable.

The vulnerability of prey is also important. A small population of grass rats are almost invisible in long rank herbage, but when abundant, at up to 200 per acre (450/ha), the rats eat down their cover and expose themselves to attack. However, they are then so abundant that all the available rat-eating avian predators (Wahlbergs and Long-crested Eagles, Augur Buzzards and Black-shouldered Kites) cannot eat enough to control them. Theoretically superabundance and exposure may have made the rats more vulnerable; but sheer numbers make them less vulnerable. Rats normally die then in large numbers; one week the place is crawling with them, the next they are gone. However, the population of eagles remains stable, and does not really affect the situation.

Some nomadic or migratory species of eagles, notably Tawny and Steppe Eagles, do concentrate in numbers to feed upon abundant mole rats and other rodents, or swarms of locust hoppers; or collect in breeding colonies, numbering millions of pairs, of Sudan Diochs (*Quelea quelea*). In highland Ethiopia, I once calculated that there could be over 100,000 rodents per square mile (38,000/sq km), and mole rats certainly abound in the Kenya Rift Valley. Even quite large flocks of Steppe Eagles could have no serious effect upon so many rats, still less upon swarms of locust hoppers or colonies of *Quelea*. All these are so abundant that the whole range of predators cannot appreciably reduce them.

Relative vulnerability of prey is also well illustrated in fish and sea eagles which cannot normally take swift or deepwater fishes, but can only catch species inclined to or forced (for instance by the receding tide) to live in shallow water; or which approach the surface of deeper water. A sluggish, bottom-feeding, deepwater fish is completely invulnerable to such eagles which can only catch fish in the upper foot or so of water. The African Fish Eagle regularly feeds on catfish and lungfish, which must sometimes or regularly surface to breathe air. The eastern White-bellied Sea Eagle eats many air-breathing sea snakes. Yet active, swift fish such as mullet, or garfish which tend to shoal near the surface, are commonly taken by both Ospreys and sea eagles. At Lake Malawi, Tilapia feeding on surface plankton, become temporarily vulnerable. Young water birds in breeding colonies are hopelessly vulnerable; I have watched one immature African Fish Eagle wipe out a colony of African Spoonbills in a few days. Adult water birds, such as dabbling ducks, which fly to escape, are comparatively seldom caught; but diving sea ducks such as eiders are very vulnerable and European Sea Eagles may catch them almost at will.

The piratical habit of fish and sea eagles enables them to obtain prey they themselves could not catch. Ospreys, which regularly catch fish swimming deeper in the water than those taken by fish and sea eagles, are frequently robbed of their prey. Herons, storks and pelicans fishing among water lilies and thick reeds probably catch fish invisible to fish eagles, which may then rob them. Thus fish eagles can have only a small effect on surface-feeding members of some fish species; and none at all on any which live more than 2ft (0.6m) beneath the surface, unless they can pirate such fish from other water birds.

These examples show how easy it is to begin with the idea that an eagle eats a known quantity of certain preferred food animals per day, and how from this it should be possible to calculate its effect upon the total population in its range; but that when the situation is closely studied it becomes so complicated that no accurate assessment of any eagle's effect on its prey is yet available. The more varied the ecology, the greater the variety of predators and prey animals, the more difficult it becomes. The difficulties multiply when other predators complicate the effect of one eagle on its clearly favoured prey. Even in the apparently rather simple case of Golden Eagles in Utah, ten or twelve other predators may be involved including coyotes, rattlesnakes and other large avian predators, feeding on young if not adult jackrabbits.

This sort of difficulty may also arise when several eagle species all feed on the same sort of prey. In the Tsavo National Park in Kenya, where dikdiks are abundant, Martial, African Hawk Eagles, Tawny Eagles and Bateleurs all feed largely on them. In fact, both the Martial and African Hawk Eagles normally eat gamebirds, the Tawny Eagle is a scavenger-pirate preferring small mammals, and the Bateleur an aberrant snake eagle. Chris Smeenck here estimated that all these eagles would kill 1017-1485 dikdiks per year in 110sq km (43sq miles), and that they caused 40-60 per cent of all dikdik mortality. Bateleurs and Tawny Eagles between them killed 765-1064 dikdiks per year, with the Tawny Eagle killing 400-480 alone. Food preferences of Bateleurs and Tawny Eagles overlapped by 78 per cent by weight, each strongly preferring dikdik in this area. However, these figures are based on a number of arguable assumptions, and on inadequate supporting figures on the total population of dikdik.

Thus, in most cases, we can only consider the effect of a particular eagle species in isolation; and even then only when the numbers of prey can be reasonably well estimated in the home-range of a resident pair of eagles. It then seems clear that the eagles alone do not effectively control the numbers of any abundant prey animals. In some cases, for instance the Golden Eagle and scarce grouse in western Scotland, the eagles may prevent any increase but do not eliminate grouse or ptarmigan. These remain rather scarce, with some cyclic population fluctuations over periods of years, though the population of eagles remains almost constant.

Unfortunately it would now be almost impossible to study the effects of Scottish eagles on their prey because of excessive human interference. The evidence from studies done elsewhere suggests that all eagles cover home-ranges or territories large enough to maintain a superabundance of preferred prey. This has also been found to be so in several predatory African mammals, including lions, leopards, hyenas and wild dogs. A single predator is seldom the main, or even an important, limiting factor on the numbers of prey, though the cumulative effect of several predators together may be considerable.

We simply do not know what may be the effect of many eagles on their prey. This would apply, for instance, to all the sea and fish eagles whose prey is hard to count, and to snake eagles, for the number of edible snakes there might be in a snake eagle's 50 square mile (130sq km) African range is unknown. In many species, for instance the harpy group and forest booted eagles, the food preferences are not even known. In these, until much more knowledge is available, conjecture is a waste of time.

One must, however, start from a reasonable estimate of the amount eaten daily by an eagle in the wild state, a function of its body-weight if it is not more accurately known from captive birds. Then, one must know the size of an eagle's range, its breeding statistics and likely mortality before sexual maturity. Thus, one can estimate that an average Golden Eagle's range must support two adults, about 0.8 young per pair per year (each young eating about as much as an adult) and about 0.4 grown young or surplus adults; in all, about 3.2 eagles per home-range. The Martial Eagle, a larger, slower-breeding, tropical species, must maintain 2.6-2.8 eagles per territory, while the small migrant Wahlberg's Eagle must support 3.2 per territory during its six-month breeding season. Given such relatively solid fact, derived from adequate data, the rest of the arithmetic is fairly simple.

Again, in no case has the number of prey been really accurately computed, though a fair attempt has been made in the Scottish Golden Eagle. No single human being can do it all; a team of co-workers is needed, including an ornithologist, a mammalogist and a herpetologist, with access to plant and geological or soil surveys. The study should also continue for several years, to observe the effects of any regular population cycles such as occur, for instance, among game birds or rodents. So far as I know no such long-term studies have yet been done.

Even if such studies are done it is not enough to assess the effects of eagles alone, without considering also other predators, mammalian, avian and reptilian, nocturnal and diurnal. In some of the simpler situations, mainly in northern latitudes, much information is already available; in others, for instance the tropical forests of South America or even in Africa (where research on individual eagles is as advanced as anywhere), even conjecture seems useless for lack of knowledge of the habits of other common but nocturnal or secretive predators.

I believe that if ever the results of such more complicated and detailed studies are available, the end result will be that no eagle alone seriously affects the numbers of its prey. The cumulative effect of all available predators will necessarily be greater, perhaps even important. However, since any prey animal must be able to persist and survive, not only from predation, but also from disease and starvation, predation by eagles alone can never really have a crucial effect on the total numbers of their prey.

14 Territorial Requirements and Regulation of Numbers

I dislike the word 'territory' in relation to eagles, because it is normally defined as 'any defended area'; but the area occupied by a pair of eagles is not always or even very often obviously defended from intruders. I prefer the term 'home range' for the area occupied or used by a pair of eagles, and though that is not entirely satisfactory either, it is probably the best available. Part, or the whole of the home range may at times be defended actively, thus becoming a true territory.

Where not persecuted, every species of eagle so far studied maintains a stable population evenly spread over the entire

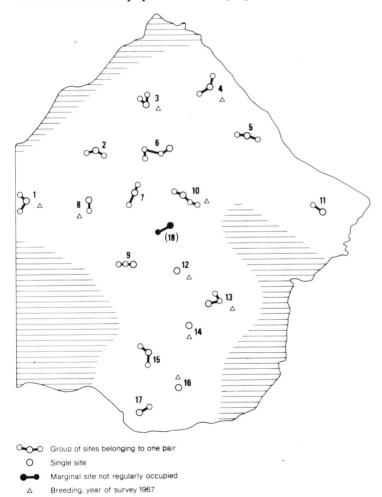

Golden Eagle territories in Scotland, showing even dispersion of breeding sites in a capacity population (from *British Birds of Prey* by Leslie Brown, published by Wm. Collins Sons & Co Ltd)

○─●─○ Group of sites belonging to one pair

○ Single site

●─●─● Marginal site not regularly occupied

△ Breeding, year of survey 1967

═══ Low ground unsuited to breeding eagles

habitat. Such a population I call a 'capacity population'; the area is supporting as many eagles as possible. The density of a capacity population of the same species may vary from area to area, but a capacity population cannot develop where there is any marked limiting factor, such as the lack of suitable nesting sites, or severe human interference. Where the Scottish Golden Eagle is not persecuted, and where there are plenty of nesting cliffs, the population reaches capacity; but in other areas it does not, rarely for lack of nesting sites, much more often because of persecution or casual disturbance. However, from the data gathered in areas lacking limiting factors, one can predict what a capacity population should be where such factors do limit numbers of eagles.

At Lake Naivasha in Kenya the African Fish Eagle population is at capacity along much of the shoreline. The birds are not interfered with, and the population of breeding pairs has been stable for at least four years. Where tall Acacia trees provide safe nest sites, pairs breed only 200-300yd (m) apart, occasionally even less. Even without the trees, pairs occupy and defend a stretch of a lagoon or shoreline without breeding. The population of adults is at capacity; but not all of them can breed. It would be interesting to erect some artificial nest sites on poles, a method used successfully in recent years to increase the North American Osprey population.

Similarly, the population of Verreaux's Eagles in the Matopos hills is at capacity level, varies little from year to year, and with almost unlimited nesting sites is rather evenly spaced over the available jumble of rocky kopjes. In Kenya, Verreaux's Eagles are much more scattered; and in many places do not breed, although the favourite prey, rock hyrax, is abundant. Here the potential capacity population is limited by lack of good cliff nesting sites. Eagles that breed in trees in forest or savanna, however, are seldom so limited. They are normally regularly spaced over the habitat at a certain distance apart, which varies somewhat within the species, and varies greatly from species to species.

Such capacity populations are usually remarkably stable, even despite considerable change in land use and ecology. In Embu district in 1948-51 I studied 146 square miles (378sq km) of savanna, locating every pair of eagles with the aid of honey hunters, and finding a final total of twenty-six pairs of eleven different species, including: one pair of Verreaux's Eagles; eleven of Wahlberg's Eagles; two of African Hawk Eagles; one of Ayres' Hawk Eagles; three of Martial Eagles; one of Crowned Eagles; one of Long-crested Eagles; two of

Bateleurs; two of Brown Snake Eagles; and two of African Fish Eagles. Mapping several of these species in the open savanna, with unlimited suitable nest sites, showed that the nest sites were nearly equidistant from one another, as in the Scottish Golden Eagle. Others were irregularly scattered, for no obvious reason.

I re-surveyed this area in 1968. In the interim the human population had more than doubled and had destroyed much riverine forest vegetation, and cultivated great tracts of land which in 1950 were wild and uninhabited. However, the eagle population had been surprisingly little affected. The Verreaux's Eagle had left in 1952, after an insecure nest built on a rock had collapsed. The nests of the two African Fish Eagle pairs in riverine forest trees had been destroyed. Of three pairs of Martial Eagles, one was breeding still in the very same tree as in 1952; the others had moved 100yd (91m) and 1 mile (1.6km) respectively. The same old sites were occupied by Ayres' and Crowned Eagles, but a new pair of Ayres' had appeared. Bateleurs had increased to three pairs, but one pair of Brown Snake Eagles had disappeared. African Hawk Eagles had increased from two to five pairs, one occupying a former Wahlberg's Eagle's nest site, another that of a Brown Snake Eagle. Wahlberg's Eagles had apparently decreased to seven pairs; but this may have been partly due to a less thorough search for one year only.

The final result was twenty-four pairs of nine species. Three pairs of two species had disappeared, mainly because of loss of nesting sites. The most surprising increase was among African Hawk Eagles, perhaps because of the increase of people and their poultry. The most surprising decrease was in Wahlberg's Eagle, from eleven to seven pairs, but a longer and more thorough survey might have revealed more pairs. The total population and variety of species had altered surprisingly little, despite drastic changes in land use.

Likewise one can return at twenty-year intervals to parts of highland Scotland, to find Golden Eagles nesting close to or even in their old known nest. Usually, the focus of an eagle's home range is the nest site, with one or a cluster of alternate nests. When these sites are mapped it becomes clear that if two sites in any given area provide an approximate idea of the usual distance between two adjacent pairs, one can predict where the next pair should be. Intervening country, however suitable as a nesting ground, can be exhaustively searched without locating any more nests. This principle applies to every eagle I know; but the actual distance between nest sites in the same species can vary. Thus, Lake Naivasha Fish

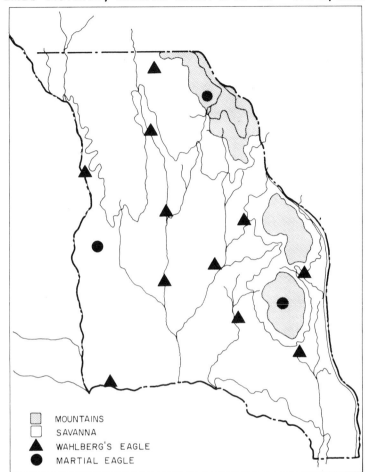

Territories of Wahlberg's and Martial Eagles

MOUNTAINS
SAVANNA
▲ WAHLBERG'S EAGLE
● MARTIAL EAGLE

Eagles nest about 250yd (230m) apart; at Lake Baringo, not far away, about 500-600yd (m); in the Okavango swamps 400-500yd (m) apart; and in the Ruwenzori National Park 600yd (m) apart.

These facts suggest that many eagles can maintain control over a large and fixed area of ground without overt or obvious territorial fighting. Large powerful predators such as eagles or lions seldom actually come to blows. If they repeatedly fought they could suffer grievous disabling wounds, which could jeopardise their survival as a species.

In most eagles that I know well, there is no obvious territorial aggressiveness between adjacent pairs, although birds with their visual powers can obviously see one another with the naked eye at the distances involved. The average distance between Scottish Golden Eagle nest sites varies from 3.0 to 4.4 miles (4.8-7.1km). Clearly soaring eagles could easily see each other and, if so inclined, make territorial

Typical distribution of Golden Eagle alternative nest sites in a Scottish valley. Sites 1 and 2 are often used and are close together; site 3—a mile away—is used occasionally, when snow lies deep at the head of the lock.

113

attacks. They very seldom do; in many months of walking I have seen only two such territorial disputes, neither causing the loss of a feather.

In the Matopos hills of Rhodesia, where conditions for such a study are ideal, Valerie Gargett has found that the territory of a pair of Verreaux's Eagles is like an inverted truncated cone of air. At the top of the territory cone the airspace used by two or more adjacent pairs may overlap; but at ground level, the pairs keep separate, sometimes with considerable tracts of 'no-man's-land'. The pairs maintain their territories without actual fighting, by perching on conspicuous rocks, by flights in and over the territory, by display flights near the boundaries and by calling. Paired eagles are territorial; single adults or immatures are not. Neighbours tolerate each other, with rare aggressive encounters, as in the Scottish Golden Eagle. However, any single adult or immature entering the territory of an established pair is immediately and vigorously repelled, usually without actual contact resulting in damage. The intruder usually leaves the area rapidly. A single unmated adult seeking a partner might thus fly from territory to territory, repeatedly repelled, till it found one where a bereaved adult did not repel it, and settle there.

The African Fish Eagle is still more strongly territorial. At Lake Naivasha the pairs can not only see, but also hear each other whenever they call. If one calls, a neighbour normally answers. Here the territories are linear, along a short stretch of shoreline extending some distance up into the air, and out into the lake, but not far inland. Pairs holding territories in lagoons, without a breeding site, hold a territory based upon a series of perches, flying from one to another.

Here one can define the shore boundary of the territory to within a yard or two, by seeing exactly how far one pair will go towards neighbours. Two birds from different pairs, or two pairs together, may perch a few yards apart near the common boundary and call at one another, but not attack. A bird making a fishing sortie out from a perch carefully avoids infringing a neighbour's territory, or it will be pursued at once. Even over water some distance from shore one may locate the territorial boundary exactly by throwing out dead fish and observing which of several eagles comes to take the prey. Even if very hungry, an African Fish Eagle normally will not go far into a neighbour's territory to obtain such fish, for neighbours will repel and attack it, even if not themselves hungry.

Fish eagles passing over other fish eagles' territories are

aware that they are doing so, and look down, apparently anxiously, at the perched birds below, which may call at the intruder but will seldom leave their perches to pursue it if it maintains height. If the intruder flies past below their perches, however, they will usually attack at once. With adjacent pairs so close, no fish eagle can move without being seen by neighbours. One would think that on small isolated islands in Lake Victoria, where a single pair of fish eagles may breed miles from any other, the need for territorial behaviour would be reduced. However, such pairs behave in very much the same way as pairs with close neighbours, calling at dawn, perching conspicuously and performing soaring or display flights. Their territorial behaviour is an inherited pattern, utilised whether or not it is needed to repel others.

The shore of Lake Naivasha with a pair of fish eagles on a fishing perch; such perches are foci of the territory (*J. S. Wightman, Ardea Photographics*)

Both sexes in eagles take part in territorial behaviour. In one of the territorial boundary displays I watched by Golden Eagles, four birds—two males, a female and an immature—took part. Likewise, in Verreaux's Eagle, both sexes defend the territory from any interloper, both take part in aerial displays and expose themselves to neighbours on conspicuous perches. In African Fish Eagles, females may even be more territorially aggressive than males. They initiate more bouts of calling than do males, perform as many territorial flights and, being larger, generally dominate males, though males may become more aggressive early in the breeding season.

A female eagle may 'see off' another female entering the territory. On 16 November 1972 a strange adult female Crowned Eagle appeared on the forested ridge opposite my house, and called from her perch to the resident male, Sambo, soaring overhead. Sambo went off westwards, displaying high up, where he was shortly joined by his mate, Lolita. Sambo disappeared; but Lolita returned to soar to and fro, calling, above our house. The stranger female then retreated; but in the next hour twice rose and displayed above the ridge, finally alighting there in a bare tree, where she was joined by Sambo. It seemed that he was willing to be unfaithful but Lolita won, for the next morning and for several days thereafter she displayed loudly over the nest site. The other, probably older female disappeared and did not return.

In Verreaux's Eagles, Golden and African Fish Eagles, the adults of adjacent pairs are usually close enough to see or hear each other easily. Territorial behaviour easily visible or audible can then keep pairs apart and territories discrete. However, it is less clear how, for instance, Martial Eagles maintain control over their very large home ranges. In Embu district, three pairs have nested year after year for more than twenty years at the points of an isosceles triangle 8 miles (13km) apart; it is unbelievable that they can regularly see each other and they are also very silent. In such cases any territorial behaviour may not be visible to inferior human eyes, but visible to and understood by the Martial Eagle's piercing sight.

No known eagle is truly colonial, as are some falcons and vultures, in that pairs occupy very small territories in a close group, but forage far outside these in the same areas as neighbours. On Lake Victoria, where many African Fish Eagle pairs nest on islands, with few or none on adjacent mainland shores, I felt at first that this was a sort of loose colony. However, later observation of the equally dense or denser populations at Lake Naivasha has shown that these pairs on Lake Victoria were occupying small, discrete, defended linear shoreline territories. Golden Eagles are reputed to nest colonially in a remote valley in British Columbia; but a well-authenticated, factual account of this area is lacking.

Territory may often be associated with food supply, the territorial bird defending or maintaining a range sufficient for its needs. There is some evidence to support the theory that the size of an eagle's territory depends on the available food suply. In the capacity population of Verreaux's Eagle in the Matopos the size of the territories varies, those with large tracts of grassland lacking hyrax being larger than those composed entirely of rocky kopjes. However, since the number of hyrax was not computed in any territory, this still rests on supposition. The Karroo Verreaux's Eagles maintain very much larger territories with a superabundance of hyrax. However, since the Karroo eagles were limited by both human persecution and lack of suitable nesting sites, the two cases are not really comparable.

In African Fish Eagles there is no real quantitative basis for supposing that food supply and territory size are interconnected. There is no evidence that there are more easily caught fish in a large territory on Lake Baringo than in a much smaller territory on Lake Naivasha; moreover, in both, fish eagles sometimes forage outside their defended territories and can apparently catch fish very easily. In Scottish Golden Eagles' territory size is certainly not directly connected with food supply. The range of a pair varies little from one part of the highlands to another; such differences as exist (15.6 square miles, 41sq km per pair in Lewis to 27.8 square miles, 72.8sq km in parts of Argyll) might well seem less striking, if the actual areas hunted by pairs were known, since not all the ground available is utilised. In Utah the areas used by breeding pairs varied from 6.6 to 11.8 square miles (10.3-19sq km) and averaged about 9 square miles (13.4sq km). In Scotland at least the average area available per pair, 11,000-12,000 acres (4,450-4,856ha) varies enormously in its food potential, abounding in grouse and hares in the drier heathery east, but lacking such prey in the wet grassy west. The total amount of preferred natural prey available can vary by thirty times from east to west; yet the territory or home range occupied remains about the same. Carrion in the west always seems to be superabundant; but since breeding pairs normally feed their young on the available natural prey, the superabundance may be less important than it seems.

In several other cases already described an eagle's home range or territory supports prey far in excess of the eagle's needs. In theory, the eagles should then increase till the prey is more efficiently controlled, and then decrease again. In fact, the numbers of breeding pairs of eagles remain remarkably steady whatever the level of food supply; and even breeding success, in Scottish Golden Eagles, varies only fractionally between areas of abundant and poor food supply. Although much more research is needed on this difficult subject, it seems clear that the dispersal of pairs of adult eagles through uniformly suitable habitat depends as much or more upon social or territorial behaviour as upon the abundance of possible prey. Since similar conclusions have been reached in the study of lions and several other mammalian carnivores, such social limitations controlling numbers may be very common among all sorts of predators.

Part IV The Breeding Cycle

15 General Aspects

The breeding biology of eagles has been studied far more intensively than has any other aspect of their lives. Of sixty-three forms, eight are intimately known and fourteen very well known. Another thirteen are well known, and fourteen little known, but the nests of the remaining fourteen have never been found, and their eggs dubiously described if at all. Thus, the breeding behaviour of almost a quarter of the world's eagles is still almost unknown.

Breeding biology is better known than other aspects of behaviour because the nest and nest site is the one place where an eagle can certainly be located during the breeding season. At the nest one can watch the eagles at close range, often a few yards, day after day, and for many years in succession. Study during the breeding period is also the best available guide to some other subjects. For instance, we assume that prey brought to the nest is what an eagle prefers to eat at other times, and most lists of food preferences are based mainly on records from nests.

The breeding behaviour of eagles is conveniently divided into five distinct phases, each discussed more fully later. They are: (i) display, which is of two types, display specifically connected with breeding (epigamic display) and other displays, such as threat or solicitation; (ii) nests and nest building; (iii) eggs and incubation; (iv) the fledging period, which can again be conveniently subdivided into the behaviour and development of the young, and the behaviour of the parents; and (v) the post-fledging period, after the young has flown but is still largely or wholly fed by its parents.

Our knowledge of these various phases of the breeding cycle varies greatly. The most studied phase is the fledging period, when there is much activity with a young bird in the nest. The incubation period, with the parents sitting quietly on eggs, is comparatively boring to watch, and has been much less intensively studied. The post-fledging period is also dif-

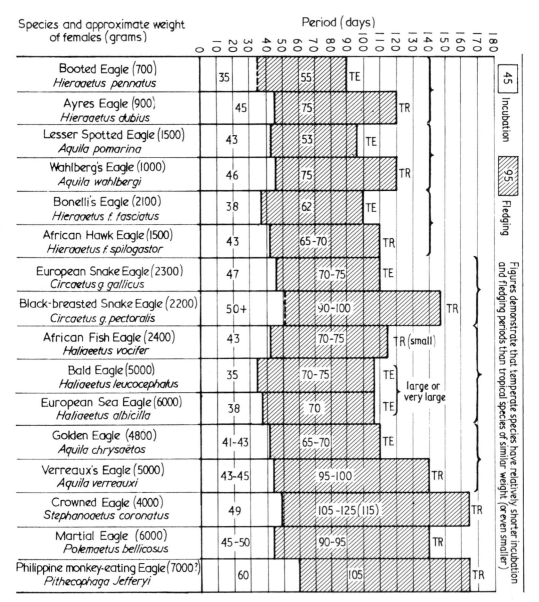

Species and approximate weight of females (grams)	Period (days)		
Booted Eagle (700) *Hieraaetus pennatus*	35	55 TE	
Ayres Eagle (900) *Hieraaetus dubius*	45	75 TR	
Lesser Spotted Eagle (1500) *Aquila pomarina*	43	53 TE	
Wahlberg's Eagle (1000) *Aquila wahlbergi*	46	75 TR	
Bonelli's Eagle (2100) *Hieraaetus f. fasciatus*	38	62 TE	
African Hawk Eagle (1500) *Hieraaetus f. spilogastor*	43	65-70 TR	
European Snake Eagle (2300) *Circaetus g. gallicus*	47	70-75 TE	
Black-breasted Snake Eagle (2200) *Circaetus g. pectoralis*	50+	90-100 TR	
African Fish Eagle (2400) *Haliaeetus vocifer*	43	70-75 TR (small)	
Bald Eagle (5000) *Haliaeetus leucocephalus*	35	70-75 TE	large or very large
European Sea Eagle (6000) *Haliaeetus albicilla*	38	70 TE	
Golden Eagle (4800) *Aquila chrysaëtos*	41-43	65-70 TE	
Verreaux's Eagle (5000) *Aquila verreauxi*	43-45	95-100 TR	
Crowned Eagle (4000) *Stephanoaetus coronatus*	49	105-125 (115) TR	
Martial Eagle (6000) *Polemaetus bellicosus*	45-50	90-95 TR	
Philippine monkey-eating Eagle (7000?) *Pithecophaga Jefferyi*	60	105 TR	

45 Incubation   95 Fledging

Figures demonstrate that temperate species have relatively shorter incubation and fledging periods than tropical species of similar weight (or even smaller)

Incubation and fledging periods for related tropical and temperate eagles

ficult to watch, because the young bird as it grows gradually moves away from the small area where hitherto it could regularly be found. It has, however, been quite intensively observed in at least two species.

The breeding cycle of any eagle is always long, varying from five to twenty-two months from the beginning of nest repair or building to the end of the post-fledging period. Since many species of eagle resident in their home ranges year-round perform epigamic display at almost any season, in

April Snow in Torridon, Scotland; such late snow forces the Golden Eagles to breed in relatively low-lying sites *(author)*

a sense their breeding cycle is continuous, for they are always performing some breeding activity, displaying after the young have become independent, and displaying or even mating well before they begin building again. However, in many species, for instance all migratory eagles and some others, there is an inactive period between cycles with no obvious breeding behaviour, during which the parents may leave their breeding range. This may also apply to some but not all members of a species. Most African Fish Eagles at Lake Naivasha remain in their territories year-round; but in the Kavirondo Gulf of Lake Victoria they often leave their breeding territories after nesting, from March to July. As they have left their nest sites and territories they are not showing any breeding activity.

The full breeding cycle does not necessarily occur annually. In virtually every eagle which has been thoroughly studied some pairs in a regular population do not actually lay eggs, though they may display, occupy a nest site and build up the nest. The cycle is arrested before egg laying, generally for reasons unknown or not understood. Such non-breeding can vary from less than a tenth to over a third of all pairs present; and failure to record cases of non-breeding together with data from pairs which lay, or rear young, can result in most misleading statistical data.

Since the shortest breeding cycle occupies at least five months, records of two successful breeding cycles by the same pair within one year are extremely rare. They cannot occur in any temperate climate, where the eagles lay in spring, the young become independent in autumn, and it would be impossible to breed again in winter, when the adults themselves may find survival difficult. Even in the tropics two broods per year would be very unlikely where six-month marked wet and dry seasons occur. Here breeding eagles normally complete their cycle in the dry season, climatically most favourable, and possibly also more favourable for food supply.

Two broods a year can only be achieved in a narrow belt on either side of the Equator, from about 4°N to 4°S. Here, because the sun passes twice across the Equator as the earth oscillates on its axis, two three-month rainy and two dry seasons occur. No eagle can complete a five-month breeding cycle entirely in dry weather. In a high rainfall near the Equator the habitat is always tropical forest, with rain in every month; but here eagles are generally rather scarce and little known.

The only proven instances I know of more than one complete brood per year are in African Fish Eagles at Lake Naivasha. In 1968-69 two pairs each reared two successive broods in the same nest; one of these reared three successive broods in eighteen months. Lake Naivasha is near the Equator with two annual rainfall peaks, but the climate is rather dry, so that there are no very wet months. One hundred and one records show that most breeding occurs in the wettest season, in April and May.

Some eagles take more than one whole year to complete a breeding cycle. African Crowned Eagles in Kenya display in any month of the year; nest building normally begins when rains give place to dry weather; the incubation and fledging periods are 49 and 105-125 days respectively; and the flying young bird continues to be fed by the parents at or near the nest for nine to eleven months after its first flight. It becomes independent about fifteen and a half months after it first began existence in an egg; and the total maximum breeding cycle in Kenya Crowned Eagles may span twenty-two months from the onset of nest building to independence of the young. No other eagle is definitely known to behave in this way; but the very large Harpy Eagle and the Phillipine Monkey-eating Eagle may do so. The somewhat larger, related Martial Eagle, which normally hunts in the savannas, apparently breeds annually as a rule, because the flying young are apparently dependent on the parents for only about four months.

Such behaviour may vary from place to place. In South Africa it is claimed (without good published evidence) that the Crowned Eagle breeds every year, actually repelling the still partially dependent and importunate young of the previous year. The potential breeding success of the same species is thus doubled by laying every year instead of in alternate years.

Although there are instances of everything from biannual to biennial breeding, most eagles complete a breeding cycle in less than one year, usually within six months. With a small clutch of usually one to two eggs, 10-35 per cent of non-breeding pairs, and further egg losses and nestling failures, scarcely any eagle can regularly rear an average of one young per pair per annum. Many average much less, over long periods and large numbers of records. Since many of the young that become independent must later die before sexual maturity, it follows that (as is generally supposed) adult wild eagles are comparatively long-lived birds.

Taking the breeding cycle as a whole, there are three possible critical stages, which I call 'points of strain', at which food supply may limit breeding success. (i) When a female lays her eggs; unless she can obtain enough food to form eggs she cannot lay. This factor is probably unimportant in eagles. (ii) When, as is usual, a male is feeding himself, his mate and one to three growing eaglets so that he must kill several times his own need, and his killing rate is not controlled by his own appetite. This critical stage is the most obvious and is the most easily observed. (iii) When the grown and flying eaglet must become independent. Wholly or largely dependent on its parents one day, it must fend for itself the next. This is the most difficult of three possible critical stages to observe, but may well be the most important of all from the viewpoint of population dynamics.

16 Display

The displays of eagles are generally rather simple, performed by one or both members of a pair. Communal, strongly ritualised displays such as those of some waders or game birds are unknown. Sometimes several eagles of the same or different species soar together in thermals or swoop and dive about the summit of a mountain. They may then have been attracted to the situation by the presence of other eagles, or merely by air currents favourable for some fancy aerobatics. I myself do not think that such aerial gatherings are true communal displays.

Display can be divided into two main types: epigamic display, which is specifically associated with the breeding cycle; and other displays, such as threat or solicitation, which may be associated with breeding, but may also be shown away from the nest. The same type of threat display is, for instance, shown by a downy nestling to a predator or its sibling; by a female to her mate when he brings prey; and by a migrant Steppe Eagle in possession of prey to another, thousands of miles from the breeding site.

In typical threat the eagle assumes the heraldic 'spread eagle' attitude, with the crest or head feathers raised, the wings spread and beak gaping. It generally leans back on its tail, freeing its powerful feet and claws to strike forward if needed. Any downy eaglet excited by a human intruder assumes this posture; and I have seen a downy Ayres' Hawk Eagle perform typical threat displays to a Grey-headed Bush Shrike *Malaconotus blanchoti*, which threatened to kill it, was not the least deterred by the eaglet's threat, and would have succeeded if I had not interfered.

The spectacle of an adult eagle at close range in threat display is unquestionably daunting; and could very well deter, for instance, mammalian predators such as foxes or arboreal cats. In threat display the eagle appears to be on the defensive, but can actually strike with lightning speed with either leg and, having obtained a hold, strike again with the other till its enemy is disabled. The display clearly means 'approach closer at your peril'. The threat is real, and the eagle means business. Even a young eagle about to fly or just flown needs a cautious approach. Its threats can usually be harmlessly absorbed in a cloth or sack, which the eagle will grip fiercely, when it can be lifted ignominiously into the air upside down, hooded with a black bag, and thereafter measured and weighed while helpless and quiescent.

One eagle often threatens another at the nest. If a male brings prey when the female is absent she usually returns quickly, at once seizes the prey, and threatens the male till he leaves. Possibly anticipating this hostile reception, many male eagles, alone on the nest with prey, seem ill-at-ease, and will seldom feed the eaglet, which begs for food just as it would from the female.

Eagles may also threaten each other in flight, either in territorial boundary disputes or in order to pirate prey from another bird. In flight-threat the eagle flies towards the intruder, with regular, deep, measured wingbeats, the head somewhat raised above the plane of the body, sometimes calling. It is as if the eagle were trying to adopt in flight (when it cannot if it is to remain airborne) something of the erect posture with wings spread of the spread-eagle threat display on the ground. When pirating prey from another eagle or bird a Tawny or African Fish Eagle flies directly at the object of

a

b

attack, sometimes calling to accentuate the threat. An eagle so attacked may drop the prey without retaliating or if on the ground, may oppose its attacker with a typical spread-eagle threat display, which may successfully repel the would-be pirate.

a. Aggressive threat posture of young Martial Eagle; b. submissive solicitation posture of White-tailed Sea Eagle.

Normal solicitation displays are sometimes confused with threat. The eagle stands in an apparently menacing attitude, the body level, staring fixedly at its mate or parent; but infantile high-pitched begging calls, whether from a large eaglet or by an adult female, reveal the true nature of the display. Eaglets can only adopt this posture after they are part-feathered and can stand steadily. When small and downy they squat on their tarsi and beg with cheeping calls for food. This solicitation posture may be assumed by adult male or female when its mate has prey; or by a female soliciting the male before copulation.

When ready to mate a female lowers her head level with the body and raises her tail to the same plane. The male then flies or jumps on to her back and mates. Actual mating usually takes place on or near the nest, and may occur many times a day just before egg laying, but can also occur many months before egg laying, and may not necessarily be followed by laying eggs at all. I have known Crowned Eagles and African Fish Eagles mate a year or more before they actually laid. In

July 1973 a male African Fish Eagle building a nest copulated
with the female seven times during a day, but she did not lay
that year. One cannot always be certain that the mating has
been successful; but equally there is often no reason to suppose that coitus was not complete. I was looking with ×12
binoculars at the rear ends of the pair of Crowned Eagles
from about 30yd away; and saw the female twist her long tail
sideways to permit union of her cloaca with his.

Before mating some eagles may perform pre-copulatory
displays in which the wings are raised high above the back,
the tail spread to display its barring, and the crest, if any,
raised. This posture is quite distinct from threat, though it
also increases the eagle's apparent size and shows off some of
the striking plumage features. I have repeatedly seen
Crowned Eagles, and one pair of Beaudouin's Snake Eagles,
perform such displays. However, this type of display so far
seems confined to conspicuously barred eagles, and has not to
my knowledge been recorded in any plainer species such as
African Fish Eagles, or even the magnificent black and white
Verreaux's Eagle.

Specific epigamic or nuptial displays vary in their intensity, and the whole possible range may not be performed by
all eagles. Some are far more inclined to display than others.
In my opinion the stages of intensity of the normal epigamic
displays are: (i) perching and calling, singly or in pairs; (ii)
soaring and calling, singly or in pairs; (iii) vigorous undulating displays in flight, by a single bird of either sex; (iv)
mutual soaring displays, in which the male normally soars or
undulates above the female; (v) rolling and foot-touching
mutual displays; and (vi) whirling or spinning, with the claws
locked. Some eagles can apparently breed without ever going
beyond the second of these stages, but many regularly perform the first five types. Whirling or spinning displays with
feet locked are recorded rarely and in only a few species; they
are commonest in sea and fish eagles.

Calling from a perch may be performed by a single bird,
such as a male Martial Eagle, or in duet, as often occurs in fish
and sea eagles, which call in different tones and syncopated
rhythm, often throwing their heads backwards over the upper tail coverts. These vocal displays are the aquiline
equivalent of passerine song from a song post. In Kenya,
where African Fish Eagles begin calling about forty minutes
before sunrise, the first calls immediately stimulate other
pairs to 'sing', and for a few minutes the whole shore rings
with the glorious sound. They then fly to fishing posts where
they readily call in challenge to a neighbour, or the passage of

another fish eagle or even an aeroplane overhead. Such calling territorial displays occur daily, whether breeding or not.

Soaring and calling is an elaboration of this display. A soaring eagle is more conspicuous than when perched, visible and audible, at long range. Martial Eagles often soar and call over the nest site, and African Fish Eagles soar and call, frequently in duet, over their territory, or in soaring flight with other fish eagles. In assessing the function of such displays in eagles as a whole, one is hampered by the almost total lack of good descriptions of the displays of many, notably the harpy group and small forest hawk eagles. Soaring and calling displays seem characteristic of almost all fish and sea eagles, including the aberrant Vulturine Fish Eagle, of all snake eagles whose display has been described at all, and many booted eagles of woodland, such as the Martial Eagle and several *Hieraaetus* species. The Long-crested Eagle can apparently breed without performing any more elaborate displays. Eagles of open or barren country, such as Golden Eagles, or Martial Eagles, usually do not call when soaring; Martial Eagles call on the wing only just before breeding.

The next, more vigorous and beautiful, phase of display is the undulating display by one or both members of a pair. In some, for instance Crowned Eagles, it is the first phase of display seen. Male or female Crowned Eagles perform this display almost daily over the breeding area; but seldom or never call from a perch, or call in flight without at the same time performing the vigorous undulating display. Typically, the male eagle circles on thermals to a height of 1,000ft (300m) or more above the ground and there hurls himself into a series of spectacular aerobatics. He dives almost vertically earthwards with closed wings for perhaps 200ft (60m), swings up again, reaching almost his previous level with his upward momentum, gives a few vigorous wing flaps towards the top of the climb, then plunges into another dive. He starts calling on his first downward swoop, and stops when he finally levels out. Voice and spectacular aerobatics are combined to draw attention to his presence from miles away—sometimes beyond the range of a naked human eye. This vigorous aerobatic and vocal display is probably an adaptation to forest life; some other small forest hawk eagles also soar and call loudly, but more elaborate displays are not described, in these or in any of the forest-loving harpy group.

Some other eagles perform these vigorous undulating displays without calling. Golden Eagles dive and swoop up again in this manner without uttering a sound. When near the ground, it appears that the eagle must be repeatedly stooping at some prey; but high above the ground the same manoeuvres clearly are display. Verreaux's Eagle performs the most spectacular undulations known, plunging nearly vertically for 1,000ft (300m) or more, swinging up again, looping the loop or rolling at the top of the upward swoop, and then sometimes repeating the series of magnificent aerial manoeuvres, swinging to and fro, like a pendulum. A Verreaux's Eagle may ascend and descend 5,000ft (1,500m) in a few minutes of such display.

These undulating displays are among the most spectacular feats of flight performed by any eagle, far more vigorous and energy-consuming than any hunting method known. Males usually display more often than do females; if females perform, their undulations are usually less deep and steep, and the display does not continue so long. This vigorous undulating display, with or without calling, is principally a means of advertising the male in his territory or home range.

The next phase, mutual soaring and rolling displays, may develop from soaring and calling, from simple soaring or from undulating displays. Typically, the male dives at the female, who turns over and briefly presents her claws to his before completing her sideways roll. In Golden Eagles this form of display develops from simple mutual soaring; but in the Crowned Eagle the male usually undulates and calls above the female for some time before diving down at her. The lighter male, because of his lower wing-loading, can always rise faster than the female on the same thermal current, so attaining the necessary height without extra effort.

These displays are typically and quite frequently performed by all well-known sea eagles; by several snake eagles, including the Bateleur; and by many, but not all, booted eagles. They may be seen in others as they become better known.

The last form of display, whirling or spinning, is apparently the most intense. In this, the two eagles, after soaring together for a time, or after mutual rolling and foot touching displays, lock their claws to one another and either come whirling down wing over wing in a series of cartwheels, or, facing one another, spin laterally and fall more gently earthwards. In either case the effect is extremely spectacular. First recognised as display by the American poet Walt Whitman (in 'The Dalliance of the Eagles'), the true nature of this performance was not again confirmed until I recorded it in African Fish Eagles on Lake Victoria. Such grappling of claws and falling to near the ground or water before separating is sometimes actual fighting. However, when one has watched a known pair of African Fish Eagles from a certain nest site first soar upwards together, calling, and then suddenly perform a whirling or spinning display of this type, there can be no doubt of its real significance. Apart from the sea and fish eagles, these displays seem very rare in eagles. They are often performed by Black Kites, which again suggests evolutionary links between kites and sea eagles, and are also rarely recorded in Tawny Eagles and Verreaux's Eagles.

These various soaring and calling displays are mainly performed before the breeding season proper; but may continue year-round. The male Crowned Eagle displays on any day when the air currents enable him to soar in mid-morning; wet weather effectively silences and grounds him. In Scottish Golden Eagles nuptial soaring displays reach their peak on fine days in midwinter and Bonelli's Eagle displays most in autumn and winter. African Fish Eagles display at any time of the year on Lake Naivasha, and even migrant eagles such as Steppe Eagles may sometimes perform undulating displays in their winter quarters. Since Golden Eagles display regularly in midwinter such displaying pairs of Steppe Eagles may have remained loosely attached even in their winter quarters. Display between successive breeding cycles could help to maintain the pair bond outside the breeding season.

Soaring displays are principally initiated by climatic factors. If the eagles cannot rise to soar on thermals or mountain wind currents they cannot perform vigorous aerial displays. In Scotland still days of steady soaking wet effectively prevent display; but on a fine sparkling day of blue sky with snowfields on the mountain tops, Golden Eagles are at their most magnificent when displaying in such surroundings.

Eagles may also be stimulated to vigorous undulating display by the presence of an intruder, whether avian or human. Verreaux's Eagles frequently display in response to the presence of another soaring pair, or after repelling a single intruder from their territory. They will also display if anxious about the nest when humans approach it too closely.

True injury-feigning or distraction displays are rare in eagles. In a very common form of behaviour (which I have called 'intruder reaction' because it is not apparently true injury feigning or distraction), the adult eagle lies flat and immobile in the nest, when incubating or with young. This certainly makes it much less conspicuous to a casual passer-by; and it may even deceive experts. What real enemy this process is meant to deceive is not clear. Though it seems to be reserved for man and though it would not nowadays deceive a determined human enemy, it could have had survival value when bands of primitive hominids ranged the plains seeking anything they could eat. Monkeys or baboons do not elicit intruder reaction but typical threat if they approach a nest, while other tall animals such as giraffes or elephants are normally ignored.

True injury-feigning or distraction displays are only recorded in the European Snake Eagle and, doubtfully, Wahlberg's Eagle. A female European Snake Eagle has been seen to drop off the nest and shuffle away on the ground as if hurt. Such distraction display seems extremely rare even in this species, which normally flies like any other when disturbed at the nest. Young eagles sometimes lie flat in the nest, as if shamming dead; but usually not.

The Bateleur performs a display alternatively interpreted as threat or distraction. When disturbed at the nest one or both of the pair sometimes perch nearby, where they jig up and down, with part-opened wings flapping, uttering sharp short barks, 'kau-kau-kau-kau'. Both R. E. Moreau, the first observer to record these actions, and African tribesmen interpret the behaviour as threatening; for instance in the Hausa *'Gaggafa chi yaro'* (lit, 'Bateleur eat boy'). However, Peter Steyn in Rhodesia considers this behaviour is distraction; and having seen it several times myself, I would agree that it is an expression of frustration and an attempt to distract rather than threaten a persistent intruder.

However, there seems to be no mistaking a Bateleur's threatening intent when it dives at an intruder with loudly flapping wings. Such displays terrify large dogs, which hide under bushes; and a human climbing the tree feels he may be struck. However, Bateleurs have not been known to strike men, and are actually shy birds, unusually likely to desert their nests when disturbed.

Some eagles, however, actually attack men at the nest. The formidably armed and very powerful female Crowned Eagle and several small hawk eagles regularly attack. Eagles may sometimes attack monkeys and baboons that approach a nest; on the other hand, Sykes' Monkeys sometimes bait Crowned Eagles on and near their nests with the insolent impunity of an expert *torero* with a bull. A female Crowned Eagle may attack persons known to her, but refuse to attack strangers, or a familiar when strangers are present. The attacks are best avoided, but can usually be warded off with a stick or leafy branch.

Much remains to be learned of eagle display. It would be

specially valuable to study the relative importance of voice and flying displays in forest species; and whether defined systematic relationships in the types of display emerge, such as, for instance in the whirling displays most often seen in African Fish Eagles. If, however, an eagle is seen performing an unusually spectacular aerial manoeuvre, it is more likely to be in nuptial display than attacking or hunting anything.

17 Nests and Nest Building

Eagles' nests or eyries are traditionally large or enormous, and occupied for many years. This is true for all the sea and fish eagles; for all the harpy group as far as is known; and for most of the true or booted eagles. However, most better known snake eagles build rather small nests, not necessarily occupied year after year. The aberrant Bateleur departs from this general rule, for its nests are as large and solid as those of a typical small booted eagle.

Most African, Asian and European snake eagles all build rather small, flimsy nests, often right on top of such trees as stunted pines or oaks growing on heathery mountainsides or among dunes, on the crown of a thorny Acacia, or the even more formidable centre of a circle of spiky Euphorbia fronds. The same general area may be frequently used by a pair of snake eagles, but they may build new nests miles from previous sites, though after a period of years may return to the same suitable tree.

The small nest, the rather secretive and unobtrusive habits of nesting snake eagles, and their way of squatting very flat in the nest in intruder reaction, makes snake eagles' nests much more difficult to find than most. They may even move one or two miles away from the nest used in a previous year. Even experts are often defeated by snake eagles until the large young reveal the situation by loud raucous yells for food. Finding one nest of the Southern Banded Snake Eagle by the yells of the young bird has not helped me to find another; and this nest was never used again.

The nests of many eastern Serpent Eagles (*Spilornis*), and of the Congo and Madagascar Serpent Eagles, are unknown; but the Crested Serpent Eagle, like African and European *Circaetus* species, builds a small slight nest. Any unknown snake eagle's nest is likely to be small, and may be very difficult to see, for instance on a thorny creeper growing over a tall tree. Some snake eagles' nests are more easily seen from an aeroplane than otherwise, for they are often open to the sky but hidden from below.

The nest and single egg of a Black-breasted Snake Eagle showing the flimsy nature of snake eagle nests (*Peter Steyn*)

All snake eagles nest in trees except, very rarely, the European Snake Eagle, which in deserts occasionally breeds on cliffs. Rarely, snake eagles, especially the aberrant Bateleur, use the nest of another bird. I have known a Bateleur use the nests of Wahlberg's Eagles and even the huge nest of a Crowned Eagle. When a snake eagle is found breeding in a large stick nest it has probably not built it itself, but has taken over the empty nest of some other bird of prey. Reports of snake eagles breeding in large stick nests of their own making are suspect.

Snake eagles make the smallest, but fish and sea eagles make the largest known eagles' nests. One of the biggest ever described, a celebrated Bald Eagle's near Vermilion, Ohio, was thirty-six years old, 12ft (4m) deep, and 8ft (2.6m) across. Probably the largest ever measured, at St Petersburg, Florida, was 20ft (6.1m) deep and 9½ft (3m) across the top. These huge nests have now disappeared; but until recently a Scottish Golden Eagle's nest 17ft (5.5m) deep existed. Like other such huge nests, it was really a series of nests built on top of each other, the lowest tier certainly dating from 1904.

The size of the nest may depend on the availability of material. Icelandic European Sea Eagles breed in completely treeless terrain, and only make a scrape on top of a rock pillar, adding some feathers and small pieces of vegetation. In Scandinavia the same species makes huge nests of sticks. Eastern Scottish Golden Eagles' nests are usually very large; but in the north-west, where trees or even heather are less luxuriant, usually much smaller. An eagle nesting near a wood may build a much bigger nest than a neighbouring pair with access only to heather.

Site and weather also affect nest size and persistence. In

hot or wet climates nests tend to disintegrate more quickly. The largest known nests of Verreaux's Eagle on cold high mountains are tower-like structures resembling many Golden Eagle's nests, up to 8ft (2.6m) deep and much deeper than those on most lowland cliffs. On a broad but overhung ledge a Golden Eagle's nest spreads laterally for lack of headroom to build upwards, and may then become 10ft (3m) across by only 1-2ft (30-60cm) deep. A deserted nest may persist for ten years in a dry overhung niche; but on a wet open ledge may grow moss and disappear in five.

The principal factor affecting nest size, however, is age. Any new nest is just sufficient to allow the eagles to lay and rear young. On a cliff it need only be a scrape, surrounded by sticks and lined with finer material, but in a tree it must be larger and more solid, though never so large as it becomes with age. Nests in regular use for many years become enormous, usually wider and very much deeper than a new one. On broad cliff ledges they tend to sprawl laterally, but in niches they may be cylindrical tower-like structures, broader at the base than across the top, and much deeper than they are broad. Ground nests of the Steppe Eagle resemble truncated cones, broader basally than at the top; but all nests in trees tend to be broader across the top than at the base, and are usually basin-shaped rather than cylindrical.

Naturally, small eagles normally build much smaller nests than big eagles, whether sea, harpy or booted eagles. However, the relatively small Bonelli's and African Hawk Eagles make very large nests for their size; and the rather large Tawny Eagle makes a relatively small nest. Sea eagles build the largest nests, relative to the size of the bird. Eagles normally build their own nests; but in less than one in a hundred cases, one species may take over and use the deserted nest of another, or of another large bird of prey.

The share of the sexes in building is very seldom accurately recorded, perhaps because in temperate or cold climates nest building or repair occurs in very cold winter or early spring weather, while in the tropics it may be spread over many months of sporadic activity. In fish and sea eagles the male commonly brings much of the material, and though the female sometimes works the material into the structure, she may leave this also to the male. In most eagles which have been much watched, both sexes bring some of the material. The female often stays in the nest while the male brings branches; but females also build alone. Better data are needed for most species.

New nests may be built very quickly; or the process may be

Nest and egg of a Wahlberg's Eagle
(Peter Steyn)

spread over many months of sporadic activity. The European Snake Eagle, a late summer migrant to Europe, normally builds a new small nest each year and completes it in two to three weeks. Other northern species, like the Sea Eagle, Bald Eagle or Golden Eagle may partially build a new nest the previous summer and autumn, add to it sporadically during the winter, and finally use it the following spring. In large tropical eagles such as the Crowned and Verreaux's Eagles a nest may be added to over one or even two years at intervals before it is finally used.

Again, the sites can affect the time taken to build a new nest. On a cliff, or on the ground, a solid base already exists and the eagle need only make a depression, place some sticks round it, and line it with dry material. In the far commoner site of a tree, however, the solid base must first be constructed, which takes longer and needs more material. So much material may fall out of the chosen fork when first placed there that the eagles give up and do not breed. A new tree nest in temperate climates takes at least three weeks to construct, but longer, up to two months, in the tropics, where climatic pressure to complete the nest rapidly are lacking.

Apart from the snake eagles, most eagles occupy their nests for several or many years; and many species also have one or more alternate nests which they repair and may sometimes use. An eagle more often repairs and uses an old nest than

135

A typical, open, very large sea eagle's nest in an isolated tree *(W. Puchalski, Bruce Coleman Ltd)*

builds a new one. Sixty pairs of African Fish Eagles at Lake Naivasha built only twenty-five new nests in three years. Not all were used, so any nest was used for at least seven and most probably for nearer ten years. Some eagles' nests are used for much longer than that, and others for shorter periods. The size of the eagle and the length of time a nest is occupied are broadly correlated—the bigger, the longer. Wahlberg's Eagles build new nests every four or five years, but very large booted eagles such as Crowned Eagles, or some of the sea eagles, very much less often. Three pairs of Martial Eagles in twenty-five years have built five new nests, but three of these nests were built by one pair in insecure sites.

Repair of an old nest may be sporadic and protracted in the tropics, or swift among migrant eagles with little time to waste in temperate climates. A pair of Alaskan Golden Eagles must get on with it as soon as they arrive in the breeding area; but in California, Mexico, Spain or Scotland, nest repair can occur at almost any season. Probably it is another activity which helps to maintain the pair bond and to hold the birds in

A close-up of a White Tailed Eagle's nest *(Viking Olsson)*

their breeding area. If eagles fail to breed successfully for any reason they frequently repair one or more nests during the breeding season, when they would normally have young. Generally, both sexes take part in nest repair; but again there is too little good data on the subject.

Most eagles occupying the same nest site over many years have several nests in the same small area, group of trees, or even the same tree. Most Golden Eagles have two to four but may have one to fourteen nests per pair. In temperate countries related eagles seem to build more nests per pair than do similar tropical eagles. Verreaux's Eagles in the Matopos hills average 1.4 nests per pair as against 2.3 for Scottish Golden Eagles. Eighty-six pairs of African Fish Eagles had one to four nests, some not used, averaging 1.48 per pair. In Norway the much larger European Sea Eagle has one to eleven nests per pair, averaging 2.4.

It is often stated that the use of alternate nest sites is connected with sanitation. The old nest in which young have been reared is supposed to be foul with parasites, and better avoided. I believe there is no substance in this view, for eagles which regularly use only one nest, or a favourite among several seem just as successful as those which move from one to another more often. In cold climates nest selection may be due more to snow conditions than previous use; a snow-free nest must be preferred. I am confident that if I examined this statistically I should get no significant indication that moving from one nest to another was biologically beneficial.

Persistent human interference with Golden Eagles in Scotland can cause the eagle to move to a new site more often than it would if left strictly alone. In north-west Sutherland in 1967 those pairs of Golden Eagles which were more likely to be interfered with had on average more nests (2.7 per pair) than those breeding in remote places free from human interference, or otherwise inaccessible (2.3 per pair). Such moves may have survival value, for an old nest is well-known, large and conspicuous, so more readily disturbed by any human enemy. A small new nest built not far away may escape observation and allow the eagle to breed successfully for at least a year or two.

Usually, nest repair or building a new nest is mainly done with dead sticks or pieces of vegetation, either broken off trees, sometimes by seizing them as the eagle passes in flight, or picked up from ground. A Golden Eagle uprooting heather flaps its wings violently to aid tearing off a piece it has grasped in its foot. The largest pieces of branch carried by big eagles may be up to 6ft (2m) long and more than 1in (2½cm) thick; and the size of sticks used can be a useful guide to the species of eagle which has built an unidentified nest, though long experience is needed to judge such points. Rarely, odd items such as a coil of wire, bones or other oddments are incorporated into the nest structure. One Golden Eagle's nest I knew was built on the base of a coil of three turns of fencing wire, which had been carried some distance.

Towards the end of the building period eagles, like many other birds of prey, add many green branches to the nest. Some have interpreted this anthropomorphically as adornment; but these green branches merely serve as a somewhat softer lining to receive the eggs. The amount of green material added varies from a few sprigs or sprays to a mass 6in (15cm) thick. Some eagles will go some distance to get favourite materials for this purpose. Scottish Golden Eagles often use the great woodrush *Luzula sylvatica*; and they prefer sprigs of pine or larch to those of broad-leaved trees, which often are not in leaf when the eagle builds. Green sprays are usually collected from close by; but a sprig of larch

Female African Hawk-Eagle bringing a spray of green leaves to the nest (*Peter Steyn*)

in one Scottish Golden Eagle's eyrie came from at least a mile (1.6km) away and 1,000ft (300m) downhill.

Sometimes other materials besides green leaves are used. African Fish Eagles often use the feathery heads of papyrus, or even weaver birds' nests, which may be attached to the eagle's own nest; I have seen an incubating African Fish Eagle lean over, seize a nest and add it to the lining of her own. Tawny Eagles use grass in semi-arid areas lacking soft green leaves. However, eagles do not regularly line their nests with wool, felt, rags or plastic bags as do Red and Black Kites.

Eagles frequently decorate several nests with green material, then lay in one of them. While the eggs are scarcely ever laid without adding some green material, green material does not infallibly indicate the nest selected for use, or definitely forecast egg laying. Generally, however, plenty of green material on one nest of several indicates that it will probably be used.

It is essential not to disturb eagles at this time in countries where they are liable to persecution, such as Scotland. However, where they are not persecuted I have never known an eagle abandon her intention to lay eggs in a nest she had lined because of a visit by a human observer. A week or two later the eagle is usually sitting or the eggs lie in their bed of green; if not, she is not going to lay at all.

18 Eggs and Incubation

More is known about eagles' eggs and the incubation period than about nests and nest building, partly because eagles' eggs have been sought by egg collectors for many years, even today when egg collecting is illegal. Eagles' eggs are not specially beautiful, usually dull white, marked with brown, but often unmarked as in all snake eagles' eggs. However, to obtain a set of eagles' eggs often means climbing a formidable tree or a cliff, and so presents a challenge to some people. As a whole, egg collecting does little harm to eagles, but is a dangerous threat to rare species.

As summarised in Appendix 3, eagles lay one to four eggs, normally one to two. Fish and sea eagles lay the largest clutches, sometimes three, exceptionally four. Most species average two or less. Of thirty-three more or less well-known eagles, ten invariably or normally lay one egg; reported clutches of two in these may need careful verification. Among sea eagles, only the Vulturine Fish Eagle lays one; this and other details of its breeding behaviour set it apart, and suggest that it is incorrectly placed here. All snake eagles lay only one egg. In the harpy group, the Philippine Monkey-eating Eagle apparently lays only one but the larger Harpy two. In the genus *Aquila*, Wahlberg's Eagle normally lays one egg; some reputed cases of two may be doubtful. Among hawk eagles, the Martial Eagle, Isidor's Eagle, several *Spizaetus* species and Ayres' Hawk Eagle normally or only lay one.

Clutch size is not related to the size and weight of the eagle. All snake eagles, and some small booted eagles, always lay one, while much larger sea or booted eagles may lay up to four. The largest hawk eagle, the Martial Eagle, and one of the smallest, Ayres' Hawk Eagle, always or normally lay one. South African Ayres' Eagles may lay two, but there are no recent good records.

Tropical eagles share the general worldwide tendency to lay smaller clutches than their relatives in temperate areas; but the difference is small, not significant in a large series. Verreaux's Eagle is not known to lay four, and very rarely three. Though its temperate counterpart, the Golden Eagle, quite often lays three, exceptionally four, the clutch in both would average about 1.8-1.9. The African Fish Eagle, under optimum conditions, lays one to three, averaging 1.8; but the European Sea Eagle, Bald Eagle and Pallas' Sea Eagle lay one to four, quite often three. Norwegian Sea Eagle clutches average 2.14, Icelandic 2.1. Florida Bald Eagles may lay three less often than those in Alaska, which also lay bigger eggs. Good data on clutch size can, however, only be based on authentic complete clutches.

Few observers record the fresh weight of eagles' eggs— essential, as they lose weight during incubation. However, the weight of a single egg or clutch is always small related to

A single Brown Snake Eagle's egg, also showing the leafy central depression characteristic of eagle nests (*Peter Steyn*)

that of the female eagle. Four Swiss Golden Eagle's eggs varied from 94 to 120g, averaging 107g; a normal clutch of two eggs thus weighs 200-220g, about 4.5 per cent of the female's body-weight of 4,700g. The Australian Wedge-tailed Eagle lays two eggs of about 115g, about 6.5 per cent of average recorded body-weight. Two fresh Verreaux's Eagle's eggs weighed 125 and 115g. The huge Steller's Sea Eagle lays eggs weighing about 160g; a normal clutch of two would weigh only about 4 per cent of the female's body-weight. A European Sea Eagle's egg weighs about 140-145g, so a normal clutch weighs about 5.5 per cent of the female's body-weight.

Egg-weight is not consistently related to clutch size and single eggs are not always relatively heavier. The single egg of the European Snake Eagle averages 135g, 7 per cent of her body-weight, more than a normal two-egg clutch in the Golden Eagle. However, among booted eagles single eggs are not unusually large. The single egg of a Wahlberg's Eagle, weighing about 2lb 6oz (1.1kg) measures on average 61.6×48.6mm nearly the same as the two eggs of the somewhat heavier 3lb 4oz (1.5kg) European Lesser Spotted Eagle which average 61.8×49.8mm. Martial Eagles, weighing 13lb 2oz-14lb 3oz (6-6.5kg), lay single eggs averaging 80.7×57.0mm, only slightly larger than those of smaller Golden Eagles, averaging 76.7×59.4mm.

The weight of a single egg varies from 7 per cent of body-weight in the European Snake Eagle to about 2-2.5 per cent in large booted eagles. A normal clutch weighs from about 2.5 per cent to about 7 per cent of body-weight; and a maximum clutch of four eggs in the Golden Eagle is about 9 per cent of the female's body-weight. Normal single egg clutches weigh 2.5-7 per cent of body-weight, and normal clutches of two weigh 4.5-6.5 per cent of body-weight. In, for instance, ducks, waders or even hummingbirds, clutches are relatively

A clutch of two Golden Eagle's eggs
(S. Roberts, Ardea Photographics)

far heavier. A guillemot's egg is the same volume as a Golden Eagle's; kiwis may lay eggs weighing altogether 25 per cent of body-weight; and a mallard lays about ten eggs each 5 per cent of body-weight, so that her clutch is relatively about ten times as heavy as an eagle's.

In an eagle's breeding cycle, I have suggested three 'points of strain' at which food requirements may limit breeding, the first when the female lays her eggs. In view of the small number and relatively low weight of a normal clutch, and the ease of obtaining food, I find it impossible to believe that actual shortage of food often prevents a female from laying. Any American or European female Golden Eagle in spring could easily gorge at will on a dead deer or sheep. Verreaux's Eagle in tropical Africa can apparently easily catch enough hyrax and African Fish Eagles, spending less than 2 per cent of the daylight actually flying to hunt, must easily obtain enough fish physically to enable the female to lay. Comparing individual cases the concept becomes still more impossible. Two adjacent pairs of Naivasha Fish Eagles, nesting 300yd apart and fishing in the same lagoon, respectively laid at least six eggs and reared three broods totalling four young in eighteen months; the other did not lay. Two other pairs, fishing adjacent stretches of shore, bred three times and not at all between 1968 and 1972.

It is probably not actual shortage of food that prevents egg laying. However, females perhaps do not lay because males are unable to or do not provide enough of the right food at the right time, not so much as actual food, but as part of the courtship ritual. In recent experiments with captive birds of prey, this 'titbitting' has seemed important. A female not fed by the male before laying might go off and hunt for herself; lose interest in the nest; and so fail to lay. This hypothesis is difficult to test, but one year the female Crowned Eagle nesting near my house was apparently not fed often enough by the male, and did not lay as expected; in the following year she was apparently fed better and did. However, I have also known cases where male African Fish Eagles certainly caught enough fish but nevertheless the females did not lay. Although there is slight evidence for a connection between failure to lay and inadequate food supply, the real reasons for such failure are unknown.

Whatever the reason, from 10 to 35 per cent, sometimes even more, of all female eagles in a population do not lay eggs when expected. They do not breed, though they may be undisturbed, have enough food, and may have repaired a nest or two. In Scottish Golden Eagles, 15-20 per cent of all females do not lay; and there is little real difference between areas of good and bad food supply. In the tropics the proportion of non-breeders is often much higher. Only 150 out of 222 pairs of Rhodesian Verreaux's Eagles actually laid over a five-year period; 32.7 per cent did not. At Lake Naivasha only 71 out of 112 pairs of African Fish Eagles laid in two years' observation; 37 per cent did not. Equally accurate figures are not available for related European and American species; but probably less than 20 per cent of female European Sea Eagles and Bald Eagles normally do not lay.

This tendency for more frequent non-breeding among tropical eagles is apparently an extension of the well-documented tendency to lay smaller clutches in the tropics. In temperate developed countries today, sound quantitative conclusions are often impossible because we are seldom dealing with a natural capacity population, rather with a beleaguered or persecuted remnant while pesticides and casual interference further mask the situation. In the Matopos hills or at Lake Naivasha, Verreaux's Eagle and the African Fish Eagle maintain capacity populations which are either not persecuted or are actually protected, whereas Golden Eagles in Scotland or France, or the Bald Eagle and European Sea Eagle in much of their ranges are persecuted, poisoned, or both. However, in temperate climates about one female in five, or 20 per cent, may not lay, as compared to about one in three, or 33 per cent in the tropics.

In the beleaguered and persecuted eagle populations in developed temperate countries, human interference now seriously aggravates the sterilising effects of pesticides. In Scotland, many pairs fail to lay because of rock climbers, casual walkers and, in one case, a ski-lift. Pleasure boats disturb European Sea Eagles and American Bald Eagles. In the tropics, eagles are apparently less affected by human interference. Naivasha Fish Eagles pay no attention to fishermen or water skiers; and the Matopos Verreaux's Eagles tolerate people climbing to their nests. This may be because these populations have never really had cause to fear man, while those in Europe or America have been conditioned to fear man over the last century or so. Bonelli's Eagle does not attack man near the nest; but its close African relative, the African Hawk Eagle, regularly does.

A female may lay at almost any time of day. Few accurate times are available; but a Scottish Golden Eagle laid the second egg of her clutch at about 2pm. The Crowned Eagle near my house laid once between 10am and noon; and once at about 3pm. Two Verreaux's Eagles laid their second eggs late in the afternoon, at about 5pm. Since careful observers try not to disturb eagles at such times, it is difficult to be certain exactly when an egg is laid. When laying, a Crowned Eagle sits with her tail raised at an angle; when she has laid she settles lower in the nest. However, to be certain of the exact time of laying one must see the egg.

In clutches of two or more, eggs are laid at intervals of two to four days, occasionally even longer. As later described, this simple fact profoundly influences the survival of the young. The first egg is incubated at once, but may be left for an hour or two just after laying, when it could be at risk from predators such as baboons or crows; this may be why eagles normally start to incubate at once. The second egg may be smaller and less heavily marked than the first. The eggs of individual females are recognisable by their markings year after year, a fact well-known to egg collectors who amass long 'series' from the same nest.

Egg collectors persistently and incorrectly state that if a first clutch is taken an eagle will frequently re-lay. Observation shows that eagles seldom re-lay if their clutch is taken, or lost through a natural disaster, though they may re-lay more readily in tropical than in temperate climates. In cold climates, once incubation has begun, they could rarely re-lay and still rear a brood before winter sets in, but in the tropics, clutches lost by natural disaster may be replaced weeks or even months later. Such re-laying is recorded in the Crowned, Verreaux's and Ayres' Hawk Eagle, but re-laying after loss of a clutch from natural causes or egg collectors is rare anywhere. The breeding cycle normally stops if the eggs are taken or lost.

Although good data on the incubation period, based on long watches, is scanty we know that in many species both sexes incubate by day. No male eagle has been observed to sit all night, though this has been suspected in the Golden Eagle and Verreaux's Eagle. In many species, and in individuals of some other species, females incubate alone. Single egg clutches are, broadly speaking, more likely to be incubated by the female only. In all snake eagles the female alone incubates, or the male very rarely does. In Wahlberg's Eagle, the Martial Eagle and Ayres' Hawk Eagle, normally or invariably laying one egg, males never or seldom incubate.

In the Golden, Wedge-tailed, Long-crested and African Fish Eagles, normally laying two or three eggs, the male takes a small share if any; he may relieve the female for a short spell when or if he brings food to the nest. In Verreaux's Eagle, the male takes a larger share, from 25 to 45 per cent of the daylight, but even then the female sits all night, so that she does about 80 per cent of all incubation. Incubation behaviour varies individually. In four pairs of Crowned Eagles at Eagle Hill in Embu District, both sexes incubated; but a female which bred near my house and laid five eggs between 1959 and 1968 always incubated alone. Perhaps it was just coincidence that she always laid one egg, whereas the Eagle Hill birds usually laid two.

Females incubating alone are normally fed on or near the nest by the male, but sometimes obtain their own prey. In Ayres' Hawk Eagle the male brings the prey and calls the female off to feed, but does not relieve her on the eggs. Should a male arrive and find the female away, he often seems ill at ease; perhaps males only feel free to incubate if the larger, normally dominant females are away. In the Tawny and Golden Eagles the female normally leaves the nest to feed and is not fed by the male. However, perhaps she locates the male somewhere in the home range and shares his kill. A female African Fish Eagle will readily leave her nest to snatch a kill from her own mate. In the rather rare cases where males take a larger share of incubation, females occasionally feed their mates. I have seen sitting male Crowned and African Hawk Eagles fed by females. However, it is always unusual for a female to feed a male.

With rare exceptions, some of which need careful confirmation, the incubation periods exceed forty days, sometimes even fifty days. The longest known is the Philippine Monkey-eating Eagle at sixty days; but the Harpy Eagle incubates for at least fifty-two days, and several tropical Snake Eagles and the Bateleur sit for fifty to fifty-three days. The shortest recorded period is twenty-eight days for the Malayan race of the Crested Serpent Eagle; but this does not agree with an earlier record of about thirty-five days for the same species in Java. Careful observers dislike approaching the nest at the onset of incubation for fear of causing desertion; and the fact that an eagle has begun to brood on a nest does not prove infallibly that it has laid. However, normally the beginning of the incubation period can be timed from the moment the eagle settles in the incubation posture, low in the nest, with only her head visible.

Incubation periods in closely allied species may be longer in the tropics than in temperate climates. The European Snake Eagle incubates for forty-seven days; its African race, the Black-breasted Snake Eagle, for over fifty days. Bonelli's Eagle incubates for thirty-seven to thirty-nine days, the smaller African Hawk Eagle for forty-two to forty-three. However, Verreaux's Eagle, incubating for forty-three to forty-five days, differs little from the Golden, Spotted or Imperial Eagles; and the African Tawny Eagle and European Steppe Eagle each incubate for about forty-two to forty-four days.

Any recorded short incubation periods of eagles need thorough checking. For many years the incubation period of American Golden Eagles was said to be thirty-five days, but recent good records are of forty-one to forty-three days. The very large Bald Eagle has repeatedly been said to incubate for thirty-five days, with a barely believable variation of thirty-one to forty-six days in captivity; a recent record in captivity confirms the thirty-five day period. Eagles incubate longer than some other birds of prey of similar weight. Wahlberg's Eagle and Ayres' Hawk Eagle, for instance, sit for forty-five to forty-six days, whereas buzzards, also weighing 1lb 12oz to 2lb 12oz (0.8-1.1kg), hatch in thirty to thirty-three days. The length of the incubation period is more closely connected with genetic relationship than with body size or latitude. The tiny Ayres' Hawk Eagle actually has a longer incubation period than the Golden Eagle, five times as heavy.

Although we know enough about the incubation period to provide a good general picture, more accurate, careful records are still needed for most species. No really complete records are available for any wild sea or fish eagle, nor for any wild member of the harpy group. Accurate records are available for several snake eagles, the Bateleur and some booted eagles, but often depend on only one nest watched throughout the period. Really good records from which one can calculate the share of the sexes accurately, and the precise length of the incubation period to within half a day, are only available for about six species, one, the Ayres' Hawk Eagle, a very rare bird. Only in Verreaux's Eagles is the incubation period known to within a matter of hours or minutes.

It is doubtful if such accuracy is really necessary, certainly not if it means disturbing the eagle only for the sake of an accurate figure. However, students of eagle behaviour could profitably concentrate more on the incubation period and less on the fledging period in some of the well-known or very well-known species; while in many nothing is known of the incubation period at all.

19 The Fledging Period: Development of Young

An eaglet normally takes several days to hatch. So-called 'chipping time' is the period between first hearing the eaglet cheeping inside the shell until it has burst completely free of the egg. In a few instances this has been accurately recorded, in others estimated. One Verreaux's Eagle chick broke its way out of the egg in sixty-nine and a quarter hours. Other estimates have varied from twenty-four to forty-eight hours. Since to obtain such accurate records repeated visits to the nest at a critical time are necessary, it is only worth collecting such figures with a very tame eagle which will tolerate repeated disturbance.

The parents may remove the eggshell, or more often trample it by degrees into the nest. If one egg does not hatch, it remains in the nest until buried in the nest lining or broken. Eagles that incubate an infertile egg or clutch continue to sit for many days or weeks after the normal hatching date. A Sutherland Golden Eagle in 1967 was still incubating eggs on 8 July; she must have sat for about 115 days. Tropical eagles have sat for over eighty days in Africa; but after a time any infertile egg is deserted.

The hatching eaglet cuts its way out of the egg with the egg-tooth, is not normally helped by its parent, and weighs less than the egg from which it hatched. Newly hatched Golden Eagles weigh 3-3½oz (95-100g), compared to about 4oz (115g) for a fresh egg. A Verreaux's eaglet weighed 3½oz (100g) twenty-two and a half hours after hatching from an egg which, when fresh, weighed 3¾oz (110g); since it had already been fed thirty-one tiny morsels of meat its hatching weight may have been about 3oz (90g). These figures suggest efficient conversion of the nutrient material in the egg into the body of the chick, for much of the difference in weight must be the empty shell.

A newly hatched eaglet may not be fed at first, or may receive a number of small meals. The same Verreaux's Eagle chick, which hatched at 10.55am on 11 June, was fed at

1.55pm, three hours later. A very young eaglet is weak, can scarcely raise its heavy head on its wobbly neck, and must be carefully coaxed to take small slivers of flesh held out to it on the hooked tip of the parent's beak. If it fails the female eats the morsel and tries again and again. Most who have watched at eagles' nests at this stage have been entranced by the fascinating contrast between the strength of the huge parent and her wonderful gentleness as she feeds the tiny chick. Settling to brood, adults clench their huge taloned feet into balls and place them carefully and gently on either side of chick or unhatched egg. If not gentle and careful, they evidently could injure or kill their offspring.

The eaglet feeds more vigorously on its second and third days, and grows rapidly. Thus, by the time a second egg in a clutch of two hatches, the first hatched eaglet (known for brevity as C1 or Cain) is several times the weight of its sibling (C2 or Abel). Three Golden Eagle chicks, the third just hatched, weighed $12\frac{1}{4}$oz (367g), 9oz (252g) and $3\frac{1}{2}$oz (98g). C1 is usually two and a half to three times as heavy as C2 when the latter hatches. It is also by now alert and vigorous, able to move about, while C2 is as weak and wobbly as C1 was a few days before.

In most eagles laying two eggs, C2 does not survive when both hatch. A violent battle may now develop between the two eaglets, first immortalised as the Cain and Abel battle by Seton Gordon. It does not necessarily begin immediately; and may even be started by C2. Usually C1 violently attacks C2, driving it to the edge of the nest, where it lies exposed to the cold wind or sun, both likely to be fatal. It may squat on or peck C2 exposing areas of raw flesh. If C1 does not actually kill its sibling, it soon dominates C2, which thereafter is always submissive; obtains food only when C1 does not want it; and often dies of starvation. It may then fall out of the nest, be eaten by the parent, or be fed to the victorious Cain.

Recent research on this by Bernd-Ulrich Meyburg suggests that C2 is often not attacked or killed by the elder, but simply lies in the nest and makes no attempt to obtain food, later dying of starvation. In one Lesser Spotted Eagle's nest observed from start to finish, C1 weighed 5oz (138g) and an unhatched egg $2\frac{3}{4}$oz (79g). C2 hatched a day later, weighed $1\frac{3}{4}$oz (49g) and was attacked by C1, now weighing $5\frac{1}{4}$oz (148g). The female fed C1 ninety-two pieces of flesh; but C2 just lay in the nest and did not attempt to obtain food. The next day C2 was dead; and on the day after was partly fed to C1 and partly eaten by its parent.

Two eaglets of identical size placed on a table struggle

The Cain and Abel struggle: aggression by a six-day-old Verreaux's Eagle eaglet which viciously attacks its day-old sibling; at the top of the picture lies a dassie which could keep them both well fed for a couple of days *(Peter Steyn)*

The only brood of four ever recorded in the Imperial Eagle (both subspecies); the weights of the chicks were $8\frac{2}{3}$ oz (246g), $7\frac{1}{4}$ oz (206g), $5\frac{2}{3}$ oz (161g) and 3oz (86g) *(B-U. Meyburg)*

towards and attack each other, each trying to drive the other to the edge. One becomes dominant in from a few minutes to twelve hours. Thereafter the other becomes supine, 'accepting intimidation'; in the nest it would make no attempt to obtain food. Meyburg concluded that death occurs as often from starvation as from actual attack and injury; but also records attack and injury in Golden Eagles, European Sea Eagles and Imperial Eagles. The hatching interval may be critical for survival. If short, say two days, C1 has a better chance of being brooded, fed and protected by the female, and may survive. With a short hatching interval, a Lesser Spotted Eagle may brood and feed both chicks; and four eaglets have been found surviving in a Spanish Imperial

Eagle's nest. However, a hatching interval of three to four days, common in larger eagles, results in such superiority in size, weight and activity in C1 that C2 usually dies, though Cain does not necessarily kill Abel. If both chicks survive the first few days, they normally fight. Cain then usually, in some species invariably, kills Abel.

The intensity and effect on survival of the battle varies from species to species. Sea and fish eagles seem less aggressive than some others, and two or three young more often survive. In several *Hieraaetus* and *Aquila* species, C2 survives in about one case in four, so that about 1.2 young are reared per successful nest. In some others, C2 scarcely ever, or never, survives. No broods of two are recorded in the Crowned Eagle; and only one in over four hundred broods of Verreaux's Eagle.

This sibling aggression and submission is the largest single cause of nestling loss, accounting for about 30-40 per cent of all eaglets hatched. Both Lack and Wynne Edwards, arguing from different standpoints, concluded erroneously that it must be a response to food supply. However, the younger chick actually dies because it does not attempt to obtain food, or because its elder sibling kills it. In every carefully observed case there has been far more food available in the nest than both the eaglets could possibly eat. There is tenuous evidence that larger average broods may be reared in areas of abundant food supply; but in Scottish Golden Eagles the fractionally higher percentage of broods of two in the east is not proportionate to the relatively enormous differences in available natural food supply, which may be up to thirty times as abundant in the east as in the west.

Strangely, the parents do nothing at all to prevent the battle. If the weak younger eaglet does not beg for food it is not fed; and a female eagle will calmly observe the elder striving to kill the younger without interfering. Fighting is usually fatal within twenty-four to forty-eight hours. A younger chick surviving this far becomes stronger, can beg for food, is fed by the parent, and has a better chance of survival, even though intermittent fighting continues for up to three weeks. An eaglet taken and hand-reared for two weeks, then returned to the nest, at once hurls itself ferociously at its sibling. Fighting becomes sporadic and normally ceases before the end of the downy stage. Though feathered eaglets do not fight, the younger always remains submissive to the elder, and is fed second if the elder is hungry.

No really convincing explanation of the evolutionary advantage of this process has yet been proposed. It appears to be biologically wasteful, since a similar effect could be produced by reducing the clutch to the single egg laid by many eagles. Meyburg suggests that the second egg acts as an insurance if the first laid fails to hatch; but this does not explain why so many successful eagles lay only one. Other suggestions regarding Verreaux's Eagle in particular, are that the struggle to dominate C2 may induce C1 to take more food and grow faster, or that sibling aggression is the first manifestation of the adult territorial behaviour. There is no good evidence for the first; and against the second, the intensely territorial African Fish Eagle quite often rears two or even three young.

The level of fatality seems to be connected with the hatching interval and the degree of aggression by C1 to C2; but the latter seems unconnected with intensely predacious habits in the species concerned. In all sea and fish eagles, C2 quite often survives, but in the rather inoffensive weak-footed Lesser Spotted Eagle it almost invariably dies or is killed. C2 survives in about one in four Golden Eagle nests, but in the very similar Verreaux's Eagle practically never. In the very powerful Crowned Eagle, C2 apparently never survives; but in both the African Hawk Eagle and Bonelli's Eagle, perhaps the most predacious of all eagles relative to their size, C2 survives in about one in five cases. The fatal effect of the battle is clear. It reduces the size of brood, individually by half, in a longer series where some eggs are infertile by 30-40 per cent.

It used to be thought that the larger eaglet, C1 or Cain, was invariably a female; and that therefore more females than males would survive. That, however, would imply an improbable non-random distribution of the sexes in the eggs. It is the elder eaglet that normally survives, whatever its sex, and any difference in survival rates of the sexes is slight. Perhaps a female hatching from a second egg might be more aggressive and better able to survive than a male; but, the second smaller, lighter egg would normally produce a smaller chick, regardless of sex. Records show that as many male eaglets leave the nest as females; age, not sex, is the crucial factor.

Human intervention in the battle to save the otherwise doomed second eaglet can be specially beneficial in some threatened species. If C1 is removed as soon as it hatches and reared by hand, C2 then has all the female's attention, and will normally survive. C1 can also be reared in the nest of some other common large raptor such as a Black Kite, which will readily accept and feed a young Lesser Spotted Eagle. In

Female Wahlberg's Eagle with her 45-day-old feathering eaglet (*Peter Steyn*)

Spanish Imperial Eagles, young with little or no chance of survival in broods of three or more have been readily adopted by other Imperial Eagles laying infertile eggs. Feathered young eagles can later be returned to their own nest, just before first flight. They do not then fight with their sibling; and the old eagle apparently accepts and feeds them in the nest, and after their first flight to independence. Such human intervention can nearly double the breeding success of a rare species.

The progress of the fledging period is normally divided into three stages:(i) The downy stage in which the eaglet is entirely devoid of true feathers. In this it is first covered with a thin coat of first down, later replaced by a thicker, woollier coat of second down. (ii) The feathering stage, beginning when the feathers break through their sheaths. In this stage the eaglet becomes first spotted, then covered with growing feathers. (iii) Finally, the feathered stage, in which the eaglet is covered with feathers, but because the wing and tail quills grow more slowly, still cannot fly.

The downy eaglet is more or less helpless, must be brooded most of the time by the parent, and must be fed. Gradually it becomes more expert at reaching up to snatch proffered food from the parent's bill, and towards the end of this stage becomes quite active, and learns to stand and defaecate over the nest rim. Rarely, as in the Crowned Eagle, it even feeds itself. The feet of a Crowned Eagle are immensely powerful; and the growing eaglet can already hold down and tear up prey while still entirely downy.

Throughout the downy stage, which lasts two to five weeks, the eaglet must normally be sheltered from sun, cold or heavy rain. In the later parts of this stage the first down is replaced by thicker woollier second down. The eaglet may not then be brooded by day; but will still normally be brooded at night, even in the tropics. Exposure to rain or cold and, especially, strong sun will quickly kill it, a fact which bird photographers should remember. Admittedly, it is easier to photograph eagles at this stage, but it is unfair to place the life of the eaglet at risk merely to obtain a photograph.

Once the first feathers burst through they thereafter grow rapidly, and the eaglet's appearance is transformed within a week. The wing and tail quills are the first to break their sheaths and the contour feathers appear on body and wings a few days later. In most eagles they grow more rapidly on the wings and body than on the head which, in fish and sea eagles and most booted eagles, remains partly downy after the body is feathered. However, in snake eagles, the Bateleur and the African Tawny Eagle, the feathers of the head, back and upper wings develop more rapidly. They effectively protect the young eagle from hot sun in an open nest before the feathers of the underside, wings and tail have developed. It is of interest that this similar adaptation to an open nest site has developed independently in the Tawny and in the otherwise very different snake eagles and Bateleur.

Most eaglets continue to be fed by their parents during the feathering stage; but usually they will also attempt to feed themselves. Young snake eagles can certainly swallow a whole snake, if it is not too big, even when downy, without parental assistance. Careful measurements of the bill and claws of the feet in several African eagles show that they attain nearly full size during the feathering stage, important since these are the instruments with which eaglets hold and tear up prey. Once the feathering stage is complete young eagles are normally left alone thereafter to feed themselves with prey brought by either parent. They will still solicit a parent which comes with food and may even be fed; but they do not need such help any longer.

During the feathered stage of its existence the eaglet grows more active, but has a very dull time. In most eagles the parents now only visit the eaglet briefly, perhaps not even once a day, to deposit prey which the unaided eaglet can now tear up or swallow whole. Remaining for hours in the nest without seeing its parent, it frequently lies on its side and sleeps. It is not brooded by day, is exposed to rain, wind and

Small downy two-week-old
Wahlberg's eaglet *(author)*

The same Wahlberg's Eaglet about
to fly at two months *(author)*

sun, and in many species the parent does not even return **at**
night. In a few, such as Ayres' Hawk Eagle, the female roosts
on the nest with the eaglet until it makes its first flight.

Although among the first to appear, the wing and tail quills
develop slowly during this stage, gradually lengthening and
becoming stronger. During the last few days of the feathered
stage the eaglet practises wing flapping, and may climb out on
branches of the nest tree, or along the ledge of a cliff into the
shade. Males are always lighter and more active than females
and can often be recognised by both activity and smaller size.
However, in broods of two the male may be C1 and so appear
larger than a female C2 up to the very end of the fledging
period.

Eaglets gain weight very rapidly during the downy and
feathering stages; but much more slowly in the feathered
stage. Just before they fly they may actually lose weight.

Young Imperial Eagle practising
wing flapping (*B-U. Meyburg*)

Since they may fly prematurely if repeatedly disturbed, they are best left alone at this stage. In recorded cases, premature flight did no harm; but it is obviously unnatural and best avoided. Eaglets are best ringed late in the feathering stage, when their legs and feet have attained almost full size, but when they will make no attempt to fly.

Through all three stages the actual gain is about forty times the hatching weight. A young Golden Eagle, weighing $3\frac{1}{4}$-$3\frac{1}{2}$oz (90-100g) at birth, weighs 7lb 10oz to 8lb 12oz (3.5-4kg) at first flight. About three-quarters of this increase is added in the first two stages, the last quarter in the feathered stage. For about a week or so before first flight the general appearance of the eaglet changes little, and the imminence of first flight is foreshadowed by increased activity such as wing flapping or climbing on branches.

Some early observers claimed that the parents coax the eaglets to make their first flight, bringing food near the eyrie and tantalising the young bird until it makes the necessary effort, but if this ever really occurs it is by accident. Young eagles normally fly without coaxing, usually in the absence of their parents. Often the first real flight is preceded by a series of short hops among the branches of a tree; but in some eagles it is a sudden direct flight of 200-300yd (m) to another tree, across a valley or down a slope to alight on the ground.

Obviously such an eaglet, which may have been reared in a cliff nest safe from predators, is now vulnerable to large mammalian predators, or to humans. However, it usually gathers itself again before long and flies to a safer perch. An eaglet forced to fly prematurely by a human intruder may have more difficulty in gaining another perch; but otherwise such premature flights differ little from natural first flights.

Factors which may stimulate the eaglet to make the essay include, especially, wind, which fills the eaglet's wings when it opens or flaps them and lifts it off the nest. Yet eaglets may also fly for the first time on perfectly windless days, for no obvious reason.

The length of the fledging period varies from about fifty days in the smallest species to well over a hundred days in the largest. It may also vary within a species. Young Crowned Eagles from the same nest have flown in 105-125 days. Broods of two may take longer to fledge than a single youngster, and males fly sooner than heavier females. As a group, snake-eagles have much longer fledging periods relative to their body-weight than any others, in African species 100-105 days. Their young are also notably cautious about making their first flights.

The fledging periods of tropical eagles always appear longer than those of their close relatives or counterparts in temperate climates. The European Snake Eagle fledges in 70-75 days, the Black-breasted Snake Eagle in 90-100 days; the Tawny Eagle in Rhodesia in 75 days, the larger Steppe Eagle in 55-60 days; the Scottish Golden Eagle in 65-70 days, Verreaux's Eagle in 95-100 days; Bonelli's Eagle in 62 days; the slightly smaller African Hawk Eagle in 65-70 days. The Scottish Golden Eagle flies in about the same time as the much smaller Tawny and African Hawk Eagles.

However, when such figures are related to day length the apparently shorter fledging periods of temperate species or races prove to be actually longer. In high summer a Scottish Golden Eagle could hunt for eighteen of the twenty-four hours, perhaps for 1,170-1,260 hours during the whole fledging period. Near the Equator, Verreaux's Eagles could hunt at best for ten of the twenty-four hours or only 950-1,000 hours in the entire fledging period. Similarly, the subtropical Bonelli's Eagle could hunt for fifteen of the twenty-four hours, the African Hawk Eagle for ten of the twenty-four, 950 and 650-700 hours respectively in the whole fledging periods.

In any case, however, the parent eagles never hunt for anything like the full available time. So long as the feathered eaglet is supplied with food on which it can feed at will, adequately provided by a snake, game bird, rabbit, hare or hyrax left in the nest, it will make normal growth in the last stages of the fledging period, and launch itself on its first flight when ready to go.

20 The Fledging Period: Parental Behaviour

More is known about this part of the breeding cycle than any other because so many bird photographers, who generally agree that the eaglet should hatch before they start work, have found watching eagles at this stage fascinating. Throughout the fledging period the parental behaviour is broadly controlled by the stage of development of the young. With experience, a mere glance at an eaglet in the nest enables an observer to predict what should happen that day.

The hatch is signalled by the sitting adult. The incubating male or female is aware of the eaglet, now audible, cheeping in the shell as it chips its way out. The parent repeatedly half-rises from the egg and looks down into the nest-cup. Normally the female, sometimes the male, is brooding at the dramatic moment when the eaglet breaks free. Few observers have watched these events at close quarters, for since small eaglets are very vulnerable the nest should be avoided or observed from a discreet distance at the hatch. Newly hatched eaglets are very easily killed by sun, cold, rain or even their own siblings if the old bird is disturbed.

In a few unusually tame eagles the full details of the hatch have been watched. In Verreaux's Eagle, the best known, males have been recorded incubating for 16-63 per cent of

Female Crowned Eagle on guard at the nest *(author)*

157

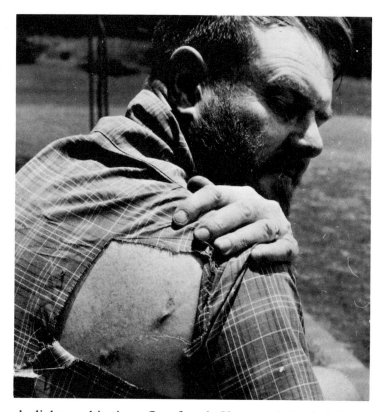

daylight at this time. One female Verreaux's Eagle left the
nest for thirty-three minutes when the chick was half
hatched. The male then took over, and picked up the half
shell, placing it beside the chick and an infertile egg. The
female returned with a hyrax, which she had killed in her
half-hour absence, took over from the male and, when she
had brooded for thirty-five minutes, stood to reveal the now
fully-hatched chick. At the hatch female Crowned Eagles,
very bold birds, will not even stand up to allow an observer to
see what goes on; but crouch in the nest and glare with real
and intended menace.

A newly hatched eaglet cannot be more or less force fed by
thrusting food into its instinctively gaping beak; but must be
gently induced to reach for and take a minute morsel of flesh
held out on the hooked tip of the parent's beak. The adult is
most solicitous, turning its beak this way and that, presenting
a completely charming picture at close quarters. The same
female Verreaux's Eagle offered her eaglet thirty pieces of
flesh in three feeds in its first twenty-four hours. It took
twenty-four of these; she ate the rest.

Either parent, most often the female, broods the young day

and night in its first few days. In this same Verreaux's Eagle parents were on the nest for 97.8 per cent of the daylight, the female for 91.8 per cent, the male for 6 per cent. The female brooded the chick for 93.5 per cent of her time on the nest. This sort of behaviour is typical. Observations at other nests with other species confirm that eagles brood their small downy young, or at least stand over them sheltering them from rain or sun, for 80-90 per cent of daylight and all night. Some eagles in warm climates voluntarily leave their small downy young for up to three hours at a time, and the eaglets normally survive such exposure and risk from predators. However, if an eagle with two hatched young is then disturbed, the elder C1 is likely to attack and perhaps kill C2— another reason for leaving the birds alone at this crucial stage.

Downy eaglets can stand a fair amount of cold; but not hot sun or heavy rain. When a rainstorm threatens, an absent parent hurriedly returns to the nest and broods, her plumage dripping. If observers *must* visit nests at this stage, the eaglet should be shaded from sun with a cloth or, if cold, kept warm inside one's shirt. Its life should never be risked just to acquire statistics.

Parental behaviour varies according to species, and between individuals within species. As a fair generalisation, if the female has incubated alone she will normally brood alone. However, male Golden Eagles which have not incubated frequently brood small eaglets. Variation between individuals makes generalisations based on only one nest unwise. A female Crowned Eagle near my house regularly laid only one egg and never shared incubation or brooding with her mate, but in all other Crowned Eagles I have observed, males have shared incubation but seldom or never brooded chicks. If I had only observed the Karen Crowned Eagles I should have assumed, wrongly, that only females incubated and brooded the young. However, I have never known a male Martial Eagle, Ayres' Hawk Eagle, any species of snake eagle or Bateleur brood small young. Results from at least three or four nests are needed to support any sound generalisation.

Towards the end of the downy stage the eaglet becomes active, learns to stand and walk about and occasionally, as in the Crowned Eagle, to feed itself. The parent then does not brood it much by day, though the female may brood at night. Few have ever watched an eagle all through the night, but one Scottish Golden Eagle stood on the nest with its downy eaglet throughout a cold summer night, and surprisingly did not brood it. I have many times watched tropical eagles settle to brood young at dusk, though they may have been exposed

Female Verreaux's Eagle with her month-old eaglet *(Peter Steyn)*

and active during the evening. An active eaglet, in hot sunshine, shuffles into any available shade, or crawls under the attendant parent; and I once watched an African Hawk Eagle deliberately spread her left wing to shade a small downy chick.

The amount of prey brought to the nest is always sharply increased immediately after hatching. During the incubation period the appetite of female eagles is apparently reduced; they are fed by the male, if at all, every few days. Detailed records show that female Crowned Eagles receive prey during incubation about once in three days. In the early fledging period, however, kills are brought on average once in 1.55 days. Since this eagle kills large mammals, each kill lasts for more than one day. In Ayres' Eagle, feeding on small birds, the male brought the incubating female eight kills in twenty-five days, about one per three days; but almost trebled his killing rate, to almost one a day, after the hatch. In seven species of Kenya eagles and the Secretary Bird, the average rate of killing by the male before hatching was 0.3 per day, and after hatching 0.8. In three, Ayres' Hawk Eagle, the Martial Eagle and the Brown Snake Eagle, the figures were 0.3 and 0.87 per day respectively. Thus, although more records are needed, it is clear that male eagles double or treble their rate of killing just after the hatch.

This is of special interest, because it is the only time when an individual eagle regularly kills more than its own needs. It also suggests that males can kill more almost at will. At all other times the frequency of killing is mainly (but not quite invariably) controlled by appetite. However, the presence of

a downy eaglet (which he must see either during or soon after the hatch) evidently stimulates the male to increased hunting effort. The small downy eaglet eats very little of the superabundance provided; Scottish Golden Eaglets are often surrounded by several kills, each much heavier than themselves.

Pair of African Hawk Eagles on the nest with young (*author*)

Such large larders are unusual among tropical eagles; normally one finds at most two kills beside a downy eaglet. In Scotland a surplus of grouse or hares will keep for a week, and could tide over a time of extreme wet when the eagles may be unable to hunt. In the tropics a large larder would simply rot in a few days, or even hours; but the daily fine weather in the dry season, when most species breed, perhaps permits more regular successful hunting.

Whether they brood young or not, some males will feed eaglets if they visit the nest, occasionally even when a female is present; a male Golden Eagle has been photographed feeding a chick, with the female calmly looking on. More often, however, the male arrives when the female is away, and he may then feed the eaglet, which automatically begs from any adult. If the female returns she may either seize the prey fiercely and prevent the male from feeding (as normally happens with the Crowned Eagle); or he may simply cease feeding and relinquish the prey without a conflict. Some males, for instance in Ayres' Hawk Eagle and Wahlberg's Eagle, apparently never feed the eaglet, even if they arrive with prey when the female is absent. They then seem ill at ease, and back away from their offspring, which automatically beg. If the female were killed or dead an eaglet dependent on such a male would starve. Biologically, it is desirable for the male to be prepared to feed an eaglet if he brings prey to the nest and is not dispossessed by the female. In short, Dad should know how to do it.

During the second, or feathering stage, brooding the eaglet normally ceases even at night, though the female often rests on the nest with the eaglet. Although it is now large, able to walk about on the nest, and sometimes attempts to feed itself if alone in the nest with prey, it usually cannot, or is unwilling. At this stage, as in many other birds of prey, the female usually perches near the nest while the male hunts and brings most of or all the prey. The male is now feeding himself, his mate, and one or more large and ravenous, rapidly growing eaglets. A feathering eaglet will attain three-quarters of its final weight by the end of the feathering stage, still growing rapidly. If a young eagle eats about the same as young buzzards of similar weight, it probably eats at least as much as an adult, if not more. A young buzzard eats about $5\frac{1}{4}$oz (150g) per day, an adult 5oz (140g) per day. Thus a male eagle, with a brood of two eaglets, must provide for at least four adult-equivalents, perhaps more; and three even if there is only one young.

This is the second 'point of strain' in the breeding cycle, when the whole family depends on the hunting efficiency of the male, who must kill three or four times his own needs. Brood losses should occur through starvation now, if at all. However, most eaglets that have reached the feathering stage survive. Brood losses are then much lower than during the early downy stage, when sibling aggression accounts for most, though the food demand is obviously far less and superabundant food is usually available. Feathering eaglets also can survive longer without food than when small and downy; if one large kill is brought even every two days a parent can feed them. Food shortage at this stage might have most effect in those eagles which, like buzzards, feed on relatively small prey such as rats. However, even in these I know of no definite evidence that food shortage reduces the brood.

Green branches are brought to the nest throughout the incubation and fledging periods, but especially at this stage of the fledging period, when the female is not actually on but remains near the nest. She tends to collect and bring more than usual from any available green tree or bank of heather or rushes near the nest. She generally leaves one branch, then brings another or several. She may drop a branch on the eaglet, and some have interpreted this as attempting to shade

Pair of Imperial Eagles with two offspring (B-U. Meyburg)

the young. However, I believe that the bringing of green branches is neither to shade the young nor to provide additional nest lining; but is a displacement reaction, which may be biologically advantageous in helping to keep the female near the nest when she is actually off it for hours, and might otherwise be more inclined to hunt than to stay on guard.

Even if not feeding young, it may be desirable that females stay near the nest to guard them. Some, not all, eagles are very aggressive to man at this stage. Golden Eagles and Verreaux's Eagles, sea or fish eagles or snake eagles never attack man, but Crowned Eagles, African Hawk Eagles, even the tiny Ayres' Hawk Eagle, regularly do attack men near the nest at this stage. Since Crowned Eagles are powerful enough to do serious damage one should not invite attack. Even an African Hawk Eagle, in a high tree shaken by the wind, can be dangerous. I have never actually seen any eagle attack a monkey or a baboon in similar situations; but when such animals approach a nest containing feathering young the female will return and perch in the nest tree, if not on the nest. The monkeys then usually retreat, and actual contact and battle is avoided.

When feathered, occasionally earlier, young eagles have developed enough strength in beak and feet to tear up their own prey. This normally releases the female from any need to remain near the nest, and she can now regularly share in hunting and killing prey. Up to the end of the feathering

163

stage, males normally bring most of the prey to the nest, but thereafter the female normally brings at least as much as or more than the male. At two Crowned Eagles' nests, males brought twenty-six kills to the female's twenty-two in the downy and feathering stages; but after feathering nine to the female's twenty-one. In some, such as Ayres' Hawk Eagle and Wahlberg's Eagle, the male continues to bring most prey right up to the end of the fledging period. A female apparently bringing more than the male may not always have killed it herself. Once free to leave the vicinity of the nest, she can locate her mate anywhere in the home range, perhaps collect prey from him and take it to the nest. She certainly does kill some prey at intervals throughout the fledging period, from the day of hatch on, in several species; but has her best chance to hunt when released by the development of the eaglet's feathers from brooding and guard duties at the nest.

The behaviour of the adults at this stage varies considerably from species to species. In snake eagles and the Bateleur the young is left wholly alone, and the parents do not even roost near it. One pair of Bateleurs ceased roosting near the nest when their thirty-one day old eaglet was just showing its first feathers; although they abandoned it unusually early it flew successfully. African Fish Eagles normally roost in their territory near but not on the nest. In three consecutive days and nights a feathered eaglet about forty-eight to fifty-two days old, watched by Dieter Plage, was left alone except for brief visits totalling 1.1 per cent of the observation time, during which the female fed it all that it ate. She roosted with the male on a tree nearby. Female Ayres' Eagles, however, roost on the nest with the eaglet until it makes its first flight, and even after it flies, when it returns to the nest to roost.

Essentially, however, once the eaglet is feathered, the parents are released from any duties except to supply food at intervals of twenty-four hours or more. Such visits last only a few seconds as a rule, seldom more than a minute. Rarely the parents may stay longer for unknown reasons. One male Crowned Eagle came four times in a day, twice with prey, once staying half an hour and the female once. Bonelli's and African Hawk Eagles are also likely to spend quite long periods on the nest with large feathered young.

Since most eaglets make their first real flight in the absence of their parents, the adults must either find the eaglet wherever it may have gone, or it must return to the nest when next they bring prey, which they will naturally continue to do unless prevented. In forest or savanna an eaglet's first flight is normally to another nearby tree, whence it can either see its parents, or they can see it. In open mountain country the eaglet probably alights within a few hundred yards of the nest; and it is no problem for the parents to find it.

In most eagles, for instance the Golden Eagle, Martial Eagle and African Hawk Eagle, the young eagle is found and fed by the parents away from the nest. In Wahlberg's Eagle the young is apparently at once fed away from the nest by its parents; its first strong flight coincides with their departure from their normal roost perch near the nest. A young Verreaux's Eagle made a clumsy first flight of only a few yards to some rocks just below the nest. The male then brought in prey, which the female ate, ignoring the young bird desperately struggling to climb back to the nest. The next day the young bird had moved 300yd (m) and was thereafter fed mainly away from the nest. Young Crowned Eagles, however, return to the nest for nine to eleven months after their first flight, and receive all prey there.

Behaviour thus varies from species to species; but the eaglet's first flight does not seem to be a very critical moment, for it or its parents. It either returns to the nest, or is found by the adults without difficulty. I know of no case where a young eagle has been reared to its first flight to be later lost through misadventure, or inability on the part of parents. Since the first flight is so often made in their absence, they evidently search for it as a matter of course; and find it within a few minutes if it does not return to the nest of its own accord.

21 The Post-fledging Period and Independence of the Eaglet

The post-fledging period is the time from the eaglet's first real flight until it becomes independent of its parents. It is now no longer confined to the nest itself, and the parents often feed it far from the nest, so naturally observations on this stage in the life of the young eagle and its parents are scanty. One can no longer locate either at a definite spot, but must find and follow them in a much larger area perhaps in difficult conditions.

Really good observations on the post-fledging period exist only in the Crowned and Verreaux's Eagles. Both are large species, but one is a forest bird while the other inhabits open rocky mountains. This partly accounts for the observed differences in their post-fledging behaviour. Partial observations of the post-fledging period have also been made for a number of other species; but very often observation soon becomes profitless as it is impossible to locate the young eagle.

In the United States attempts have been made to study post-fledging behaviour of young Golden Eagles with small radio transmitters. By bleaching or cutting out a pattern or cutting out a 'window' in the wing feathers the young bird can also be recognised easily. Bleaching is preferable to window-marking for although, so far as is known window-marking has not yet caused the loss of any young eagles, it evidently must affect flying ability more than bleaching, or the attachment of a radio transmitter. None of these methods has yet provided good published evidence on the post-fledging period.

In the early post-fledging period the young eagle (as it should now be called) usually stays near the nest since, when it makes its first considerable flight, its wing and tail quills are still enclosed in soft blood-rich sheaths, and the firm quill base has not yet fully formed. In falconers' parlance, the flight feathers are 'in the blood'. These big quill feathers take ten days to three weeks, sometimes even more, to become really strong; and only then can the young eagle fly well.

In all snake eagles the fledging period is relatively very long and the young bird makes its first flight at an advanced stage of maturity. Its plumage development seems hardly different from that of its parents, though the colours may differ. Young snake eagles are very cautious about making their first flights; but once they leave they do not remain long near the nest. Brown and Black-breasted Snake Eagles normally leave the nest area within a few days of first flight and Bateleurs do not usually stay more than a few days near the nest. Probably, most young snake eagles soon follow their parents about in the neighbourhood, and receive prey from them away from the nest. A very long fledging period could have the advantage of producing an eaglet able to fly far and easily a few days after first flight. Though young tropical snake eagles apparently remain in the general area of the nest and the parental home range for up to six months, the young European Snake Eagles must migrate.

In the better known fish and sea eagles, the young remain close to the nest for about the first two weeks; and in the neighbourhood for six weeks to two and a half months. Young European Sea Eagles remain near the eyrie for thirty-five to forty days, and the parents simply deposit prey there for them. Young African Fish Eagles at Lake Victoria and Lake Naivasha remain near the nest for from one to nearly three months, usually between six and ten weeks. They are fed by their parents on or near the nest; but probably return to the nest only because it is a convenient feeding platform.

Though little is known of post-fledging behaviour in the harpy group, in the Harpy Eagle itself the post-fledging period is certainly very long. Young Harpies thought to be eight months old in worn plumage were still near the nest, being fed there by the parents at five- to fourteen-day intervals, evidently not yet independent. This behaviour resembles that of the African Crowned Eagle; and may be associated either with forest life and a diet of large mammals, or with sheer size. The almost equally large Philippine Monkey-eating Eagle is said, unlike the Harpy, to breed every year, but its very long recorded incubation and fledging periods make this doubtful.

In most booted eagles the young apparently remain near the nest for a period and then wander more widely, being seen often with their parents, and presumably sharing in their kills. In Wahlberg's Eagle the young bird is absent by day but returns to roost at the nest for about ten days after its first flight. After ten days (perhaps the time needed for the quills to harden) it no longer comes near the nest. Young Bonelli's and African Hawk Eagles soon leave the nest area to accompany their parents in the home range. Young Golden Eagles are usually found near the nest for two to three weeks after their first flight, their resting and roosting places marked by numerous tufts of stripped down. Young Lesser Spotted Eagles stay close to the nest for about three weeks, but must migrate from Europe only about two weeks later. Young African Tawny Eagles apparently roost, perch and feed near the nest for up to six weeks after their first flight, but do not necessarily return daily. The young Ayres' Hawk Eagle, a forest species, remains near the nest and roosts in it for up to three weeks, thereafter remaining in the neighbourhood with its parents for up to three months. Young Martial Eagles may return to roost in the nest for a few days, and remain loosely attached to the general area for up to six months. When four months old they can certainly soar several miles from the nest site, and behave very differently from their near relatives, Crowned Eagles.

One young Verreaux's Eaglet, and four young Crowned Eagles, have been studied throughout their post-fledging periods. The latter were all reared in the nest near my house, and were observed almost daily during their nine and a half to eleven and a half month adolescence. All behaved in a similar way. They perched somewhere in the forest, gradually moving farther away, but seldom more than about half a mile

Immature Martial Eagle *(Peter Steyn, Ardea Photographics)*

(0.8km) from the nest, remaining always within earshot of the adult's food call. During adolescence they were fed at intervals of two to thirteen days, averaging in two complete post-fledging periods three days between feeds, almost the same as the feeding rate in the late fledging period.

Using a standard procedure, the food was taken to the nest by the parent. Usually the female, sometimes the male, would arrive with prey, perch on a large tree, and start to call loudly, 'Quee-quee-quee-quee'. If the young eagle was close by, it heard at once and responded shrilly. It would then fly into the nest and solicit the adult with lowered head and loud shrieks. Then, and only then, would the adult fly into the nest to leave the prey. The young would continue calling while the adult remained in sight, and begin to feed only when it had gone. In four complete post-fledging periods the young was only once given prey away from the nest, when it was very nearly independent.

These young Crowned Eagles all learned to kill for themselves before the parents stopped feeding them at the nest. Different individuals certainly killed for themselves on the 61st, 125th, 188th and 219th day after their first flight; other kills were suspected. Thus, although mainly dependent on their parents for 285-350 days after their first flight, they did kill even large, agile animals for themselves. The 1962 eaglet killed an adult Sykes' Monkey only sixty-one days after its first flight; and an adult white cat on its 219th day. Thus, though the parents normally feed the young Crowned Eagle for up to eleven months, it *can* kill for itself before they cease to feed it. It should therefore have a better chance of survival if something happens to the parents before the normal end of the post-fledging period.

In the very different Verreaux's Eagle, the post-fledging period, in one case, lasted ninety-eight days. In the first sub-stage of twenty-eight days the young bird spent 56 per cent of its time in the nest and 42.7 per cent on the nest kopje; 98.6 per cent of its day was spent on or close to the nest and it roosted there. It made only weak short flights, becoming gradually stronger on the wing. In the next sub-stage of twenty-eight days it spent only 20 per cent of daylight on the nest, flew much more (6.7 per cent of observed time), and was away from the nest and nearby rocks for 15.4 per cent of daylight, though it still spent about 40 per cent of its time on the nest kopje. During the final sub-stage of forty-one days it spent 17.6 per cent of its time away from the nest kopje, only 2.5 per cent of its time on the nest, and 6.2 per cent in flight. It began to fly to perch near its parents in its second twenty-eight days, and made longer and longer flights thereafter. It last roosted on the nest ledge six days before it finally disappeared.

These observations indicate that the young Verreaux's Eagle remains in the neighbourhood of the nest for about three months after its first flight, gradually becomes less and less attached to the nest, but never spends more than 6-7 per cent of the day on the wing. Young Crowned Eagles, by comparison, soar and fly very little, even late in their protracted post-fledging period, while young Martial Eagles probably soar and fly more than do young Verreaux's Eagles. Such differences reflect the general behaviour of the adults, the Martial Eagle being the most aerial of the three, and the Crowned Eagle spending most of its time perched in forest.

Parents bringing food to young Crowned Eagles had always fed first. Entire kills were not brought, and parents seldom remained at the nest after depositing the prey for the young eagle. Occasionally a parent would return and remove a portion of prey lying in the nest, and once a female robbed her own offspring. On rare occasions, once for thirteen days, the adults did not bring prey for long periods. The young eagle then became extremely hungry; and the longest of these foodless gaps, from 16 to 28 August 1960, ended with the eaglet's first known unaided kill.

The parents did not normally provide the young bird with more prey than it could use, and often it lacked food for several successive days. Rarely the parents brought more prey than the young could eat; and on one such occasion the young bird, which could clearly see its parent with prey, did not respond normally to the adult's call; the adult eventually departed with the prey.

The adult Verreaux's Eagles, in contrast, regularly provided the young eagle with more prey than it could consume. Moreover, it had a priority right to prey, even if the parents themselves were not full fed. It was never known to kill for itself during the post-fledging period. The female claimed all prey brought by the male during the period, but relinquished it if the young wanted it. When bringing the prey the adults called, and the much more vocal young responded. The differences in the amounts of prey brought and the frequency of killing in Verreaux's and Crowned Eagles reflect not only differences of habitat and abundance of prey, but also some basic behavioural differences between species.

Young eagles approaching independence are often said to be driven away by their parents, but observed results conflict on this point. The four young Crowned Eagles certainly were not driven away; rather, they released their parents from their duty to supply prey. Late in the nine and a half to eleven and a half month period of adolescence, the young became increasingly difficult to attract with calls to the nest. Finally, one day the parent arrived and the young simply did not respond or appear. The parent remained, calling and calling, for up to two hours; but when the young still did not appear the parent left, with the prey, not having received the expected hungry response. The adults might repeat this process once, but not a second time. They seemed to know that the young bird had gone its way; and soon began a new nesting cycle. The young bird might be located in the forest later, apparently healthy, and evidently young Crowned Eagles leave of their own volition when ready, and are not driven away by their parents.

Similarly, young male tigers and lions gradually attain independence, and are not repelled; young lionesses stay with their pride. Young African Fish Eagles probably also become independent of their parents of their own accord. At Lake

Victoria two young remained on their breeding island after the parents had left the territory. However, such behaviour probably varies from place to place, and recently independent young fish and sea eagles tend to be social. Up to six young fish eagles may associate, and young Bald Eagles may gather near any available easy source of food, such as an army rubbish dump or a dead whale. Young African Fish Eagles are also more likely than adults to come to carrion.

In the single detailed observed case of Verreaux's Eagle, the parents did drive their offspring away. They attacked it first on 20 November, seventy-three days after first flight. It then remained unmolested until 15 December, when it was again attacked and this time left the territory, never to reappear. Though the attack on 15 December was less violent and protracted than that on 20 November, it occurred near the nest. E. G. Rowe also recorded adult Verreaux's Eagles driving away a nine-month old young bird, believed to be their own, when they were incubating their next clutch of eggs.

Which of these two processes—painless independence when the young is ready or violent repulsion by the parents—is normal can only be ascertained by more observation. My view, to which I shall stick till proved wrong, is that most young eagles gradually become independent of the nesting area without being repelled. In migrant eagles in Europe or North America this must almost certainly occur.

It is clear, however, that recently independent young usually leave their parents' home range or territory, and move to any available area of no-man's-land without breeding adults, there to survive if they can. Young Scottish Golden Eagles often move to lower grouse moors, where they are in danger. On Amchitka Island the young Bald Eagles collect at the army rubbish dump; and at Lake Naivasha young African Fish Eagles move to large lagoons of waterlilies devoid of breeding pairs. Here, if not entirely free from molestation by adults, they are not subject to the incessant attack they would suffer in the small breeding territories.

The percentage of fledged young which become independent is unknown in most eagles; but it may be high. Between July 1959 and late December 1967, our Karen Crowned Eagle laid five eggs and hatched and fledged five young. The 1967 young died prematurely in August before it was independent, so triggering a new breeding cycle. The female laid again in late December, and hatched her fifth young in February 1968; it flew in June 1968, and became independent in May 1969. Of her five known eggs, all produced young which flew, and four independent young, a record of which a human mother might be proud. Other observations suggest that such success is typical of the Crowned Eagle; and I think it likely that most young eagles, once fledged, reach independence. After that, once on their own, they are subject to all the hazards of inexperience and youth, but forced to fend for themselves.

22 Reproductive Potential, Replacement Rate and Longevity

In any stable population of eagles, enough young must be reared to independence and thereafter survive through immaturity to replace natural losses among the adults. Unmolested populations of eagles are generally very stable; total numbers change little. Man interferes with the natural situation; but only within the last 150 years, especially the last thirty years, has the natural order of events been much upset anywhere in the world.

Since very little is known about young eagles after they can fly, and even less after they become independent, a population's reproductive potential is normally calculated from the number of young flown from nests. This can be calculated per pair overall; per pair which breed (lay eggs); and per successful nest (rearing young). The rate per successful nest, or per pair which laid, is often claimed as a more precise and reliable figure than the rate per pair overall, which includes non-breeding pairs. However, since the fundamental figure needed is the replacement rate per adult in the whole population, it is misleading to calculate ignoring non-breeding pairs.

Eminent ornithologists such as the late Dr David Lack have argued that true non-breeding pairs cannot exist, and that any bird must breed whenever it can, that is, when it has a place to nest and enough food. However, among African Fish Eagles, pairs certainly exist with a good nest site, which can and do catch fish, but which do not breed while near neighbours apparently no better off do. Non-breeding thus certainly occurs in these Fish (and other) Eagles; and is not connected either with nest sites or food supply. Non-breeding occurs more often in the tropics, so is more readily accepted by observers there than in temperate lands, where human interference also has much more effect. However, most experienced observers in North America and Europe now also accept that non-breeding occurs.

The causes of non-breeding are not really known. It is

sometimes due to lack of a nest site; and sometimes may be due to poor food supply, though good direct evidence is lacking, and this seems unlikely because of the small size of the eagles' eggs. There is no concrete evidence that it is due to age, or sickness; African eagles known to be young or quite old seem able to breed. Building a new nest, or a natural disaster to an old one, does not regularly prevent breeding, though sometimes one suspects such causes. The only possibly consistent cause is success in a previous year. In Verreaux's and several other African Eagles a pair rearing young one year is less likely to breed again the next.

Eagles laying one egg can never rear more than one young per successful nest. Those laying two or more eggs sometimes produce two or more young; the number reared per successful nest is 1.2-1.4. The maximum number produced per adult never exceeds 0.5-0.7 per successful nest. The actual number reared per adult overall is often only about half this because some pairs do not lay and others fail after laying. In 112 African Fish Eagles, the number of young per successful nest was 1.28, that per pair which bred 0.74, and 0.47 per pair overall. In 223 Verreaux's Eagles' nests the figures were 1.00 per successful nest, 0.67 per pair which bred and 0.51 per pair overall. In 312 Alaskan Bald Eagle territories the number per successful nest was 1.61, and that per territory 1.02, a territory here equivalent to a pair which bred; non-breeding was not counted.

Thus, in natural conditions without human interference, the reproductive rate of Verreaux's Eagle is 0.51 young per pair or 0.26 per adult; that for the African Fish Eagle 0.47 and 0.24; that for the Alaskan Bald Eagle about 1.02 and 0.51. African Fish Eagles rear overall less than half the young produced per successful nest (0.47:1.28) and Verreaux's Eagles do little better (0.51:1.00). These figures demonstrate how misleading it is to use only figures from successful nests, or from pairs which have laid, to calculate the overall replacement rate per adult.

In Europe and North America, human interference now often masks the true situation. The actual figures in 489 records of Scottish Golden Eagles were 1.17 per successful nest, 0.58 per pair which bred and 0.47 per pair overall. Severe human interference reduced the number of young reared per pair which bred and per pair overall, but scarcely affected the young reared per successful nest—again showing how this particular figure can mislead. Eliminating human interference, and allowing proportionately for pairs that failed, the real potential replacement rate in Scottish Golden

Eagles is about 0.83 per pair per annum overall—much higher than for the similar-sized but tropical Verreaux's Eagle.

In a few eagles, for instance African Crowned Eagles in Kenya, the replacement rate is even lower, since the fifteen-month nesting cycle permits breeding only in alternate years. Even with 100 per cent success it cannot exceed 0.5 young per pair, since in this species any second-hatched young either die or are killed by their siblings. Failures reduce the replacement rate; in fifty-four good records it is 0.39 young per pair per annum overall, or 0.19 per adult.

Such statistics may even suggest why an eagle may be rare. Ayres' Eagle, apparently a very efficient predator on abundant small birds, breeding in unlimited forest and woodland habitat, is yet rare or very rare throughout its wide African range. It is apparently a thoroughly incompetent nest builder, breeding regularly in secure sites but often building nests on insecure lateral branches, where they fall off. The replacement rate in this eagle (which lays only one egg) is reduced, mainly from this cause, from a potential of 1.0 to 0.34 per pair overall, even less than in the Crowned Eagle, and among the lowest figures recorded for any eagle. Ayres' Eagle may only just rear enough young to maintain a small stable population. However, since all the available figures come from the pairs known to me in one small area, they need confirmation elsewhere.

Replacement rates, of flying young reared per pair or per adult per annum overall, are presumably geared to the survival of a stable natural capacity population. They are higher or much higher for temperate species than for similar tropical eagles. Scottish Golden Eagles rearing 0.83 per pair per annum, or 0.415 per adult, may be compared with 0.51 per pair and 0.26 per adult in Verreaux's Eagle; and 0.47 per pair in the African Fish Eagle with about 1.02 per pair in the Alaskan Bald Eagle. Few such direct comparisons can be made because there are far fewer eagle species in temperate than in tropical climates, and also because most figures from temperate climates do not include non-breeding pairs. However, the available data agrees nicely with the now well-documented evidence that temperate birds lay larger clutches and rear larger broods than their tropical counterparts.

From the replacement rate one can calculate potential longevity at any subsequent mortality rate. If all young Naivasha African Fish Eagles survived to sexual maturity, adults would only need to live for an average of four and a quarter years to replace themselves ($2:0.47 = 4\frac{1}{4}$). This seems

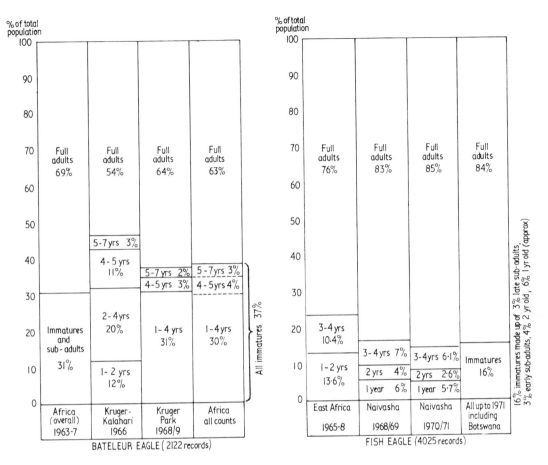

BATELEUR EAGLE (2122 records)

FISH EAGLE (4025 records)

an improbably short life for a large eagle; and certainly some young die before they become adult and sexually mature at perhaps five years old. If half the young die, adults must live on average for eight and a half years; and if three-quarters die adults must live for seventeen years. This seems likely to be too long, so that probably between 50 per cent and 75 per cent of immatures die before sexual maturity.

The age adult eagles can attain is of general interest, but is very rarely even approximately recorded in the wild state. I know of no good records in any temperate eagle, though one American Golden Eagle was believed to live for over twenty years. Captive Golden Eagles have lived for over forty years, and potentially any large eagle may live forty to fifty years. The average lifespan of even captive adults is probably much lower, since zoos often do not record all lifespans, but only the longer and more outstanding. In any case, such records mean little applied to wild eagles, because captives live an unnatural life, never exposed to normal stresses and dangers.

Histograms showing proportion of adult and of different age classes of immatures in Bateleurs and African Fish Eagles to show population make-up (see pp 183-4)

I have recorded a number of known complete Crowned Eagle lifespans. Two females lived eight and a half and nine years and a male twelve; the average is about ten to eleven years. Ayres' Eagle lives for five to seven years, averaging about six. However, I do not know if these birds were adult, but unmated for several years before they appeared at the breeding site; or whether, when they disappeared, they died, as I assume. The average observed lifespan of known Crowned Eagles agrees well with observed changes of mates, which occur about once in six years, giving each adult an average breeding life of about twelve years. Since an adult can only replace itself as a member of a breeding pair, this is the important figure.

The known replacement rate of young reared per pair per annum is 0.39 in Crowned Eagles. If 75 per cent of the Crowned Eagle's young died before sexual maturity at about four years old, too few young would reach sexual maturity to maintain the population. Adults would have to live twenty-two years to replace themselves. Accordingly, to fill any vacancies the death rate must actually be lower. Likewise, in Ayres' Eagle, living about six years as an adult, a replacement rate of 0.34 young per pair per annum (0.17 per adult) and 75 per cent pre-maturity mortality would necessitate an average adult life of about twenty-three years, more than four times that observed in the wild state. Even 50 per cent pre-maturity mortality would not maintain the population.

Although such figures and arguments show how little we really know about the population dynamics of eagles, I think they demonstrate clearly that estimates based only upon the young reared per successful nest are certain to be wrong. If this figure (1.00) is used in Crowned Eagles, at 75 per cent mortality of young, adults need only live four years, whereas their actual life spans about eleven years. Moreover, any assessment of population dynamics and reproductive potential based only on successful nests, or even on pairs which breed, can easily lead to a false sense of security about eagle populations. Non-breeding pairs must be recognised and counted as well if the true reproductive potential of a population of eagles is to be assessed correctly.

Part V The Young Eagle

23 Plumage, Moult and Development to Maturity

When finally independent the former eaglet has become a young eagle, now obliged to fend for itself, but inexperienced, and liable to die before it can enter the adult population at sexual maturity. Very little is known about this stage of an eagle's life, for such young are hard to follow. In some other birds of prey, ringed specimens of known age reveal the stage of moult and plumage changes. However, few eagles have been ringed in any numbers; and most of these recovered were first-year birds, while the body may not be kept and only the ring reported.

The young eagle sometimes appears even bigger than adults because the plumage may be looser and some feathers longer. Young Bateleurs have much longer tails and broader wings than adults. The plumage may be very different, or almost identical. In young Martial, Crowned and Harpy Eagles, the grey and white juvenile plumage is totally unlike the adult; but a young Wahlberg's Eagle is scarcely distinguishable from an adult. Several other young *Aquila* eagles are darker than adults, but with more white in their plumage. However, young Verreaux's Eagles are much paler than the adults, and in the Indian Black Eagle young are so much paler that some authorities have thought they must be kites. Young fish and sea eagles are generally brown or dark brown, whereas adults have white heads and/or pure white tails.

The colours of the eyes, cere and feet also differ. Most adult eagles with yellow eyes have brown eyes when young; but young snake eagles acquire yellow or whitish eyes in the nest. The cere, at the base of the beak, is often grey or greenish in young, yellow or even bright red in the adults. Similar colour differences apply to feet and legs. Such differences are often very imperfectly described in standard works, making identification difficult.

First-year eagles are normally easily recognisable, but moult into full adult plumage over a period of three to eight years, passing through a series of often very confusing subadult plumage phases which are not understood in most species. Even very experienced observers cannot always identify sub-adult eagles. In all the rarer species the sequence of moult is unknown or poorly known. Good details are available for less than ten species, the best-known being the Golden Eagle, Verreaux's Eagle, Bateleur and African Fish Eagle. Several moult studies have yet to be published.

Detailed study of captive birds is the best available guide to these changes. Zoo keepers and falconers could make a great contribution here but seldom do. Though one can argue that if a young captive is not precisely aged such studies are of little value, in most species any information would be better than none. A captive tropical species in North America, with a bitter sub-zero winter, might also moult in different sequence. An assured supply of food, lack of exercise and the natural stresses of wild life are also factors known to affect moult in some birds. However, the sequence of plumage moult in captive birds is still the best available guide to that of wild eagles.

Though information on plumage changes in wild eagles can also be derived from museum skins, some such studies appear highly misleading. For instance, it is estimated that both the Steppe Eagle and Imperial Eagle acquire definitive adult plumage over eight years. Yet the larger Golden Eagle in captivity acquires full adult plumage in four years, an estimate confirmed by Seton Gordon's studies of wild birds. Similarly, Richard Brooke estimates that a Crowned Eagle would only acquire full adult plumage in twenty years, about five times as long as a single young female watched from egg to maturity, and twice the known average lifespan of breeding wild individuals.

The best published studies of moult are for the Golden Eagle and Bateleur. A first-year young Golden Eagle is easily recognised by its generally darker colour and large areas of white at the base of the tail and carpal joint of the wing. It attains adult plumage by a two-stage moult; first into an immature plumage in which the areas of white are reduced; second, when about three and a half years old, into plumage closely resembling an adult's. In a third moult the few remaining immature-looking feathers are shed. A young Golden Eagle is thus mature, and can probably breed, when four years old, a figure substantiated by Seton Gordon's observations in Skye. A young pair occupied a nest cliff in 1942, when probably fifteen months old, and bred in 1946, when they were probably five.

Captive young Bateleurs taken from nests and reared to maturity at Cornell University retain a similar pale brown, streaky or mottled first juvenile plumage for three years, with

looser softer feathers than in adults, and a longer tail. The tail
has shortened by the third year and tail length is thereafter
the best guide to exact age. In the late fourth and fifth years
the underwing coverts darken, and the young can be sexed by
the different shading of their wing quills; the tail shortens
again. In the third pre-adult or sub-adult plumage, at six to
seven years old, the underwing coverts become partly white,
and the width of the dark band at the trailing edge of the wing
differentiates the sexes, as in adults; the feet now just project
beyond the tail tip. In the eighth year the full, magnificent,
black chestnut and white adult plumage, with scarlet cere and
legs, is acquired. The period of sexual immaturity in young
Bateleurs is thus very long, and may not be typical of snake
eagles since the Bateleur is so highly specialised. Other young
snake eagles either resemble the adult or differ less markedly.

Immature African Fish Eagles apparently pass through
four plumage stages. They are, the first immature, mainly
brown juvenile, at two months to one year; second-year immature, much paler, basically white and streaky below, at
thirteen months to two years; early sub-adult, with streaky
white head and neck and black belly at two to three years; and
late sub-adult, probably three to four years, with chestnut
feathers emerging in the black wing coverts and belly.
Finally, when the bird otherwise appears adult, the cere turns
from pinkish to bright yellow. With a little practice, any
competent observer can distinguish these changes, as
presumably can other African Fish Eagles.

Young Martial and Verreaux's Eagles moult in very
different ways. A young Martial Eagle retains the first immature plumage through successive gradual moults until it is
five. In the sixth year dark adult-type feathers blotch the

Juvenile Tawny Eagles (*V. E. M. Burke*)

179

white breast, and the small black dots of the adult pepper the thighs and abdomen. At seven, the plumage is adult; and the eye now changes from pale brown to the adult's glaring golden-yellow.

A young Verreaux's Eagle moults at two to three years to a plumage resembling the adult. At two it is almost black; and at three has only a scatter of brown-tipped feathers. The late sub-adult is practically indistinguishable from an adult. This pattern essentially resembles the two-stage moult of the Golden Eagle, but almost reverses the colour changes. The young Verreaux's Eagle changes from brown and black to black and white, but the young Golden Eagle becomes paler brown.

Assumption of adult plumage does not necessarily mean that an eagle is sexually mature and can breed, though we assume it is. Conversely, some young eagles breed successfully, laying fertile eggs, in immature plumage, for instance an obviously immature Spanish Imperial Eagle.

A young Crowned Eagle which began life as an egg in late December 1967 hatched in February 1968, left the nest in June 1968, and became independent in May 1969, at about fifteen months. When about two and a half she moulted into a paler version of adult plumage, and in August 1971, when about three and a half, actually laid an egg and incubated it for over forty days. She still had a few immature-looking feathers, and her egg was infertile, suggesting she was not fully mature. She finally laid again and reared her first young in 1974-5, when about seven years old. Without colour ringing, certainty that it was the same bird is impossible; but repeated sightings and careful notes on plumage at intervals made me confident that it was.

From the number of young eagles wearing different stages of immature plumage, survival rates can be estimated. However, we must first know the age of the young birds observed, which is possible only when the sequence of moult to maturity is understood. The examples given show how different it can be; and it is impossible when adult and immature plumages are much alike. However, in several species the immatures can be recognised as first, second, third and fourth year birds, as in African Fish Eagles; and in others as first immatures or juveniles, immatures, and sub-adults or pre-adults of known age, as in the Bateleur.

Probably no young eagle except perhaps young Crested Serpent Eagles or some small forest booted eagles is sexually mature at less than three years. Several are not mature until seven or eight years old. Age at maturity is not necessarily correlated with size, for the specialised Bateleur, much smaller than Verreaux's or Golden Eagles which apparently mature earlier, and only about a quarter the weight of the Martial Eagle which apparently matures in a year less, has the longest known immature period. However in general, smaller eagles mature sooner than larger close relatives.

Since in most eagles plumage changes between first flight and sexual maturity are not understood, while in many not even the first immature plumage is well described, it will be many years before such plumage changes are well enough known to permit reasonably accurate ageing of any young eagle encountered. However, the available detailed studies suggest a few useful guidelines; much more knowledge could quickly be gained if zoos and falconers kept better records of plumage changes in young eagles they acquire. Even colour photographs taken about every three months would go far to remedy our present ignorance.

24 Mortality, Survival and Entry into the Adult Population

Once young eagles leave the parental breeding territory, our knowledge of their habits depends largely on conjecture supported by scraps of fact. A few species have been ringed in considerable numbers; but the few recoveries are generally from unnatural causes. Radio transmitters have been attached to some; but if small enough to be carried easily without affecting survival, their range and life is so far too short to follow a young eagle's wanderings for several years. Window-marking or bleaching of wings and tail permits instant identification at long range, but the young eagle inevitably moults and replaces these feathers, so contact is usually soon lost.

All these methods show that a young eagle tends to wander at random after leaving the parental territory. In the population of Bald Eagles that breeds in winter in Florida and migrates *northwards* to avoid the hot summer, the ringed young eagles revealed the unusual flight path of the adults. The few British Golden Eagle recoveries indicate that the young eagles may travel in almost any direction, usually to lower ground. The few African recoveries of young Verreaux's and Martial Eagles indicate a random dispersal in almost any direction up to 110 miles (180km) from the ringing site. Young eagles of migrant northern species evidently migrate along the same routes as adults, passing through well-known concentration points such as Suez or the Bosphorus. Some young winter in different areas to the adults; most Steppe Eagles found in Africa south of Tanzania and Zambia are immatures.

Some eagles, for instance the very intensively studied population of Verreaux's Eagles in the Matopos or the Naivasha Fish Eagles, seem to offer better chances, but results have so far been rather disappointing. Of quite a large number of ringed or window-marked Verreaux's Eagles, most are never seen again. Although it might appear relatively easy to colour-ring or radio-tag and follow young Naivasha Fish Eagles, the obstacles proved formidable. Since they nest on the higher branches of extremely inaccessible Acacia trees I have so far been unable to ring any in the nest, nor can I catch and ring them later. They come readily to a fish bait festooned with nooses, but drop it instantly when they feel the pull of the attached line. Two young colour-ringed on Lake Victoria left the parental territory after two and a half months and were never seen again. So far no good information has been gathered from abundant, tame African Eagles.

The treatment a young eagle receives from its parents during the post-fledging period and at independence should affect its ability to survive. The extremely protracted post-fledging period during which a young Crowned Eagle learns to kill for itself, and is not driven away by its parents but leaves of its own accord, should give it an advantage over young African Fish Eagles which are apparently deserted by their parents before they have learned to kill, and may be attacked and driven to other areas. Young Verreaux's Eagles are also driven away by their parents before they have ever killed for themselves. The figures for replacement rates in these species suggest that a young Crowned Eagle does in fact survive more easily than a young Verreaux's Eagle, fed by its parents one day, but forced to fend for itself the next, and probably harried by other adults if it tries to remain and survive in familiar terrain. The biological advantage of the extraordinarily protracted post-fledging period of the Crowned Eagle, and perhaps some other large forest eagles such as the Harpy, may be a better chance of survival.

The manner of independence may be connected with the type, abundance, availability and size of prey. Since young Crowned Eagles and Harpies must kill relatively agile monkeys or quite large antelopes on the forest floor, it would be advantageous to be strong enough to kill without hesitation. Young Verreaux's Eagles may not have tried before; but they at once find an abundant population of rock hyrax, while

young Scottish Golden Eagles become independent in October when populations of grouse, hares and rabbits are highest. Young Steppe and Tawny Eagles can possibly find carrion, termite swarms or locusts if they cannot catch a field rat. Young fish and sea eagles can frequently find cast-up dead fish or carrion if they cannot catch their own fish. Against that, young wild African Fish Eagles are almost certain to be attacked and robbed by piratical adults and older immatures or sub-adults, including their own parents, and may have to catch several fish before retaining one.

The first few months of independence may be a crucial time for young eagles, the third 'point of strain' in the breeding cycle. Not enough data are available from any ringing studies to prepare survival life-tables for eagles similar to those available for ospreys or several species of buzzards (*Buteo* spp). All such studies show that 65-80 per cent of all young die before sexual maturity, especially in their first year. Hence, we estimate that about three-quarters of all young eagles reared die before they become mature. Most of this mortality may occur in the first few months, before the young eagle has gained enough experience to be able to catch the prey it needs to survive.

All life-tables based on ringing returns suffer from two disadvantages. First, all have so far been done in developed countries where birds of prey are directly persecuted, or subject to unnatural dangers, such as electrocution or being killed by cars. Ninety-eight per cent of American Golden

Two young eagles look at the Lesser Spotted Eagle female expecting prey; one of the young was raised for most of the nestling period by a pair of Black Kites *(B-U. Meyburg)*

Eagles electrocuted on power lines are recently fledged, clumsy young birds. Secondly, almost all the reported recoveries are of birds that have been shot, found dead (often a euphemism for shooting) or have died of some other unnatural cause. Even in Africa several ringing recoveries are clearly of shot birds. Very few healthy eagles have been caught and released again; while in northern latitudes the risk of dying of natural starvation in winter is high. Lost rings, especially on old birds, could complicate the problem. Though ringing studies are valuable and often the only or the best guide to survival we have, results must be accepted with some reserve.

In the Bateleur and African Fish Eagle, where moult studies permit reasonably accurate ageing of immatures in the field, attempts have recently been made to assess the number of young eagles of different ages surviving to maturity. Since both are common and widespread, a large total of individuals in different stages of plumage can be counted, either over wide areas, or by repeated counting of a smaller area. Since little or no unnatural interference is involved, such counts should tell us the number of eagles in adult, sub-adult, second- or first-year plumage; and, in theory, should give a more accurate picture of mortality and survival than any study based on unnatural death and ringing records. Although this method shows promise, it is not applicable to eagles in which the young closely resemble adults, and has also led to some conflict of facts. (see p175.)

In the Bateleur, a long series of counts showed that of 1,661 identified Bateleurs 1,015 were adults, and about 31 per cent of the whole population was immature. Fifty-one of 646 immatures were in the pre-adult six or seven year old plumage; and since such late sub-adults are the only age-group capable of providing replacements for dead adults, 1,000 adult Batelurs have available about fifty potential mate-replacements per year. Adult Bateleurs therefore *must* live about twenty years *as adults*; and twenty-seven or twenty-eight altogether, to maintain population stability.

Available evidence suggests that the replacement rate in the Bateleur is low, probably 0.5 per pair, perhaps only 0.3. Since the Bateleur also is immature for up to eight years, it is safe to assume that it is a very long-lived bird in addition to its other remarkable attributes. An average age of twenty does not seem unlikely; and a magnificent Bateleur streaking across the African sky may be a veritable aquiline Methuselah.

The proportion of immature African Fish Eagles may vary

in the same area. In 1968-9, of 1,391 Naivasha Fish Eagles 1,155 were adults and 236 immatures; of these 103, or 4.3 per cent, were sub-adults three to four years old. In 1970-1, of 2,210 African Fish Eagles 319 were immatures, 14.4 per cent as opposed to 17 per cent in 1968-9. Of the 319 immatures, however, 134, or 4.2 per cent, were sub-adults, almost the same as in 1968-9. In 1970-1 the sub-adults were distinguished by plumage as early or late sub-adults; the late sub-adult segment of the population was about 4 per cent of the adults. Thus, adult African Fish Eagles at Lake Naivasha *must* live for an average of twenty-five years as adults to find a mate on the lake itself; and so long a life seems unlikely. Other counts of fish eagles suggest that on average about 25 per cent of the population is immature; but probably a much larger series of counts is needed before a good figure is obtained. Such counts and other data so far suggest that African Fish Eagles must live for sixteen to twenty-five years as adults, or twenty to twenty-nine years altogether. (See p175.)

This method of estimating survival in immature eagles so far conflicts with theoretical figures worked out from the breeding statistics and the known lifespans of wild eagles. In Naivasha Fish Eagles, 0.47 young per pair per annum will produce 0.12 sexually mature replacements per adult at 50 per cent mortality, and 0.06 per adult at 75 per cent mortality. On this basis adult African Fish Eagles must live a little more than eight or less than seventeen years as adults to replace themselves. Even this second figure is much lower than the twenty-five years calculated from the proportion of late sub-adults in the population. Either, therefore, this method is misleading; or more than 75 per cent of young African Fish Eagles die before sexual maturity. The figures in fact suggest that about 96 per cent die before maturity.

This method requires further study and proving before it can provide reliable survival estimates. It can only be used for those eagles easily recognised at different stages of immature moult, and common enough to give large figures, but these will probably be a reliable guide for other species. In temperate climates this method might, with practice, serve for the Bald and European Sea Eagles, the Golden, Lesser and Greater Spotted and Imperial Eagles, in all of which at least first-year immatures can easily be distinguished from the adults. A massive aerial count over two years on the plains of Wyoming in 1972-3 produced a total of 11,008 adult and 4,385 definite immature Golden Eagles. In the winter population there were about 0.80 immatures per pair, or 40 per cent, a much higher ratio than in any tropical eagles. This may, however, be compared with a higher replacement rate of about 1.46 per successful nest and 1.0 per pair overall in this part of the USA.

Adult African Fish Eagles, Bateleurs or Verreaux's Eagles cannot be recognised with certainty without colour-ringing or similar identification. However, Crowned Eagles and Ayres' Eagles can be recognised by plumage and habits. At two sites which I have watched for twenty-five and fifteen years respectively, I am confident that I have identified individual Crowned Eagles year by year. At least I know when a new adult appears and I assume that this only occurs when an adult dies. Two female Crowned Eagles at Eagle Hill lived for eight and a half and nine years, and a male for twelve; and a female, 'Loosefeather', lived near my house for at least twelve years as an adult. The second of her two mates in that time was killed; and she then disappeared when at least fifteen to sixteen years old.

Loosefeather and her two mates reared four young to independence from the five eggs she laid between 1959 and 1968. The last was flying but still dependent when her second mate was killed by a neighbour's gardener, allegedly when killing a goose—an unnatural prey for a Crowned Eagle. Loosefeather reared the flying young bird to independence in May 1969. We expected this young to leave and Loosefeather to attract a new adult male. A new male did shortly appear in the territory, a rather small, unusually black individual whom we called Sambo. However, astonishingly he did not mate with Loosefeather (who may have died), but with the recently reared immature, whom we instantly dubbed Lolita after her precocious namesake.

Sambo assiduously courted Lolita, but she did not respond when he ran round and round her on the nest, raising his wings in pre-copulatory display. However, the pair remained loosely attached, and were sometimes seen singly or together. After two and a half years with little change, Lolita moulted into a pale version of the full adult plumage, retaining a few immature-looking feathers, and at about three and a half she laid an egg, in the abandoned nest of a Harrier Hawk, which the pair built up in 1971. She incubated for over forty days, but the egg was apparently infertile, for she abandoned it.

In 1972 and 1973 she and Sambo attempted to build up the old nest, now largely collapsed, and also added to the Harrier Hawk's nest. However, although apparently fully adult in 1972, Lolita did not lay another egg in either year. She successfully repelled another adult female, which entered the territory and with which Sambo appeared inclined to dally, in

November 1972. After December 1973 we did not see her for some time. Then, in September 1974, the Harrier Hawk's nest was again repaired, and in early October Lolita was sitting. She was now six and a half; and this time the egg was fertile, and she reared a young bird which flew in February 1975, almost exactly seven years after Lolita herself hatched from the egg.

This little story, scientifically accurate if told in somewhat anthropomorphic manner, suggests that immature eagles can sometimes enter adults' territories and pair with adults, even though they cannot yet breed. Other instances are recorded. Several immature Scottish Golden Eagles have been found living in breeding territories, even building nests, sometimes mated to adults and sometimes alone, or with other immatures. Seton Gordon's celebrated Skye pair were both immatures when they first occupied their nesting cliff in 1942; they bred successfully from 1946 until 1954 at least. In Sutherland in 1967, two immature females were apparently living alone in regular breeding territories; one of these was building two new nests close together. In the upper Findhorn Valley a second-summer female Golden Eagle was trapped on a nesting ledge in a 'fox trap'; she had been bred in a nest near the Cairngorm Chair Lift, and may only have been able to live in this territory because persecution by grouse moor gamekeepers had eliminated the rightful adult.

As Lolita proved, such things can happen even where eagles are not persecuted, though here too the premature killing of the resident adult male appeared to precipitate the extraordinary chain of events. Immatures in breeding areas are not normal, and most have been seen in species which are for some reason endangered. Eagle experts generally consider that a high proportion of immatures in pairs means that the species is in trouble. The Spanish Imperial Eagle, which numbers less than a hundred pairs altogether, is one such case. Egg collectors at one time robbed so many of the few nests that few young survived and a high proportion of the eagles nesting in the Coto Donana were immatures. However, this species, and perhaps others, can breed when still obviously immature. Recently a female Imperial Eagle not more than three years old mated with a fully adult male and laid two fertile eggs, both of which hatched and resulted in fledged young. This young, perhaps inexperienced female did not, as would be normal, take the major share of feeding the young, but left this duty largely to the much older male.

Though we know little of how it comes about, young eagles surviving to sexual maturity must some day find a mate and become a member of an adult pair resident in a territory or home range. In the African Fish Eagle at Lake Naivasha, late sub-adults pair and display to one another, with all the vocal repertoire of full adults. They seem unable to occupy a breeding territory, however, and usually perch side by side in a lagoon lacking a nesting tree. Occasionally, an adult African Fish Eagle mates with a sub-adult, or even a two year old, but such unions are not permanent. In two observed cases such sub-adults were later replaced by a full adult.

Adult pairs of Verreaux's Eagles tolerate established neighbours, but instantly repel immatures and strange adults entering their territory. Such strange adults might well be recently matured birds seeking a mate, and be driven from territory to territory until they enter one where a vacancy has been caused by the death of one of the adults. Then, if of the right sex, they might be allowed to stay—though no such case has yet been proved.

In any healthy, wild, unpersecuted, capacity population of eagles, for instance the Naivasha Fish Eagles or the Verreaux's Eagles of the Matopos, all pairs holding breeding ranges or territories are normally composed of full adults, though in one pair establishing a new territory in the Matopos an adult male was paired with two different sub-adult females; this pair did not breed. Immatures and sub-adults can find no place among these, though, as I observed in at least six species, they often appear in adult home ranges early in the breeding season. In temperate climates, too, immature eagles often appear in an adult's breeding territory in spring. They may have been loosely attached to the parent adults all winter; or they may be total strangers. Where the adults are subject to direct persecution or unnatural losses, for instance through pesticides, such young birds, too young to breed, may remain, and may thereafter have a better chance of survival than if forced to live alone in no-man's-land. Some unnatural adult losses might thus be partially balanced by better survival of immatures to maturity, though a mature breeding adult is not adequately replaced by a sexually immature bird.

Between independence and sexual maturity, and in capacity populations perhaps for some time after sexual maturity, immatures are generally forced to live somewhere well away from the focus of the adult home range or territory, the nesting area. On the relatively crowded shorelines of tropical African lakes where African Fish Eagles breed only 200-300yd (m) apart, this is not easy. In others, notably migrant species in their winter range, immatures are not

Young Spanish Imperial Eagle adopted by an adult with infertile eggs *(B-U. Meyburg)*

subject to territorial repulsion, but compete on nearly equal terms with adults. Sometimes young African Fish Eagles can congregate on tracts of shore devoid of breeding trees. At other times they must live among the adults by a combination of more retiring habits and opportunism. They then perch out of sight well within the canopies of big trees, and keep a wary eye on their elders when flying through or over adult breeding territories.

Adults are sometimes so concerned with maintaining their territory that an immature, by opportunism, can snatch a fish right in front of an adult. In Botswana, on two successive mornings, a two year old African Fish Eagle swooped from high up, snatched fish set out for an adult female, and escaped before the adult could overtake; she would not go far from her territory. Perhaps it was this same immature that later successfully fought off two adults that tried to rob it of a fish; if so it deserved to win through and rear many families.

The young eagle's life between independence and entry into the breeding population is the most obscure and difficult of all periods to study. Probably not until radio telemetry or a similar technique enables us to follow the young continuously for years shall we know what happens. It seems certain that it is a period of difficulty and heavy mortality in all eagles, temperate or tropical, migrant or sedentary. However, the whole territorial behaviour and breeding biology of any species in the natural state must be nicely adjusted to ensure that enough young do survive to maintain a stable population. It is only when twentieth-century man—comes on the scene—for not even nineteenth-century man was as bad—that the natural balance is upset and eagle populations decline.

189

Part VI The Conservation of Eagles

25 The Threats to Survival: Eagles and Economics

Before one can conserve eagles in their natural state, the threats to their survival must be identified, examined and if possible dealt with. For practical purposes, *all* threats to eagles are due to man. Being large, powerful, predatory birds, they have few natural enemies, though naturally a few are lost to mammalian and avian predators, disease and starvation, or climatic effects. However, the reproductive biology of all eagle species is adapted to such natural checks; an undisturbed population not threatened by some activity of mankind is usually healthy, thriving and stable. Such healthy and thriving populations, which have been studied most intensively in tropical Africa, suggest what should be normal in other populations which are not thriving, or are decreasing.

I have listed the species which are or may be threatened in Appendix 4. Of fifty-nine species, including sixty-three distinct forms, twenty-six forms in twenty-five species—nearly half of all eagles—are more or less threatened in the whole or some part of their range. Although the level of threat may be ill-defined, perhaps not immediate, to be on the safe side one should regard a species as threatened until proved otherwise. Since eagles are large birds requiring large home ranges per pair, they are never common and are among the first to be affected by the generally prevalent worldwide destruction of habitat, which is proceeding apace with no practical check, since its basic cause is young human mothers who already exist.

An eagle with a restricted range on one or more relatively small islands is automatically more severely threatened than a wide-ranging continental species. Ten of the twenty-five threatened species are insular. They include one sea eagle, five snake eagles, one of the harpy group, and three small eastern hawk eagles. However, the status of eight of these is really unknown; so we cannot definitely say that they are threatened with early extinction. In Sanford's Sea Eagle, and the two small snake eagles inhabiting the Andaman Islands, there is no good evidence of immediate threat, and some to the contrary. In the three small eastern hawk eagles, our ignorance is almost complete, but all three are mainly or entirely forest birds. Since forest is generally being destroyed *pari passu* with rapid human population increase in the east, they probably are threatened, unless adequate forest habitat is conserved.

The Madagascar Serpent Eagle and the Philippine Monkey-eating Eagle are acutely threatened with extinction. The Madagascar Serpent Eagle may even be extinct already, having gone into oblivion unnoticed. It has not been seen for some years in forested areas of Malagasy. Almost nothing is known of its habits but the paucity of records suggest that it is a very retiring or rare bird. There is reason to hope it may not yet be extinct, for considerable blocks of suitable forest habitat still exist in Malagasy.

The Philippine Monkey-eating Eagle suffers not only from a restricted island range and limited forest habitat, but also from direct persecution. Very large and spectacular, it has been in demand for zoological collections and for sporting trophies in the Philippines themselves. Feeding on monkeys, it is basically beneficial to agricultural man; though powerful, it is not reported to eat domestic stock. Its forest habitat has been greatly reduced in the last half-century by the swift, continuing population increase in the Philippines. However, action has now been taken to save the remnant by the passage of legislation completely protecting it; prevention of capture for zoos; and a special project to rehabilitate known captives to the wild. Even if successful, these measures can now only save a remnant since much of the original habitat has been destroyed.

The next category of three threatened species includes those with a fairly wide continental range, but restricted to threatened forest habitat; the Southern Banded Snake Eagle of Africa, the Chestnut-bellied Hawk Eagle of India and the east and Isidor's Eagle, a magnificent and little-known species of the Andean slopes. The Southern Banded Snake Eagle is not immediately threatened; but since its habitat is coastal forests and thick bush, generally in densely populated country, it is automatically threatened by accelerating habitat destruction. Fairly rare throughout its range, it is little known, but commoner than supposed. It can survive alongside not-too-numerous man, for it lives on snakes often caught in human cultivation.

I include the Chestnut-bellied Hawk Eagle here merely because it is a forest bird, apparently rather rare throughout its range, so automatically threatened by the widespread forest destruction in the east. Though its status is obscure, it is probably not really threatened. Isidor's Eagle has aroused some concern in South America. Again its range and status are obscure; but in South America, where population explosion and feckless destruction of habitat are unequalled, this eagle is automatically threatened by destruction of habitat, perhaps also by active persecution.

Twelve other wide-ranging continental species, mostly large or very large, are not, as species, immediately threatened with extinction, but have become rare or extinct in parts of their range through human persecution, pesticides or both. These include the Bald Eagle, the European Sea Eagle, Pallas' Sea Eagle and Steller's Sea Eagle; the nominate race of the European Snake Eagle; and seven booted or true eagles, the Lesser and Greater Spotted, the Imperial Eagle (two races), the Golden Eagle, Wedge-tailed Eagle, Verreaux's Eagle and Bonelli's Eagle. The level of threat posed varies from slight to acute, most acute in countries of western Europe and North America, where persecution has exterminated some populations within the last century, and where pesticides and pollution have recently accelerated population decline. The threat is least acute in thinly inhabited non-industrialised areas (eg the Bald Eagle in Alaska), or in underdeveloped, mainly rural countries. As human population in such underdeveloped countries increases, and industry and agriculture develops, some eagles not now obviously threatened may become threatened, but for the moment some populations of these eagles evidently thrive in such countries.

I have included Pallas' and Steller's Sea Eagles only to be on the safe side. Steller's has a rather restricted range in north-eastern Siberia and Kamschatka; but was until recently fairly common here. Its Korean race has certainly declined and it no longer breeds in Korea. Pallas' Sea Eagle has a very wide range in central Asia, northern India, etc; but parts of this range are now badly polluted. Since other sea eagles are sensitive to organochlorine or mercury pollution, Pallas' Sea Eagle must be regarded as threatened unless the contrary is proved. It is at least not in immediate danger of extinction.

The Bald Eagle and the European Sea Eagle have attracted more attention because they have been acutely affected by human persecution and by pesticide effects in this century. Though the Bald Eagle has been most studied, the remnant population of European Sea Eagles in Sweden, East Germany and Norway has also been fairly well documented. Six populations of the Bald Eagle, in Alaska, Wisconsin, Florida, Michigan, Maine and the Great Lakes, have been studied from 1961 or 1963 to 1970. Three populations, in Alaska, Wisconsin and Florida, are stable; the other three are decreasing, due to falling productivity per nest. If less than half the pairs breed and productivity falls below 0.7 young per pair per annum overall, the species will decrease.

Of three discrete populations quite close to one another, in Wisconsin, Michigan and the Great Lakes, that in Wisconsin is stable, that in Michigan decreasing and that around the Great Lakes almost gone. These differences are clearly correlated with the level of pesticide residue and pollution in the Great Lakes, the Michigan lakes and the comparatively clean lakes of north Wisconsin. The stable population of Bald Eagles in the Everglades National Park in Florida reproduces more slowly than that in Alaska or Wisconsin (0.73 per pair overall compared to 1.02 per nest for both Alaska and Wisconsin), perhaps because of the warmer climate.

The European Sea Eagle was exterminated in Britain in this century by gamekeepers and shepherds, on the grounds that it ate lambs. In western Europe it has greatly decreased in Sweden and East Germany, and in Sardinia and probably in other Mediterranean haunts is now apparently extinct, but it holds its own and has recently been protected in Norway and Greenland (where it was until recently persecuted). In western Europe its recent decline is due to a combination of pesticides and human persecution, often not deliberate.

Southern Swedish Sea Eagles barely hold their own, and are heavily loaded with mercury and organochlorine pesticides. Sixty times as much mercury is present in their feathers now as at the beginning of this century (as determined by analysis of feathers from old specimens). The use of organochlorine pesticides is now restricted or banned, but mercury will disappear very slowly from the nearly tideless Baltic, which is a sump of industrial poison. The now enormous numbers of people who visit the Swedish Sea Eagle's breeding haunts in spring in pleasure boats may not mean any harm, but they disturb the eagles at a vital time, and prevent some otherwise fertile pairs from laying. Some Bald Eagle populations in America are similarly affected. The combination of organochlorine pesticides, mercury and inadvertent human interference has more effectively reduced the eagles since 1945 than the active persecution prevalent earlier this century.

In the Bald Eagle and European Sea Eagle the danger spots

have at least been identified, and active steps are being taken to redress past damage and minimise future threat. However, the European Snake Eagle is still senselessly persecuted in Mediterranean countries. Persecution of this species in southern France may have reduced the total population from around 1,200 pairs in 1945 to 500 pairs in 1966. Laws have at last been passed in France protecting raptors; but their effectiveness depends on active enforcement.

Since the European Snake Eagle ranges widely from southern France to China, and its two African races are certainly not at present threatened, it is not threatened as a species, but only locally, in one of the most civilised parts of the world. Persecution of this species by sportsmen and gamekeepers is unusually senseless because the European Snake Eagle feed entirely on snakes and reptiles and could only be beneficial or neutral to stocks of sporting birds or mammals.

The remaining more or less threatened eagles include some of the commonest and most widespread species, which are not therefore threatened as species, but only locally and by certain groups of people, usually sheep farmers and sportsmen who still detest anything with a hooked beak and claws. Verreaux's Eagle is included only because it is sometimes persecuted by sheep farmers in South Africa; for practical purposes we can neglect but not forget it.

Both the Lesser and Greater Spotted Eagles have declined in Europe since the end of World War II, which had a generally beneficial effect on persecuted eagles. The extent of the decline is rather obscure; but might be about 50 per cent of the former population. Large numbers of both Spotted Eagles still pass annually over the Bosphorus and Suez, and better counting methods may make the decline more apparent than real. In parts of their eastern European and Asian range these species have probably declined little; and in western Europe the threat is recognised and some positive steps are being taken to redress the damage.

The most threatened large European species is the Imperial Eagle. The Spanish race, reduced to about a hundred pairs, is the only eagle besides the Philippine Monkey-eating Eagle in the ICBP red data book. Even the commoner nominate eastern race is certainly very much rarer than either of the Spotted Eagles. The Imperial Eagle often prefers lowlands to mountains, so comes into conflict with man, though there is no evidence that it damages man's interests. Though it is probably the least common and most endangered of all large booted eagles, both the small Spanish population and the eastern European and Asian populations are said to be stable.

The Golden Eagle and Wedge-tailed Eagle are both much more numerous than the Spotted or Imperial Eagles, probably commoner than Verreaux's Eagle. The Golden Eagle has undoubtedly suffered locally from both persecution and from pesticide effects, but in its huge range throughout the mountainous subtropical and temperate northern hemisphere is certainly not endangered as a species. The small Scottish population is much more threatened than the much larger North American population. Of about 280 pairs of British Golden Eagles, all but one are in Scotland. Of these about 220 breed each year; and of these perhaps 90 are lost annually through active or inadvertent persecution. The chief cause is undoubtedly illegal shooting and poisoning by gamekeepers and shepherds; but many unpersecuted pairs have ceased to breed *since 1960* because of the swelling flood of hikers, climbers, fishermen and bird photographers, who prevent certain pairs from laying or cause desertion. In some of the less-frequented western highlands Golden Eagles may still be at capacity numbers.

American Golden Eagles have been severely persecuted in recent years by sheep farmers. This persecution received much publicity because it was done by shooting the eagles from aircraft; and also because it was completely unjustified. Thousands were shot from aircraft before a reluctant Congress passed legislation outlawing or restricting the practice. A survey by Walter Spofford in 1964 suggested that there might be only 10,000 Golden Eagles in all North America, so that shooting 1,000 a year was a very serious loss. Local resident populations in Texas were actually exterminated. However, a recent survey revealed over 10,000 Golden Eagles in 1972-3 in Wyoming alone; so the total population in North America is probably 50,000-100,000, perhaps even 200,000. Shooting 1,000 a year, mainly immatures, would then have relatively little effect; and was even more pointless than it appeared.

The Australian Wedge-tailed Eagle, also a very numerous and widespread species in Australia, has almost certainly increased in the last two centuries because of the introduction of sheep and rabbits, the one providing abundant carrion under hard range conditions, the other easily-caught prey of ideal size. This eagle has been worse persecuted than any other; scores of thousands were killed annually. Yet it apparently holds its own. The indiscriminate killing has now been stopped, at least officially; and a full survey not yet published will certainly confirm earlier views that it was never necessary.

Bonelli's Eagle, the only hawk eagle to be appreciably persecuted, again mainly in Mediterranean countries, especially France, is not threatened as a species in its very wide range; its African race, the African Hawk Eagle, is not threatened. Bonelli's Eagle unquestionably kills game birds and rabbits, so that sportsmen and gamekeepers have better reason for persecuting it than some others. It has decreased in France from about 120 pairs in 1945 to 35 in 1966; yet it still breeds literally on the outskirts of Marseilles. Legal protection and a somewhat more enlightened attitude in France may now permit some increase.

This survey of the recent man-made threats to eagles shows that only a few species and races are in real danger. Some other local populations of more widespread species are severely threatened, but the species as a whole are not endangered. The most alarming threats to widespread species are persecution and pesticides in developed countries; but the most threatened species and races exist in underdeveloped island countries (the Philippines and Madagascar) or in less intensively industrialised countries such as Spain. For all but the Madagascar Serpent Eagle among acutely threatened species, the threats have generally been recognised and can be combated. Some others need status surveys before the situation can be understood. When such status surveys are done by an expert they often reveal that the eagle is not as rare as was thought.

Man also, having done so much positive harm to eagles in the last sixty years, is now bending his brain to improve the situation. Although many pairs of eagles are prevented from laying by human interference, recent work shows that man can play an active part in bettering the breeding performance of threatened species by reducing sibling strife.

The number of young reared per pair of Spotted and Spanish Imperial Eagles has been substantially increased by adoption of eaglets by other birds of prey until they can be returned to the nest without danger of being killed by their siblings; or by placing otherwise doomed younger eaglets in the nests of eagles with infertile eggs. Such methods, first proved with the relatively common Lesser Spotted Eagle, have obvious application in very rare species. The breeding performance of nine pairs of Spanish Imperial Eagles was thus improved by 43 per cent, equivalent to a 4 per cent increase in the whole Spanish population. If such methods were applied to the whole population of the Spanish Imperial

Direct persecution: an illegal poletrap in Scotland (*John Marchington, Ardea Photographics*)

Eagle, man would have done what he could to save this threatened race.

The Philippine Monkey-eating Eagle breeds naturally every year, or, like the Crowned Eagle and apparently the Harpy, may, if successful, breed only once every two years. In the latter case, by capturing recently flown young, so depriving the parents of an offspring needing food, one might stimulate the parents to double their breeding rate. The captured young could be reared in captivity and later returned to the wild. However, this eagle is so rare that the hitherto untried effect of strict protection should be assessed first.

It should also thus be possible to restore breeding populations of species that have been locally rendered extinct. One unsuccessful attempt has already been made to restore the Sea Eagle to Britain by releasing four Norwegian immatures on Fair Isle. The number of eagles and the habitat chosen were far too small, but a sustained effort to establish young sea eagles in Golden Eagles' nests near the west highland and Hebridean coasts over ten years or so might well establish a small but viable adult breeding population. This would require a complete and far from evident change of heart on the part of local landowners, crofters and shepherds.

The best methods of combating any threats to eagles are the simplest and most obvious; protection of habitat, prevention of unnecessary and often illegal persecution or disturbance, and the control of the pesticides and pollutants. Without the general application of these simpler and more obvious remedies the desperate efforts of a few keen individuals to rear more young in eagles' nests, or provide pesticide-free food for wintering birds, will have little long-term effect. Without man-made threats, eagles can look after themselves very well; and they thrive where no man-made threats exist.

Thus it is evident that few of the world's larger eagles are actually threatened by direct human persecution. More often the threat to survival is indirect, by destruction of habitat or the reduction of breeding success through eating contaminated food. Though these threats are man-made, they are not deliberate persecution. Deliberate persecution, however, still continues in many areas of the developed world and if legal protection is afforded there is very soon a demand that the laws should be modified; laws against shooting eagles from aircraft in the United States have now been modified in certain states.

Since sheep and goat raising, or the management of tracts of country in order to produce game birds, are likely to continue, we must know whether the complaints against eagles are economically justified. Eagles have been exterminated or severely reduced because they do, or are said to, eat fish, game birds or lambs. The fact that a few lambs may be eaten is often seized upon as a legitimate excuse to persecute an otherwise protected eagle. The species so threatened are all large and generally widespread, and none is actually threatened as a species by such persecution. However, some local resident populations of the Golden Eagle, Wedge-tailed Eagle and European Sea Eagle have been wiped out or sharply reduced in the last century by such persecution, which often continues clandestinely, despite legal protection.

Where such damage has been inflicted on an eagle species it has always been done by unthinking people without any good evidence that it is necessary. Generalised complaints unsupported by figures are made of wholesale slaughter of lambs or grouse or salmon. When such complaints are carefully investigated by competent naturalists, they are invariably found to have either very flimsy foundation or none at all. The eagles actually do no damage or very little.

In America, according to a 1964 Audubon Conservation report by Walter Spofford, Golden Eagles were killed from aeroplanes as early as 1936; and the real shoot-off began in 1940, when a certain Willie McCutcheon lost nineteen yearling sheep weighing 75lb (33kg) each. It would of course be physically impossible for a Golden Eagle to kill *one* large active animal seven to ten times its own weight, let alone

Ewe and lamb near Loch Torridon, Wester Ross, Scotland *(Su Gooders, Ardea Photographics)*

nineteen in a short time. Between then and 1947, however, 4,818 eagles were killed. Clubs were formed to kill eagles, and certain pilots became very expert and successful, killing the eagles with a shotgun from a slow-flying aircraft. At least 1,000 Golden Eagles per year were shot down; and many others were trapped with pole traps on the ground—a practice outlawed in Britain in 1904 because of the vile cruelty involved.

The claims of ranchers are often quite demonstrably ludicrous. For instance, Golden Eagles were accused of killing lambs and kids weighing 50-60lb (23-27kg), even full-grown deer—certainly abnormal or physically impossible. Moreover, several ranchers claimed to have 100 per cent lamb crops on poor semi-arid range land, also impossible in practice. The most modest claimed that eagles had taken a proportion of total lamb losses; for instance 122 lambs in a total of 167 lost from 3,500 born, equivalent to 3.5 per cent of the lamb crop, if the eagles actually killed all 122 lambs. This rancher, however, admitted that he had never actually *seen* an eagle kill a lamb. Even his more sober estimate illustrates nicely the wild fluctuations of conjecture on which the persecution of American Eagles was based, and the lack of concrete evidence even when a more reasonable claim was made.

The area concerned supported some 6 million sheep and 4 million goats. A 75 per cent crop of young would produce some 7 million kids and lambs, each weighing about 8lb (3.6kg), or 56 million lb (25 million kg) altogether. In the same area, probably a main wintering area for migrant eagles, Spofford estimated that there might be 5,000 in the main lambing season from October to March. If all these eagles ate absolutely nothing but lambs and kids, at their known requirement of 8oz (230g) per day, they would still consume less than 500,000lb, under 1 per cent of the total weight of lambs and kids available, and very easily provided by the certainly large numbers of dead lambs and kids and by many dead adult sheep and goats. Moreover, the eagles did *not* only eat lambs; they fed largely on jackrabbits.

In subsequent years studies of the food of Golden Eagles in the western United States, some financed by the wool growers themselves, have all shown that the main food of the Golden Eagle in the American west is jackrabbits and cottontail rabbits. Probably more than 20,000 food items have now been recorded, but they have not been fully analysed and published. Of 5,328 items I have myself extracted from reports, only 100 could have been lambs or kids, about 0.02 per cent. Even that figure is heavily biased since one report recorded all large bones, some undoubtedly deer, as lambs or kids. Of the 5,328 items, 4,018 were jackrabbits or cottontails, which collectively would eat as much fodder as 800 adult sheep. Thus, in sheep ranching country in America, the eagle is actually beneficial, not harmful.

Even more vicious persecution has been directed against the Wedge-tailed Eagle in Australia, again on the basis of ill-informed opinion. Even nineteenth-century ornithologists stated that most lambs taken by Wedge-tailed Eagles were picked up dead. The single food-study of the Wedge-tailed Eagle so far published records twenty-five lamb remains among 369 items, about 7 per cent, many probably picked up dead. More recent unpublished evidence confirms that Wedge-tailed Eagles feeding mainly on rabbits do little harm and much good on Australian sheep runs. At two eyries recently studied on sheep ranches, one pair fed entirely on rabbits and the other on large lizards and other native mammals in a rabbit-free area. They took no lambs at all; but the pair that fed on rabbits killed over 100 in the breeding season. Before myxomatosis, rabbits reduced the value of the Australian wool crop by several million dollars annually.

Similarly, in Scotland, there is frequent outcry against the Golden Eagle as a lamb killer, but when complaints have been carefully investigated they have proved largely baseless. Of 1,993 Scottish food items, 123, or 6.1 per cent, were lambs or kids (of wild goats). Most of the lambs were recorded from Wester Ross. Both J. D. Lockie and workers in Texas have shown that the amount of bleeding and bruising establishes whether a lamb was killed or picked up dead. On a lamb picked up dead there is none; but if an eagle strikes and kills a lamb the talons cause bleeding and bruising at the site of the wound. Lockie concluded that, of twenty-two lambs found in one eyrie over five years, ten of which could be positively identified by such wound criteria, three had been killed by the eagle and seven picked up dead. Since this particular eagle regularly had 4,500-5,000 alive or dead lambs available in her range each spring, the seven she actually killed in five years amounted to about 0.004 per cent of the lambs available. Some that were actually killed may have been lambs deserted by the ewe, or alive after the ewe was dead.

Although careful investigation of such complaints shows that they are generally entirely baseless, or very greatly exaggerated, eagles certainly do kill some lambs or kids. Kids, which are normally hidden in cover by the nanny-goats when they go off to feed, may be more vulnerable to eagles than are lambs, which run with the ewes from birth. If many nannies with kids are concentrated for kidding in one area, one or more eagles may cause appreciable local depredation. However, the occasional depredations of an individual are not a good excuse for destroying most members of a species which, as a whole, is beneficial since it feeds largely on rabbits and hares.

The European Sea Eagle was exterminated in Britain on the grounds that it fed upon lambs, not, apparently, because it ate salmon or trout—the sole reason for the nearly simultaneous extermination of the Osprey. Of 1,646 food items in Norway and other parts of Europe only eighty were parts of lambs or kids, about 5 per cent; again, most were probably picked up dead, not killed. Though proof is now impossible, there probably was never any good ground for exterminating the European Sea Eagle in Britain. Likewise, there is probably no ground for the opposition which would certainly be raised to its reintroduction as a British breeding species. Nevertheless, the prejudice against eagles as alleged lamb-killers continues, even in Britain or North America where carefully gathered facts, and much propaganda effort, have been devoted to proving their real harmlessness. An article on predators in the April 1971 issue of the *Ranch Magazine* shows that American sheep ranchers are just as ignorant and prejudiced against eagles as ever, despite the published results of a survey they paid for themselves.

Sportsmen have, on the whole, better grounds than do sheep ranchers for complaint about eagles. Some eagles, for instance the African Martial Eagle, Bonelli's, the African Hawk Eagle and some Golden Eagles, certainly kill many game birds. Martial Eagles prefer game birds to mammals. Bonelli's Eagle prefers rabbits, but also eats partridges; and the African Hawk Eagle feeds mainly on game birds and poultry. Even Tawny Eagles and Bateleurs kill many francolins. In Scotland as a whole Golden Eagles took 751 game birds in a total of 1,996 recorded items—37.6 per cent by number, but only 14 per cent by weight in the diet. In some parts of wooded northern Europe, for instance Estonia, Golden Eagles live mainly on large game birds. However, they prefer mammals; 5,328 American food items include only 247 game birds.

Animosity against eagles because they eat game birds is practically confined to civilised Europe. I never met an African or an American who worried about it. In Europe, especially in France, intense persecution has reduced eagles and other birds of prey by up to two-thirds since 1945, mainly by indiscriminate shooting by hunters and gamekeepers. Of about 220 breeding pairs of Scottish Golden Eagles, fifty or more fail annually because of gamekeepers and shepherds. Most of this loss is on eastern Scottish grouse moors, where eagles regularly fail to breed despite abundant food supply of mammals and birds. The animosity towards, and the threat to, several species of European eagles because they eat game birds is very real; but elsewhere it can generally be ignored as unimportant.

In this case, too, careful examination shows that the damage is exaggerated. In a Scottish Golden Eagle's home range of about 11,400 acres (4,613ha), on an eastern grouse moor, there would be 5,000-15,000 grouse. A pair of Golden Eagles might take 150 grouse-sized birds, not all Red Grouse, per year, and many grouse are taken on seldom-visited high ground. In autumn and winter many of these grouse are 'surplus'. birds bound to die anyhow. Thus, the actual damage done to the grouse population is less than appears at first; and is mainly important in relation to the spring breeding population. Where hares or rabbits are scarce Golden Eagles do undoubtedly feed on grouse and ptarmigan in spring; and these must often be breeding birds.

Even here, however, studies have shown that the potential damage is much exaggerated, at least on the well-stocked moors where the persecution of eagles is most intense. On one eastern Perthshire moor the eagles took 0.6-2.0 per cent of the grouse in their home range, a rate that would obviously not seriously affect the number of grouse shot annually. Using a more recent estimate of the average proportion of grouse and ptarmigan taken, 14 per cent by weight of the Scottish

Red Grouse in Scotland (*John Marchington, Ardea Photographics*)

Golden Eagle's diet, the total taken in a home range would be about 87lb (39.5kg) of grouse and ptarmigan, of which about a third, say 32lb (14kg) would be taken in the breeding season. This amounts to about twenty-five adult grouse and ptarmigan between March and June. This could make no practical difference on a well-stocked moor; but an appreciable difference in a West Highland area where grouse are relatively scarce. Paradoxically, gamekeepers do not normally persecute the eagles in western Scotland, but persecute them worst in eastern Scotland where the damage they can do even to breeding stocks is relatively small.

Sportsmen in Scotland also complain, with some justice, that when an eagle appears over a moor all the grouse, knowing they can be caught on the ground but seldom on the wing, rise and fly away. If this happens just before or during a grouse drive the expected bag, after considerable effort, organisation and expenditure, is not realised. This can evidently be very annoying and disappointing. However, the odds are theoretically equal that the eagle will drive grouse on to a moor as off it; at least the eagle should be given credit for some unexpectedly large bags. The sporting organisations concerned now generally accept that this sort of nuisance is not a valid reason for exterminating a rare and magnificent bird, though this does not prevent persecution by selfish individuals.

Eagles are often positively beneficial, even to the very people who persecute them. The staple food of the Golden Eagle is medium-sized mammals, which compete with sheep. It also kills quite a number of carnivores, notably fox cubs; 40 of 1,996 Scottish items were carnivores, nearly all fox cubs, 1.4 per cent of the food by number and 1.6 per cent by weight. If these foxes grew up they might in theory eat more lambs than the eagles. In practice, to equate predation of foxes by eagles with damage they might or might not have done if they lived would be extremely difficult, perhaps meaningless.

Many eagles are almost entirely beneficial, for instance any which feed mainly on small mammals, though among these the Imperial and Tawny Eagles are occasionally accused of taking lambs or kids. Eagles feeding largely on fish, such as the African Fish Eagle, could potentially damage human interests. However, two assessments of their effect show that it is negligible. On Lake Mobutu Sese Seko (Lake Albert) the entire population of African Fish Eagles perhaps took 0.3 per cent of the total human catch, itself far lower than the potential. In the Ruwenzori National Park, African Fish Eagles take at most 0.8-1.1 per cent of the fish harvested by man, and only 0.2-0.3 per cent of the potential. Even these estimates are too high; and African Fish Eagles do eat some fish-eating birds and carnivorous catfish and lungfish. American Bald Eagles were formerly persecuted in Alaska because they ate salmon; but most of all the salmon were dead and dying Pacific salmon kelts which had already spawned. Eagles could not catch healthy active fish in deeper water, and had no effect on the stocks.

Some eagles pose a nice ecological problem in assessing whether they are beneficial or not. Most Africans regard all snakes as abominations, to be destroyed whenever possible; and if they discriminate at all, regard snake eagles as highly beneficial. African snake eagles do kill venomous cobras, mambas and puff-adders, and so kill reptiles potentially dangerous to men and domestic animals. However, few people or livestock actually die of snake-bite. Some snakes, however, eat many young rats in burrows, or catch them in the open, and so are theoretically beneficial to mankind. If snake eagles have any calculable effect it may be adverse; but they may safely be regarded as neutral. This also applies to any forest bird or mammal-eating eagle.

Thus, although there are some legitimate complaints against eagles which a naturalist should not deny, but investigate and assess carefully and sympathetically, when such complaints are examined they always have little or no economic foundation. The largest number of eagles possible can safely be left unmolested without seriously affecting any human interests. An increasing number of people in developed countries now regard eagles as magnificent birds well worth seeking out, and are prepared to spend money visiting certain areas to see eagles. Although I do not suppose that one could compute exactly how much money is so spent, I do know that I myself am the poorer by several thousand pounds because of my own passionate interest in eagles. Some of this has been repaid by small research grants, and from writing. The rest has been repaid a hundredfold in pleasure and excitement in wild places I might not otherwise have visited.

I wrote, years ago, 'I have been frozen, lashed by hail and sleet, torn by thorns, hot, thirsty, hungry, and in fear for my life on a lonely crag'. Since I wrote that I have been all these things many times again; but I have been far more often exalted or entranced by the eagles I see and watch, some of which have become old friends over many years. I like to think I understand them better than most people. Life would certainly be the poorer for me and for many others if we could not sometimes see an eagle and revel in its aerial mastery, as people did in Biblical times. The way of an eagle in the air is as wonderful today as ever it was; and since there is no good reason for destroying any of them, or their habitats, I hope that they may be allowed to live into a more enlightened age. I certainly do not want to outlive them.

Appendix I Summary of present knowledge: all eagle species

Notes

(i) All forms generally considered as races but which some consider full species are listed separately.

(ii) Column heads are (1) General Habits, (2) Detailed Diurnal Behaviour, (3) Hunting Methods, (4) Food Needs and Preferences, (5) Breeding Biology, (6) Survival and Longevity.

(iii) They are assessed as: A, intimately known, 10 points; B, very well known, 8 points; C, well known, 6 points; D, little-known, 4 points; and E, scarcely or unknown, 2 points. 'A' does *not* mean that no problems remain; only that a thorough working knowledge of this aspect is available.

Species	(1)	(2)	(3)	(4)	(5)	(6)	*Overall rating*/60	
GROUP I SEA AND FISH EAGLES								
1 White-bellied Sea Eagle								
Haliaeetus leucogaster	C	E	C	C	C	E	28	D+
2 Sanford's Sea Eagle								
Haliaeetus sanfordi	E	E	E	E	E	E	12	E
3 African Fish Eagle								
Haliaeetus vocifer	A	A	A	B	B	A	56	A−
4 Madagascar Fish Eagle								
Haliaeetus vociferoides	C	E	D	D	C	E	24	D
5 Pallas' Sea Eagle								
Haliaeetus leucoryphus	C	D	D	C	C	E	28	D+
6 Bald Eagle								
Haliaeetus leucocephalus	B	B	C	A	B	A	50	B+
7 European Sea Eagle, Erne								
Haliaeetus albicilla	B	B	C	A	B	B	48	B
8 Steller's Sea Eagle								
Haliaeetus pelagicus	C	D	D	C	C	D	30	C−
9 Lesser Fishing Eagle								
Ichthyophaga nana	D	E	D	D	D	E	20	D−
10 Grey-headed Fishing Eagle								
Ichthyophaga ichthyaetus	C	D	D	D	C	E	26	D+
11 Vulturine Fish Eagle								
Gypohierax angolensis	B	D	C	C	C	E	32	C−
GROUP II SNAKE EAGLES								
1 European Snake Eagle								
Circaetus gallicus gallicus	A	B	B	B	A	C	50	B+
1 (a) Beaudouin's Snake Eagle								
Circaetus g. beaudouini	C	D	D	C	D	E	26	D+
1 (b) Black-breasted Snake Eagle								
Circaetus g. pectoralis	B	C	B	B	B	C	44	B−
2 Brown Snake Eagle								
Circaetus cinereus	B	C	C	B	B	C	42	B/C
3 Smaller Banded Snake Eagle								
Circaetus cinerascens	C	D	D	D	D	E	18	D/E
4 Southern Banded Snake Eagle								
Circaetus fasciolatus	D	E	E	D	D	E	18	D/E
5 Bateleur								
Terathopius ecaudatus	A	B	C	B	B	B	48	B
6 Philippine Serpent Eagle								
Spilornis holospilus	D	E	E	D	E	E	16	E+

7 Celebes Serpent Eagle *Spilornis rufipectus*	D	E	D	D	E	E	18	D/E
8 Crested Serpent Eagle *Spilornis cheela*	C	D	C	C	C	E	30	C/D
9 Nicobar Serpent Eagle *Spilornis klossi*	D	E	E	D	E	E	16	E+
10 Andaman Serpent Eagle *Spilornis elgini*	D	E	E	D	E	E	16	E+
11 Congo Serpent Eagle *Dryotriorchis spectabilis*	D	E	E	D	E	E	16	E+
12 Madagascar Serpent Eagle *Eutriorchis astur* (? exists)	E	E	E	E	E	E	12	E

GROUP III HARPIES AND ALLIES

1 Black Solitary Eagle *Harpyhaliaetus solitarius*	C	E	E	D	D	E	20	D−
2 Crowned Solitary Eagle *Harpyhaliaetus coronatus*	C	E	E	D	E	E	18	D/E
3 Guiana Crested Eagle *Morphnus guianensis*	D	E	D	D	D	E	20	D−
4 Harpy Eagle *Harpia harpyja*	C	D	D	C	C	E	28	D+
5 Philippine Monkey-eating Eagle *Pithecophaga jefferyi*	C	E	C	C	B	B	36	C
6 New Guinea Harpy Eagle *Harpyopsis novaeguineae*	D	E	E	E	D	E	16	E+

GROUP IV TRUE OR BOOTED EAGLES

1 Indian Black Eagle *Ictinaetus malayensis*	C	E	C	C	D	E	26	D+
2 Lesser Spotted Eagle *Aquila pomarina*	B	C	B	B	A	B	48	B
3 Greater Spotted Eagle *Aquila clanga*	C	D	C	B	B	D	36	C
4 Tawny Eagle *Aquila rapax rapax*	B	D	B	A	B	D	42	B/C
4 (a) Steppe Eagle *Aquila r. orientalis*	C	D	B	B	B	D	40	C+
5 Imperial Eagle *Aquila heliaca*	B	D	B	B	B	B	44	B−
6 Wahlberg's Eagle *Aquila wahlbergi*	B	C	B	A	A	A	52	B+
7 Gurney's Eagle *Aquila gurneyi*	E	E	E	E	E	E	12	E
8 Golden Eagle *Aquila chrysaetos*	A	C	B	A	A	A	54	A/B
9 Wedge-tailed Eagle *Aquila audax*	B	C	C	A	B	C	44	B−
10 Verreaux's Eagle *Aquila verreauxi*	A	B	C	A	A	A	54	A/B
11 Bonelli's Eagle *Hieraaetus fasciatus fasciatus*	A	B	B	A	B	C	50	B+
11 (a) African Hawk Eagle *Hieraaetus f. spilogaster*	A	C	B	A	A	B	52	A/B
12 Booted Eagle *Hieraaetus pennatus*	B	D	C	C	C	D	34	C−
13 Little Eagle *Hieraaetus morphnoides*	C	C	B	B	C	D	38	C+
14 Ayres' Hawk Eagle *Hieraaetus dubius*	B	C	C	B	A	A	48	B

15 Chestnut-bellied Hawk Eagle *Hieraaetus kienerii*	C	E	E	D	D	E	26	**D+**
16 Black and White Hawk Eagle *Spizastur melanoleucos*	D	E	E	D	E	E	16	**E+**
17 Long-crested Eagle *Spizaetus (Lophaetus) occipitalis*	B	D	C	C	C	C	36	**C**
18 Cassin's Hawk Eagle *Spizaetus africanus*	D	E	E	E	D	E	16	**E+**
19 Changeable Hawk Eagle *Spizaetus cirrhatus*	C	E	D	C	C	E	26	**D+**
20 Mountain Hawk Eagle *Spizaetus nipalensis*	C	E	D	C	D	E	24	**D**
21 Java Hawk Eagle *Spizaetus bartelsi*	E	E	E	E	E	E	12	**E**
22 Celebes Hawk Eagle *Spizaetus lanceolatus*	D	E	E	D	D	E	18	**D/E**
23 Philippine Hawk Eagle *Spizaetus philippensis*	E	E	E	E	E	E	12	**E**
24 Blyth's Hawk Eagle *Spizaetus alboniger*	D	E	D	D	E	E	18	**D/E**
25 Wallace's Hawk Eagle *Spizaetus nanus*	E	E	E	D	E	E	14	**E+**
26 Tyrant Hawk Eagle *Spizaetus tyrannus*	D	E	E	D	D	E	18	**D/E**
27 Ornate Hawk Eagle *Spizaetus ornatus*	D	E	D	D	D	E	20	**D−**
28 Crowned Eagle *Stephanoaetus coronatus*	A	C	C	A	A	A	52	**B+**
29 Isidor's Eagle *Oroaetus isidori*	D	E	E	D	C	E	20	**D−**
30 Martial Eagle *Polemaetus bellicosus*	B	D	C	A	B	A	46	**B−**

SUMMARY

Above broken line = C, well known, or better

Group		(1)	(2)	(3)	(4)	(5)	(6)		Overall situation
I Sea and Fish Eagles	A	1	1	1	2	0	2	7	36/66
11 species	B	3	2	2	1	3	1	12	54%
11 forms	C	5	0	2	4	6	0	17	
	D	1	4	5	3	1	1	15	30/66
	E	1	4	1	1	1	7	15	46%
II Snake Eagles	A	2	0	0	0	1	0	3	31/84
12 species	B	2	2	2	4	3	1	14	37%
14 forms	C	3	2	3	2	1	3	14	
	D	6	3	3	7	3	0	22	53/84
	E	1	7	6	1	6	10	31	63%
III Harpies and Allies	A	0	0	0	0	0	0	0	10/36
6 species	B	0	0	0	0	1	1	2	28%
6 forms	C	4	0	1	2	1	0	8	
	D	2	1	2	3	3	0	11	26/36
	E	0	5	3	1	1	5	15	72%
IV True Eagles: well-known genera *Aquila*, *Hieraaetus*, *Polemaetus*, *Stephanoaetus*	A	5	0	0	9	7	6	27	86/108
	B	8	2	9	6	7	3	35	80%
	C	4	8	7	1	2	2	24	
16 species	D	0	6	0	1	1	5	13	22/108
18 forms	E	1	2	2	1	1	2	9	·20%

V True Eagles: little-	A	0	0	0	0	0	0	0⎫	14/84
known genera *Ictinaetus*,	B	1	0	0	0	0	0	1⎬	17%
Spizastur, Spizaetus,	C	3	0	2	4	3	1	13⎭	
Oroaetus									
14 species	D	7	1	4	7	6	0	25⎱	70/84
14 forms	E	3	13	8	3	5	13	45⎰	83%
All Eagles	A	8	1	1	11	8	8	37	177/378
59 species	B	14	6	13	11	14	6	64	47%
63 forms	C	19	10	15	13	13	6	76	
	D	16	15	14	21	14	6	86	201/378
	E	6	31	20	7	14	37	115	53%

Best-known species

50+	*Haliaeetus vocifer* (56), *H. leucocephalus* (50), *Circaetus g. gallicus*
8 sp	(50), *Aquila wahlbergi* (52), *A. chrysaetos* (54), *A. verreauxi* (54),
9 forms	*Hieraaetus f. fasciatus* (50), *H. f. spilogaster* (52), *Stephanoaetus*
	coronatus (52)
40–49	*Haliaeetus albicilla* (48), *Circaetus g. pectoralis* (44), *C. cinereus*
10 sp	(42), *Terathopius ecaudatus* (48), *Aquila pomarina* (48), *Aquila r.*
11 forms	*rapax* (42), *A. r. orientalis* (40), *A. heliaca* (44), *A. audax* (44),
	Hieraaetus dubius (48), *Polemaetus bellicosus* (46), all others less
	than 40 (well known at best)

Appendix II Nest sites, dimensions, share of sexes, occupation time

Species	Nest site preferred	Size (in feet) if known	Sexes building	Years occupied	No. per pair
1 *Haliaeetus leucogaster*	Trees; occ rocks	6′ × 3′; occ 10′ × 6′	Both, poss F most	Many	1–3
2 *Haliaeetus vocifer*	Trees; occ rocks, ground	Max 6′ × 4′; usu smaller	Both; M most	7–10	1–4; usu 1–2
3 *Haliaeetus leucoryphus*	Trees: cliffs	Usu 4′ × 1′; max 6′ × 4′	Both	Many	
4 *Haliaeetus leucocephalus*	Trees; cliffs; ground	Usu 6′ × 6′; max 20′ × 9½′	Both	10–30; occ more	1–6 (?); usu 2–3
5 *Haliaeetus albicilla*	Cliffs; trees; ground	Usu 5′ × 3′; max 10′ × 6′	Both; F most	10–50	1–11; av 2–3
6 *Haliaeetus pelagicus*	Trees; cliffs	Up to 8′ × 6′–12′ deep	?	Many	?
7 *Ichthyophaga nana*	Trees	3′ × 1′ new; max 4′ × 5′	?	?	?
8 *Ichthyophaga ichthyaetus*	Trees	3–4′ × up to 6′ deep	?	Many	Usu 1
9 *Gypohierax angolensis*	Trees	3′ × 15′	Both	3–5	Usu 1
10 *Circaetus g. gallicus* & races	Trees; occ rocks	3′ × 6″; always small	Both; F most	1	1
11 *Circaetus cinereus*	Trees	3′ × 6″	Both	1	1
12 *Circaetus fasciolatus*	Trees	2′ × 6″–12″	?	1	1

13 *Circaetus cinerascens*	Trees	Reported large; (?) own nests	?	1	1
14 *Terathopius ecaudatus*	Trees	2'×1½'; max 3'×2'	Both	Up to 5	Usu 2–3
15 *Spilornis cheela*	Trees	2'×6"; always small	Both	1	1
16 *Harpya harpyja*	Trees (tall)	5'×4'	?	Many	1 (?)
17 *Pithecophaga jefferyi*	Trees (tall)	5'×5' or larger	Both; F most	Many	1
18 *Ictinaetus malayensis*	Trees	4'×1½'–2'	?	Many	1–2 ?
19 *Aquila pomarina*	Trees	1½'×1' new; max 3'×2'	Both	Several	1–3
20 *Aquila clanga*	Trees: occ on ground	2½'×1' new; grows larger	?	?	1–3
21 *Aquila rapax rapax* & tropical races	Trees	3'–4'×1' new	Both	1–5	1–3
21 (a) *Aquila r. orientalis* & *Aquila r. nipalensis*	Ground; cliffs; low bushes; trees	4'×2' new; max 5'×8'	?	Many	?
22 *Aquila heliaca*	Trees	4'×2' new; max 6'×8'	Both; F most	Up to 30	1–3
23 *Aquila wahlbergi*	Trees	2'×6" new; max 3'×2'	Both	1–6	1–3; usu 2
24 *Aquila chrysaetos*	Cliffs; trees; ground	4'×1' new; max 5'×17'	Both; F most	10–50	1–14; usu 2–4
25 *Aquila audax*	Trees; rocks; ground	4'×3'; max 6'×8'	Both; F most	5–20?	Usu 1
26 *Aquila verreauxi*	Cliffs; occ trees	6'×2' new; rarely 5'×8'	Both; F most	5–20?	1–5; usu 2
27 *Hieraaetus f. fasciatus*	Cliffs; trees	6'×2'; max 6'×6'	Both	5–10+	1–5; usu 2–3
27 (a) *Hieraaetus f. spilogaster*	Trees; occ cliffs	5'×2'; occ 5'×4'	Both; F most	5–10	1–4; usu 1–2
28 *Hieraaetus pennatus*	Trees; cliffs	3'–4'×1'–2'	?	2–5?	1–3; usu 2
29 *Hieraaetus morphnoides*	Trees	2½'×2'	Both	?	1–2
30 *Hieraaetus dubius*	Trees	2½'×1'; max 3'×2'	Both	1–10	Usu 1
31 *Spizaetus occipitalis*	Trees	2'×6" new; max 2½'×1'	Both	1–5	Usu 1
32 *Spizaetus cirrhatus*	Trees	max 3½'×2'	Both	?	?
33 *Spizaetus nipalensis*	Trees	Up to 6'×4'	Both; M brings material	Many	1–2
34 *Stephanoaetus coronatus*	Trees	5'×2' new; max 5'×8'	Both; F most	10–50+	1
35 *Oroaetus isidori*	Trees	6'×3'	?	Many	1
36 *Polemaetus bellicosus*	Trees	5'×3'; max 6'×5'	Both; F most	3–30+	1–3; usu 1

Appendix III Summarised breeding data: better-known eagles

Column heads
(1) Clutch size (normal), (2) Incubation period (days), (3) Sexes incubating, (4) Fledging period (days), (5) Young per successful nest, (6) Young per pair overall.

Species	(1)	(2)	(3)	(4)	(5)	(6)
1 *Haliaeetus leucogaster*	1–3 (2)	?	Both; F does most, occ M	65–70	1–2	?
2 *Haliaeetus vocifer*	1–4 (2)	41–44	Mainly F, occ M	65–70	1–3 (1.2)	0.60–0.47
3 *Haliaeetus leucoryphus*	1–4 (2+)	40+ ?	Mainly F, also M	70–105?	1–2 (? 3)	?
4 *Haliaeetus leucocephalus*	1–4 (2)	35–46 ?	Both; F mainly	65–80	1–3 (1.4)	0.7–1.2 (0.9)
5 *Haliaeetus albicilla*	1–4 (2)	37–40 ?	Both; F mainly	70±	1–2 (1.5)	? 1.2–1.1
6 *Haliaeetus pelagicus*	1–3 (2)	38–45 ?	?	ca 70	1–3 (1.2)	?
7 *Ichthyophaga ichthyaetus*	2–4 (2.5 ?)	?	?	?	?	?
8 *Gypohierax angolensis*	1	ca44	F only	90+	1	?
9 *Circaetus g. gallicus*	1	47	F mainly, occ M	70–75	1	Less than 1
9 (a) *Circaetus g. pectoralis*	1	50+	,,	90–100	1	c0.3–0.4
10 *Circaetus cinereus*	1	52–54	F only	100–110	1	c 0.4
11 *Terathopius ecaudatus*	1	52–55	Mainly F, occ M	90–125	1	c 0.5 or less
12 *Spilornis cheela*	1	28–35 ?	F only	60±	1	?
13 *Harpya harpyja*	1–2 (2)	52–54	Both; esp F (captivity)	?	1 ?	Less than 0.5 ?
14 *Pithecophaga jefferyi*	1	60	Mainly F, some M	105	1	Less than 1
15 *Aquila pomarina*	1–3 (2)	43	Mainly F, some M	50–55	1 (occ 2)	c0.8 ?
16 *Aquila clanga*	1–3 (2)	42–44	F only	60–65	1–2 (1.1 ?)	c0.8 ?
17 *Aquila r. rapax*	1–3 (2)	41–43	F mainly, M sometimes	70–75	1–2 (1.3)	Less than 1 (c0.8)
17 (a) *Aquila r. orientalis*	1–3 (2)	45	F only ?	55–60	1–2 (1.4 ?)	?
18 *Aquila heliaca*	1–4 (2+)	43	Both; mainly F	60–65	1–3 (1.4 ?)	c0.7
19 *Aquila chrysaetos*	1–4 (2)	41–45 (43)	Mainly F, rarely M	65–80	1–3 (1.2–1.4)	0.83–1.2 (c0.9)
20 *Aquila wahlbergi*	1 occ 2	46	Usu F, rarely M	62–80 (75)	1	0.6–0.7

21	*Aquila audax*	1–3 (2)	?	F only reported·	63–70	1–2	?
22	*Aquila verreauxi*	1–3 (1.8)	43–46	Both; mainly F	90–100	1 (1 rec of 2)	0.51
23	*Hieraaetus f. fasciatus*	1–3 (2)	37–39	Both; mainly F	60–65	1+ (cl. 2)	? c0.7
23 (a)	*Hieraaetus f. spilogaster*	1–3 (2)	42–43	Both; mainly F	55–80 (70)	1–2 (1.3)	0.5– 0.8 (0.7)
24	*Hieraaetus pennatus*	1–2 (2)	?	Both; usu F	50 ?	1	Less than 1
25	*Hieraaetus morphnoides*	1–2 (2)	?	F only	45–50	1–2	Less than 1
26	*Hieraaetus dubius*	1–2 (1)	45–46	F only	70–75	1	0.29
27	*Spizaetus occipitalis*	1–2 (2)	43±	Mainly F; occ M	50–55	1–2 (1.3)	c0.8
28	*Spizaetus cirrhatus*	1	?	F only	?	?	?
29	*Stephanoaetus coronatus*	1–2 (2)	49	Both; F mainly	105–125 (112)	1	0.38 (0.4)
30	*Polemaetus bellicosus*	1	52 ?	F mainly, M rarely	90–100	1	0.53– 0.55

Appendix IV List of threatened species with main threats outlined

A ISLAND SPECIES WITH RESTRICTED RANGE

1 *Haliaeetus sanfordi* Solomon Islands. Status obscure, but no evidence of immediate threat.

2 *Spilornis holospilus* Philippines. Status obscure, but probably not immediately threatened.

3 *Spilornis rufipectus* Sulawesi (Celebes). Status obscure, but probably not acutely threatened.

4 *Spilornis klossi* Great Nicobar Island. Status obscure, but probably no immediate threat.

5 *Spilornis elgini* Andaman Islands, forests. Status at present said to be satisfactory.

6 *Eutriorchis astur* Madagascar, forests. Status unknown, perhaps already extinct; acutely threatened by habitat destruction.

7 *Pithecophaga jefferyi* Philippines. Acutely threatened, less than one hundred alive; habitat destruction and persecution. Now specially protected.

8 *Spizaetus bartelsi* W. Java, woodlands. Rare; status obscure, but probably severely threatened by habitat destruction.

9 *Spizaetus lanceolatus* Sulawesi, Buton. Status obscure; forest habitat threatened with destruction.

10 *Spizaetus philippensis* Philippines. Rather widespread; possibly not acutely threatened.

B SPECIES OF CONTINENTAL RANGE THREATENED BY HABITAT DESTRUCTION

1 *Circaetus fasciolatus*   Coastal E. and S. Africa. Destruction of habitat; not immediately threatened.

2 *Hieraaetus kienerii*   Widespread but rare, India–Malaysia. Threatened by habitat destruction, but status obscure.

3 *Oroaetus isidori*   S. America, Andes. Status obscure, believed rare and decreasing through destruction of habitat.

C SPECIES OF WIDE RANGE THREATENED IN PART BY HUMAN PERSECUTION AND PESTICIDES

1 *Haliaeetus leucoryphus*   Central Asia and E. Europe. Status uncertain, probably affected by pesticides but not immediately threatened.

2 *Haliaeetus leucocephalus*   N. America. Some populations extinct, others declining, mainly through pesticides, some persecution. Not immediately threatened as a species.

3 *Haliaeetus albicilla*   Europe and Asia. W. European and Mediterranean populations threatened by pesticides, British population extinct; not immediately threatened as a species.

4 *Haliaeetus pelagicus*   E. Siberia, Kamschatka. Status not clear; probably not immediately threatened.

5 *Circaetus g. gallicus*   Widespread Europe, Asia. Persecuted in Mediterranean, especially France. Not threatened as a species.

6 *Aquila pomarina*   Central Europe, Asia. Apparently decreasing, not immediately threatened; human interference.

7 *Aquila clanga*   Eastern Europe, Asia. Decreasing, not immediately threatened, status unclear.

8 *Aquila heliaca* (2 races)   Spanish race *adalberti* acutely threatened, less than one hundred pairs; *A. h. heliaca* also uncommon. Persecution and pesticides, apparently fairly stable.

9 *Aquila chrysaetos*   Widespread, Holartic. Not threatened as a species; persecuted Europe, America. Locally affected by pesticides, Britain.

10 *Aquila audax*   Australia. Severely persecuted, now protected. Not now threatened.

11 *Aquila verreauxi*   Israel, E. and S. Africa. Not threatened; only locally persecuted, S. Africa.

12 *Hieraeetus f. fasciatus*   Europe, Asia. Not threatened as a species; locally reduced, especially S. France, by persecution.

Bibliography

The list of references given below cannot, for reasons of space, be fully comprehensive, for this would necessitate listing hundreds of titles. There are, for instance, 1,450 listed by R. Olendorff in 'An Extensive Bibliography on . . . eagles . . .' published in 1968 and that is neither comprehensive nor up to date. I have attempted instead to select a few major works or key papers dealing with each chapter. So far as possible, titles have been selected which also contain bibliographies reviewing the literature up to their date of publication, although some titles refer only to a subject of particular interest mentioned in the text.

In many instances, a title may be referred to at different stages in the text, and after the first mention, these are referred to in shortened form, eg in Ch 26, see also Willgohs, J. F. 1961, Ch 2. Data derived from letters not published elsewhere is acknowledged where appropriate.

Chapter 1
Brown, L. H. *Eagles* (1955, 1970)
——. and Amadon, D. *Eagles, Hawks and Falcons of the World* (1969)
Grossman, M. L. and Hamlet, J. *Birds of Prey of the World* (1964)
Peters, J. L., *et al Check-list of Birds of the World* Vol 1 'Falconiformes' (USA, 1931-68)
Steyn, P. *Eagle Days* (South Africa, 1973)
Stresemann, V. and Stresemann, E. 'Die Handschwingenmauser der Tagraubvögel' *J fur Orn* 101; 373-403 (1960)
Much general information on eagles in various parts of the world is also contained in regional or national handbooks; eg Witherby, *et al, Handbook of British Birds* (1943) or, more recently, Glutz von Blotzheim, *et al, Handbuch der Vogel Mitteleuropas* Band 4, (Germany, 1971)

Chapter 2
Brown, L. H. 'The African Fish Eagle *Haliaeetus vocifer,* especially in the Kavirondo Gulf' *Ibis* 102; 285-297 (1960)
Fischer, W. *Die Seeadler* (Germany, 1959)
Imler, R. H. and Kalmbach, E. R. 'The Bald Eagle and its economic status' *Circular 30, Fish and Wildlife Service* (USA, undated, now very much outdated, but no more recent survey published.)
Thomson, A. L. and Moreau, R. E. 'Feeding habits of the Palm-nut Vulture *Gypohierax*' *Ibis* 99; 608-613
Willgohs, J. F. 'The White-tailed Eagle *Haliaeetus albicilla* (Linne) in Norway' (Bergen, Norway, 1961)
There are numerous other short papers on individual species in this group, some listed later.

Chapter 3
Boudouint, Y., *et al* 'Etude da la biologie du Circaete Jean le Blanc' *Alauda* XXI; 86-119 (France, 1953)
Brown, L. H. 'Supplementary notes on the biology of the large birds of prey of Embu District, Kenya Colony' *Ibis* 97; 38-64 and 183-221 (1955)
Moreau, R. E. 'On the Bateleur, especially at the nest' *Ibis* 87; 224-249 (1945)
Steyn, P. 'Observations on the Brown Snake Eagle' *Ostrich* 35; 22-31 (1964)
——. 'Some observations on the Bateleur *Terathopius ecaudatus* (Daudin)' *Ostrich* 36; 203-213 (1965)

——. 'Observations on the Black-breasted Snake Eagle' *Ostrich Suppl* 6;
141-154 (1966)

——. 'Further observations on the Brown Snake Eagle' *Ostrich* 43; 149-164
(1972)

Also short papers on *Spilornis cheela* by Kooiman, J. G., *Ardea* 26; 77-88
(1937); and Cairns, J. *Ibis* 110; 569-571 (1968)

Chapter 4

Fowler, J. M. and Cope, J. B. 'Notes on the Harpy Eagle in British Guiana'
Auk 81; 257-273 (1964)

No other papers of any note appear to have been published on this group;
other references are short oddments.

Chapter 5

A large number of papers concerning booted eagles are listed under later
chapters, chiefly under breeding biology, since that is the main aspect
which has been studied. The following are more comprehensive works:

Arnold, L. W. 'The Golden Eagle and its economic status' *Circular 27 US
Fish and Wildlife Service* (1954) USA

Gordon, S. *The Golden Eagle, King of Birds* (1955)

Wendland, V. *Schreiadler und Schelladler* (1959) Germany

Chapter 6

Weights and measurements are quoted from the standard works listed
under individual chapters.

Chapter 7

Pumphrey, R. J. 'The sense organs of birds' *Ibis* 90; 171-199 (1948)

Walls, G. L. *The vertebrate eye and its adaptive radiation* (USA, 1942)

Also articles on sight and hearing in *A New Dictionary of Birds,* ed
Landsborough Thomson (1964) and in Welty, J. C., *The Life of Birds*
(USA, 1962). No comprehensive account specifically referring to the sight,
hearing, and other senses of eagles seems to have been published.

Chapter 8

Barlee, J. *Birds on the Wing* (1947)

Cone, C. D., 'Thermal soaring of birds' *Amer Scientist,* 50; 1-30 (1962)

——. 'The soaring flight of birds' *Scientific American* 206; 130-142 (1962)

Goslow, G. E. 'The attack and strike of some American raptors' *Auk* 88;
815-227 (1971)

——. 'Adaptive mechanisms of the raptor pelvic limb' *Auk* 89; 47-64 (1972)
(Although not specifically related to eagles these two papers are essential
for an understanding of how raptors kill.)

Gray, J. *Animal Locomotion* Ch 9 (1968)

Hankin, E. H. *Animal flight* (1913)

Pennycuick, C. J. 'Animal Flight' *Institute of Biology, studies in biology* 33
(1972)

——. 'Soaring behaviour and performance of some East African birds,
observed from a motor glider' *Ibis* 114; 178-218 (1972)

See also article on flight in *A New Dictionary of Birds* ed Landsborough
Thomson (1963)

Chapter 9

Brooker, M. G. 'Field observations on the behaviour of the Wedge-tailed
Eagle' *Emu* 74; 39-42

Cheylan, C. 'Le Cycle annuel d'un couple d'Aigles de Bonelli *Hieraaetus
fasciatus* (Vieillot)' *Alauda* XL; 214-234 (1972)

Murphy, J. R., *et al* 'Nesting ecology of raptorial birds in Central Utah'
Biol Ser X. 4 1-36 (1969) USA

Southern, W. E. 'Additional observations on winter Bald Eagle populations, including remarks on biotelemetric techniques and immature plumages' *Wilson Bull* 76.2, 121-137 (1964)
Also numerous unpublished observations on diurnal behaviour in African Fish Eagles by L. H. Brown.

Chapter 10
There is an extremely voluminous literature on migration, much of it concerning other than raptorial birds; recent papers referring specifically to eagles and other large soaring raptors are:
Broley, C. L. 'Migration and nesting of Florida Bald Eagles' *Wilson Bull* 59; 3-20 (1947)
Evans, P. R. and Lathbury, G. W. 'Raptor migration across the straits of Gibraltar' *Ibis* 115; 572-585 (1973)
Nisbet, I. C. T. and Smout, T. C. 'Autumn observations on the Bosphorus and Dardanelles' *Ibis* 99; 483-499 (1957)
Safriel, U. 'Bird Migration at Elat, Israel' *Ibis* 110; 283-320 (1968)
Simmons, K. E. L. 'Raptor migration in the Suez area, autumn 1949-spring 1950' *Ibis* 93; 402-406 (1951)
Tennent, S. R. M. 'Spring migration of birds of prey near Suez' *Ibis* 109; 273-4 (1967)
On speed and other special aspects refer to:
Darling, F. F. 'Speed of a Golden Eagle's flight' *Nature* 134 (3383); 325-6 (1934)
Lorenz, K. *King Solomon's Ring* (1952)
Meinertzhagen, R. 'The speed and altitude of bird flight' *Ibis* 97; 81-117 (1955)

Chapter 11
Broun, M. *Hawks aloft* (1948) USA
Brown, L. H. 'The relations of the Crowned Eagle *Stephanoaetus coronatus* and some of its prey animals' *Ibis* 113; 240-3 (1971)
Jensen, R. A. C. 'The Steppe Eagle *Aquila nipalensis* and other termite-eating raptors in South West Africa' *Madoqua* Ser 1.5; 173-176 (1972)
Meinertzhagen, R. *Pirates and Predators* (1959) Edinburgh
Murie, A. 'The Wolves of Mt McKinley' US Nat Parks Fauna Ser 5; 1-238 (1944)
Schaller, G. B. *The Serengeti Lion* (1972) USA
Vaucher, C. A. 'Notes sur l'éthologie de l'aigle de Bonelli *Hieraaetus fasciatus*' *Nos Oiseaux* 31; 101-111 (1971) France
Zastrov, M. 'On the distribution and biology of the Golden Eagle in Estonia' *Var Fagelvarld* 5; 64-80 (1946)
See also works already quoted for Chs 9 and 10.

Chapter 12
Arnold, E. L. and MacLaren, P. I. R. 'Notes on the habits and distribution of the White-tailed Eagle in Iceland' *British Birds* 34:4-10 (1939)
Brown, L. H. 'Observations on some Kenya eagles' *Ibis* 108; 531-572 (1966)
——. and Watson, A. 'The Golden Eagle in relation to its food supply' Ibis 106; 78-100 (1964)
Craighead, J. J. and Craighead, F. C. *Hawks, Owls, and Wildlife* (1956) USA
Fevold, H. R. and Craighead, J. J. 'Food requirements of the Golden Eagle' *Auk* 75; 312-17 (1958)
See also Steyn, P., Ch 1, for observations on digestion in snake eagles.

Chapter 13

Brown, L. H. *African Birds of Prey* (1970)

——. *British Birds of Prey* (1976)

Dharmakumarsinhji, R. S. and Lavkumar, K. S., 'White-bellied Sea Eagle of Karwar, *Haliaeetus leucogaster* (Gmelin)' *J Bomb Nat Hist Soc* 53(4); 569-580 (1956)

Gargett, V. 'Black Eagle survey, Rhodes-Matopos National Park; a population study 1964-68' *Ostrich Supp* 8; 397-414 (1969)

Green, J. 'Numbers and distribution of the African Fish Eagle *Haliaeetus vocifer* on the eastern shores of Lake Albert' *Ibis* 106; 125-128 (1964)

Smeenck, C. 'Comparative ecological studies of some East African Birds of Prey' *Ardea* 62; 1-87 (1974)

See also Brown and Watson (1964) Ch 12; Craighead J. J. and F. C. (1956) Ch 12; Murphy, J. R., *et al* (1969) Ch 9.

Chapter 14

Eltringham, S. K. 'Territory, size and distribution in the African fish eagle' *J Zool* 175; 1-13 (1975)

Gargett, V. 'The spacing of Black Eagles in the Matopos, Rhodesia' *Ostrich* 46; 1-44 (1975)

Lockie, J. D. and Stephen, D. 'Eagles, Lambs and Land Management on Lewis' *J Anim Ecol* 28: 1; 43-50

Material also derived from D. Merrie's unpublished mss on eagles in Argyll, and from many papers and books quoted under earlier chapters.

Chapters 15-22

Many papers on eagles cover several aspects of breeding biology, and to separate data into component parts as in this section would be impracticable. Summaries of breeding biology are also usually given in standard reference works, and some works covering breeding biology have already been listed, eg Chapter 1. The list which follows includes some early papers, but since much of the early work was done by photographers, inevitably causing some disturbance, most of the best work is post 1950.

Bent, A. C. 'Life Histories of American birds of prey' *Part 1 Bull US Nat Mus* 167 (USA, 1937)

Berg, B. *Die letzten Adler* (Germany, 1927)

Blondel, J., *et al* 'Deux cents heures d'observation auprès de l'aire de l'Aigle du Bonelli *Hieraaetus fasciatus*' *Nos Oiseaux* 30; 37-60 (France, 1969)

Brown, L. H. 'On the biology of the large birds of prey of the Embu District Kenya Colony' *Ibis* 94; 577-620 and 95; 74-114 (1952-3)

——. *ibid* Ch 2 (1955), Ch 3 (1960), Ch 12 (1966)

Calaby, J. H. 'Notes on the Little Eagle with particular reference to rabbit predation' *Emu* 51; 33-56 (1951)

Camendzind, F. Z. 'Nesting ecology and behaviour of the Golden Eagle *Aquila chrysaetos* L.' *Biol Ser* X. 4; 4-14 (USA, 1969)

Fleay, D. 'With a Wedge-tailed Eagle at the nest' *Emu* 52; 1-17 (1952)

Gargett, V. 'Observations on the Black Eagles in the Matopos, Rhodesia' *Ostrich Supp* 9; 91-124 (1971)

——. 'Observations at a Black Eagle nest in the Matopos, Rhodesia' *Ostrich* 43; 77-108 (1972)

Gordon, S. *Days with the Golden Eagle* (1927)

Herrick, F. B. 'Life History of the Bald Eagle' *Auk* 41; 89-105, 213-231, 389-422, 517-541 (1924)

Knight, C. W. R. *The Book of the Golden Eagle* (1927)

——. *Knight in Africa* (1937)

Lack, D. *The Natural Regulation of Animal Numbers* 40-41 (Oxford, 1954)

MacPherson, H. B. *Home Life of a Golden Eagle* (1909)

Meyburg, B.-U. 'Zur Biologie des Schreiadlers (*Aquila pomarina*)' *Deutscher Falkenorden* 32-66 (Germany, 1969)

——. 'Quatre poussins dans un nid de l'Aigle Imperial d'Espagne *Aquila heliaca adalberti*' *Alauda* 42; 1-6 (France, 1974)

——. 'Sibling aggression and mortality among young eagles' *Ibis* 116; 224-228 (1974)

——. and Garzon-Heydt, J. 'Sobre la Proteccion del Aguila Imperial (*Aquila heliaca adalberti*) aminorando artificialmente la mortandad juvenil' *Ardeola* 19; 107-128 (Italy, 1973)

McGahan, J. 'Ecology of the Golden Eagle' *Auk* 85; 1-12 (1968)

Mountfort, G. *Portrait of a Wilderness* (1958)

Plage, D. 'A three-day watch at a Fish Eagle's nest in Botswana' *Ostrich* 45; 143-144 (1974)

Rowe, E. G. 'The breeding biology of *Aquila verreauxi* (Lesson) *Ibis* 89; 387-410 and 576-606 (1947)

Siewert, H. 'Der Seeadler' *J fur Orn* 76; 204-235 (1928) Germany

Steyn, P. 'Observations on Wahlberg's Eagle' *Bokmakkierie* 14. 1; 7-15 (1962)

——. 'Observations on the Tawny Eagle' *Ostrich* 44; 1-22 (1973)

——. 'Breeding of the African Hawk Eagle' *Ostrich* 43 (1975)

Suetens, W. and van Groenendaal, P. 'Note succincte sur la nidification d'un couple d'Aigles Imperiaux (*Aquila heliaca adalberti*) dans la Province de Caceres' *Aquila*; Vol Especial; 573-580 (France, 1971)

——. 'Notes sur l'écologie de l'Aigle de Bonelli (*Hieraaetus fasciatus*) et da l'Aigle Botte (*Hieraaetus pennatus*) en Espagne méridionale' *Ardeola* XV; 19-29 (France, 1969)

Whitman, Walt; quot in Armstrong, E. A. *Bird Display* (1942)

Wynne-Edwards, V. C. *Animal Dispersion in relation to Social Behaviour* (Edinburgh, 1962)

Chapter 23
Brown, L. H. and Cade, T. J. 'Age classes and population dynamics of the Bateleur and African Fish Eagle' *Ostrich* 43; 1-16 (1972)

Jollie, M. 'Plumage changes in the Golden Eagle' *Auk* 64; 549-576 (1947)

Stowell, R. F. 'Notes on the behaviour in captivity of the African Fish Eagle *Cuncuma vocifer*' *Ibis* 100; 457-459 (1958)

Information from W. R. Spofford on the moults of Verreaux's and Martial Eagles; and from R. Brooke and P. Hayman on those of Steppe, Imperial and Crowned Eagles is also acknowledged.

Chapter 24
Brown, L. H. 'Some factors affecting breeding in eagles' *Ostrich Supp* 8; 157-167 (1969)

——. 'Natural longevity in wild Crowned Eagles *Stephanoaetus coronatus*' *Ibis* 114; 263-271 (1972)

——. 'Data required for effective study of raptor populations' *Research Report 2* 7-20 of Raptor Research Foundation (USA, 1974)

——. 'Is poor breeding success a reason for the rarity of Ayres Hawk Eagle?' *Ostrich* 45; 145-146 (1974)

——. and Hopcraft, J. B. D. 'Population structure and dynamics in the African Fish Eagle *Haliaeetus vocifer* (Daudin) at Lake Naivasha, Kenya' *E Afr Wildl J* 11; 255-269 (1973)

Everett, M. J. 'The Golden Eagle survey in Scotland, 1964-68' *British Birds* 64; 49-56 (1971)

Mead, C. J. 'Movements of British Raptors' *Bird Study* 20; 259-286 (1973)

Miller, D., *et al* 'Suggested practices for raptor protection on powerlines' 1-21 (USA, 1975)

Snelling, J. C. 'Some information obtained from marking large raptors in the Kruger National Park, Rep of South Africa' *Ostrich Supp* 8; 415-427 (1970)

Sprunt, A. (IV), *et al* 'Comparative productivity of six Bald Eagle populations' *Trans N Amer Wildl and Nat Res Council* 38; 96-106 (1973)

See also Brown, L. H. (1966) Ch 12, and Gargett, V. Ch 13, and papers quoted in Ch 23; Gargett, V., Ch 14.; Gordon, S., Ch 5; Suetens and van Groenendaal (1971), Chs 15-21.

Chapter 25

Baxter, E. V. and Rintoul, L. J. *The Birds of Scotland* (Edinburgh, 1953)

Bolen, E. G. 'Eagles and Sheep; a viewpoint' *Journal of Range Management* 28; 1, 11-17 (1975) (quot also Alford, J. R. and Bolen E. G. *Wilson Bull* 84; 487-489)

Curry-Lindahl, Kai. *Let them Live* (USA, 1972)

Fisher, J., Simon, N. and Vincent, J. *The Red Book; Wildlife in Danger* (1969)

(Also more recent information from World Wildlife Fund, Switzerland on Philippine Monkey-eating Eagle)

Helander, B. 'Havsornen i Sverige' *Svenska Naturskydds-foreningen* (Sweden, 1970)

Higby, L. W. 'The Eagle Survey in Wyoming' (paper submitted to the conference on Raptor Research, Colorado, 1973, forthcoming in *Raptor Research*)

Leopold, A. S. and Wolfe, T. O. 'Food habits of nesting Wedge-tailed Eagles *Aquila audax* in south-eastern Australia' *CSIRO Wildlife Research* 15; 1-17 (1970)

Lockie, J. D. 'The breeding density of Golden Eagle and Fox in relation to food supply in Wester Ross, Scotland' *Scot Nat* 71: 2; 67-77 (1964)

Oehme, G. 'Die Seeadler verluste in unserer Republik' *Der Falke* 13; 40-47 (1966) Germany

Ridpath, M. G. 'The Wedge-tailed Eagle' *Australian Nat Hist* 16; 209-212 (1969)

Spofford, W. R. 'Golden Eagle in the Trans-Pecos and Edwards Plateau of Texas' *Audubon Conserv Rep* 1 (1964)

Terrasse J-F. 'La diminution récente des effectifs de Rapaces en France et ses causes' *Terre et Vie* 112;3, 273-291 (France, 1965)

Thiollay, J-M. 'Essai sur les rapaces du Midi de la France' *Alauda* 34; 210-227, 35; 140-150, 36; 52-62 (1966)

Many c her papers on decreasing status of species concerned have been published eg in the Proceedings of the first conference on Birds of Prey at Caen (1964). Information is also acknowledged from Humayun Abdulali (in litt) on Snake Eagles in the Andaman Islands. See also papers by Meyburg, B.U., and Meyburg and Garzon-Heydt listed under Chs 15-21; anonymous articles entitled 'Predators, the Number One Problem' in *Ranch Magazine* (USA, April, May 1971); see also data in Brown, L. H. (1976) Ch 13 for summary of effect of Eagles on sheep etc; Green, J. (1964) Ch 13; Spofford, W. R. (1964) Ch 25; Willgohs, J. F. (1961) Ch 2, etc for additional factual data on these subjects.

Index